The Image of a Company

The Image of a Company

The Image of a Company

MANUAL FOR CORPORATE IDENTITY

Architecture Design and Technology Press
London

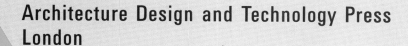

017344

First published in Great Britain in 1990 by
Architecture Design and Technology Press
128 Long Acre
London WC2E 9AN
A division of Longman Group UK Limited

© 1990, V+K Publishing, P.O. Box 144,
1250 AC Laren, The Netherlands

British Library Cataloguing in Publication Data
A CIP record for this book is available from the
British Library

ISBN 1 85454 404 7

Printed and bound in Ghent, Belgium

Contents

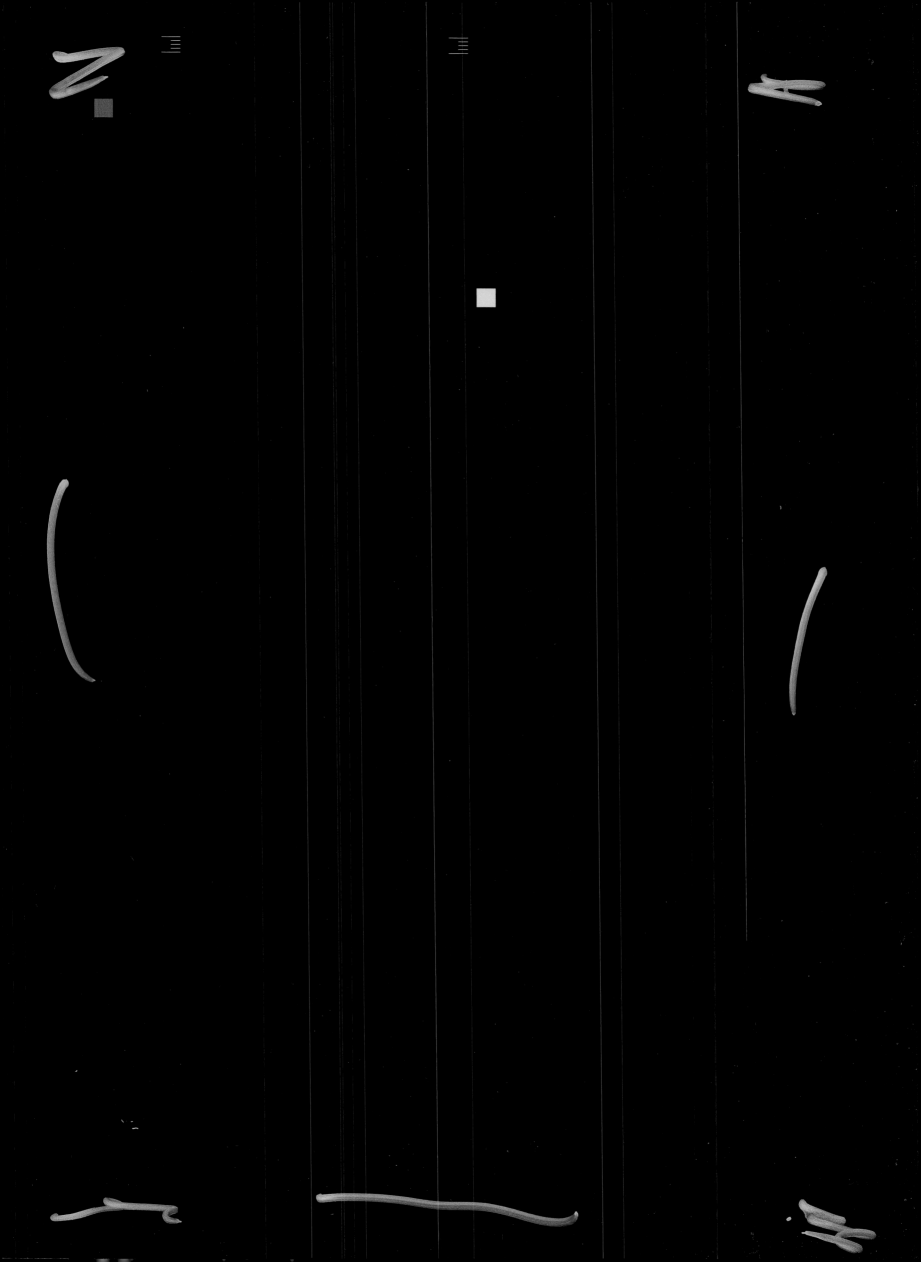

Foreword

Corporate Identity has become a frequent topic of discussion. This is hardly surprising if one considers the vital role it can play in establishing and enhancing the public image of a company or institution and in creating an essential added value. The latter has special relevance in an age hallmarked by equality of product and standard and by an increasing flow of information. More than ever, an organization needs to distinguish itself from others and above all to stand out. A carefully constructed identity and hence market position are invaluable aids for an organization to be successful in the marketplace.

An array of experts, from managers to designers, is involved with corporate identity. For all those concerned with this phenomenon today, THE IMAGE OF A COMPANY can be an elucidating as well as a practical guide, which reflects the accumulated expertise of a number of different authors.

Paul Hefting's essay outlines corporate identity as it has evolved through the ages. He is followed by F.H.K. Henrion, whose long-standing experience with corporate identity as a designer and consultant serves to illuminate the subject. Eleven world-famous company identities are subsequently reviewed – Braun, Dutch PTT, London Underground, Adidas, Coca-Cola, Esprit, IBM, Erco-Leuchten, KLM, Kodak and Volkswagen. In a series of colourful essays Jaap Huisman, Jaap Lieverse, Colin Wells and Gert Staal tell us how these companies deal with corporate identity.

This brings us to the practical plane. Alex Visser discusses how to go about organizing corporate identity – an area few before him have explored. He compiled a set of guidelines for developing a corporate identity, focusing on the visual aspect, on the corporate design or housestyle. The book closes with a presentation of a comprehensive housestyle designed for a fictitious company called Image. It offers us useful tools for solving problems likely to crop up when visualizing a corporate identity programme. The visual section was realized by Ernst Schilp and the present writer. The practical and technical information that it includes is a distillation of our many years of practice in this field. Ben Bos wrote the accompanying commentary.

In short, THE IMAGE OF A COMPANY is far from being a theoretical work; words and images initiate the reader into the workings of corporate identity. Hopefully the book will be an inspiration to many.

It is always a special moment when an idea – conceived in this case several years ago – finally appears in print. We would therefore like to thank all the authors and Ronald de Nijs, who edited the book, for their contributions to THE IMAGE OF A COMPANY.

Cees de Jong

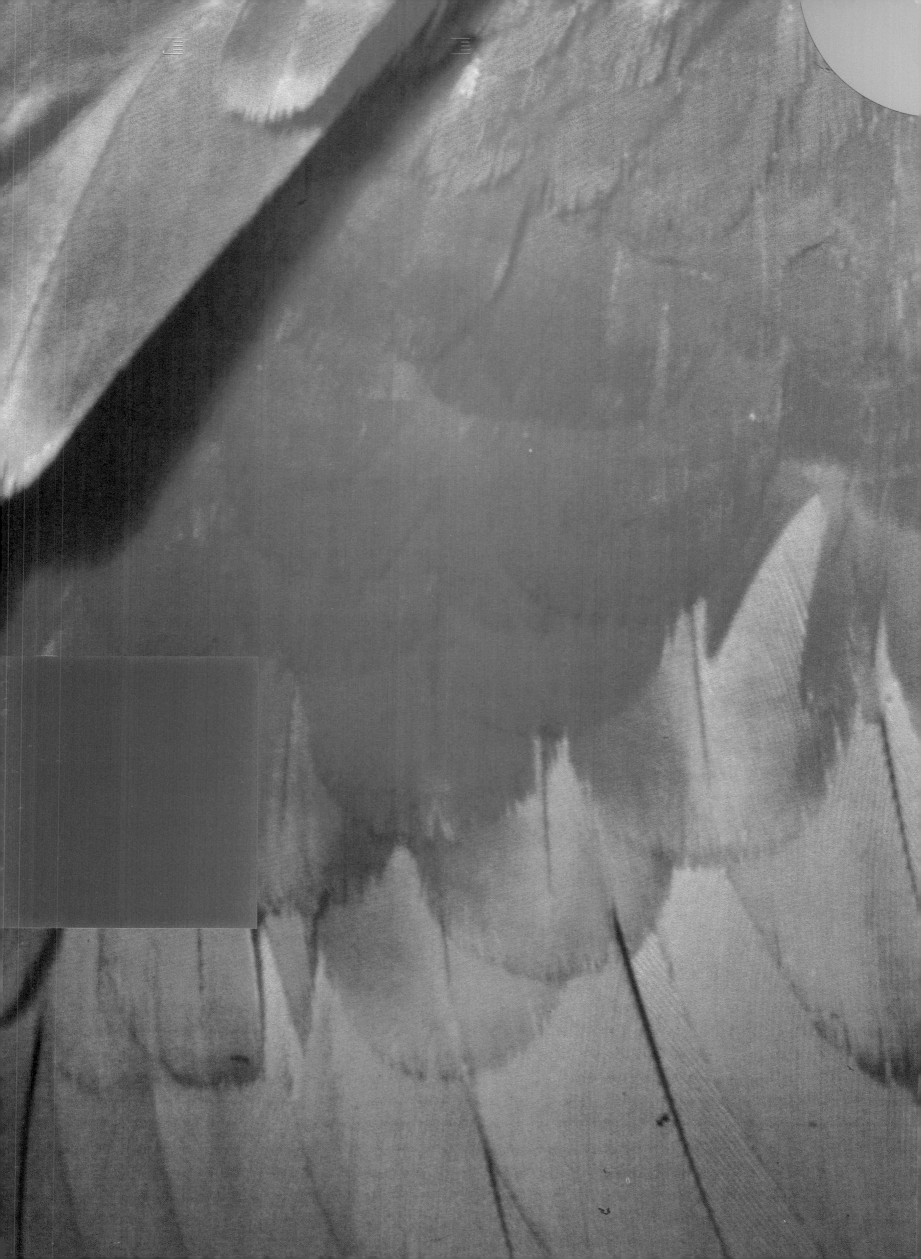

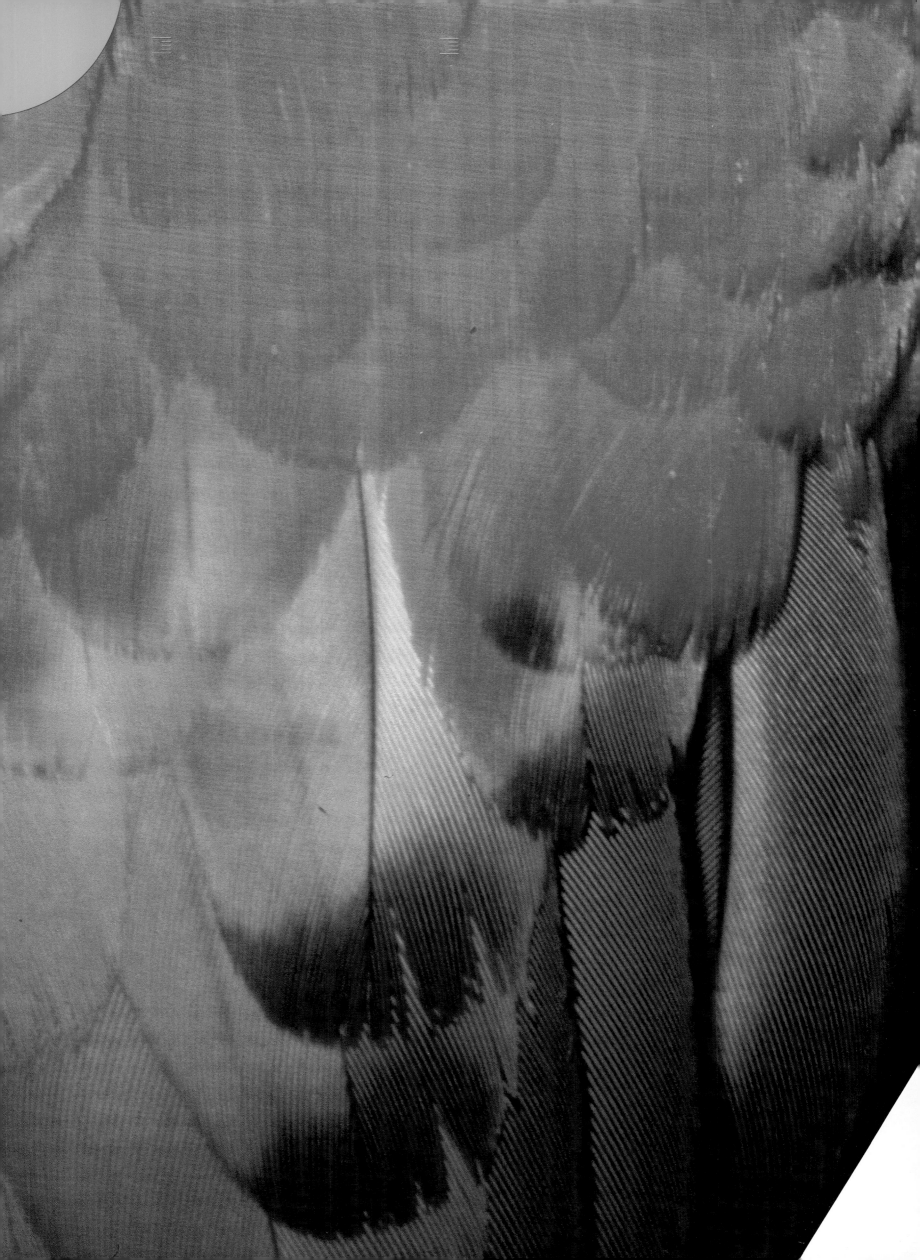

In search of an identity
So obvious yet so complex

The past few years have seen an influx of publications on the subject of corporate identity. This is closely connected with the growing competition and awareness, indeed knowledge, in the business world that a corporate image is of major importance. As new companies are set up every day and existing corporations merge to form multinationals, new images are sought to express their identity.

There is also a general tendency towards privatization and even in government-run companies we see the urge towards independence. Examples of this are British Telecom and more recently the Dutch PTT. And in national bodies such as ministries or museums there is also talk of going private – of creating units with a measure of autonomy over content, organization and financing, that are recognizable from their own flag, their own corporate identity.

Clearly, this tendency is connected with shortages in the state treasury, apparent in many countries; economic and national interests are usually interrelated and there are almost always close links between political leaders and industrial magnates. At the moment the economy has gained a new importance: it is now used as a weapon. Nations challenge each other in the economic arena, jostling over imports and exports, for a market position. And in this context the corporate banners are ever more visible.

Some definitions

In the above section I have introduced the terms corporate image and corporate identity. 'Corporate image' refers to the image that a company has (acquired) with the public.

The frequently-used term 'corporate identity' refers to the image a company strives to achieve, in order to build a good reputation with its clients. These concepts developed during or after the Second World War.

Where formerly people spoke of 'invention' and 'creation' for all manner of objects ranging from paintings or sculptures, to buildings or domestic appliances, for the past forty years or so the term 'design' has been used to designate items that would previously have been classified as 'arts and crafts'. These items now form part of the large area covered by the general term 'design'. This refers to industrially produced objects for which the maker has only created instructions concerning the appearance, the actual production being turned over to others in a factory. Thus factory production could be said to have fathered what we now call the designer.

Around 1900 industrially produced art products began to make their appearance and after 1946, in the postwar years in Holland, this production really began to take wing. In those days too the terms corporate identity and image were born, and the designers – as yet largely unspecialized – were roped in to produce a well-defined identity for a company. This work soon became too much for them to handle as one-man companies, and they grouped themselves into design offices. They could thus work not only at an ever faster tempo, but could also deal with the designs of such matters as architectural signposting, exhibitions, or particular promotional or organizational activities. The number of design offices spiralled and they became steadily more multidisciplinary.

In Britain in 1943 the multidisciplinary Design Research Unit was founded, while the first large design offices in the Netherlands were Total Design and Tel Design. Such names as Total Design or 2D3D implied that a range of design work was undertaken. Not only graphic, but also industrial, organizational or marketing aspects of design were considered and implemented at international level. At and even swifter pace the number of advertising and marketing agencies mushroomed, and took over design work, thereby introducing new competition for design offices.

There is a delicate balance between marketing agencies, designers and commissioners, that frequently results in a fair amount of confusion, difficult for the business world to resolve. Also, the benefits these disciplines offer lie in very different areas and are generally used indiscriminately. For the marketing agent, design is the final touch; for the designer, on the other hand, priority goes to the quality of the aesthetic appearance, the image in the broad sense of the word. At the moment we can discern tendencies towards the integration of these vastly differing disciplines that will ensure that both fully retain their own character.

A complex process, a corporate image develops as a matter of course and is determined by the general attitude of the employers and employees in a business. Riccardo Musatti, Olivetti's adviser, once wrote that companies that are most aware of their own responsibilities and goals – resort to a great many means in an endeavour to achieve an ever–clearer expression of their company's identity. However, such attempts were all too often restricted to standardized visual manifestations, eye-catching forms and expressions, aimed at quick, easy and superficial effects as propounded in mass-psychology.

'BUT THE IMAGE OF A COMPANY IS NOT ONLY SHAPED BY THE DESIGN OF ITS PRODUCTS, BY ADVERTISING, INDUSTRIAL RELATIONS AND WHAT IS SOMEWHAT ABSTRACTLY TERMED "PUBLIC RELATIONS". THE IMAGE SHOULD NOT BE A DISTORTING MIRROR, NOR A SYMBOL OF WELCOME, BUT THE TOTAL EXPRESSION OF A COMPLEX WHOLE. IT SHOULD NOT BE DIRECTED OUTWARDS IN ONLY ONE DIRECTION: IT SHOULD BE UTTERLY CLEAR, COHERENT AND COMPREHENSIBLE – BOTH FOR A CONFUSED AND DISTANT PUBLIC AS FOR THOSE WHOSE LIFE AND WORK IS INTIMATELY CONNECTED WITH THE COMPANY. IN BRIEF: WE BELIEVE IN A HOUSESTYLE THAT IS NOT ONLY VISUALLY AESTHETIC, BUT PRIMARILY SOCIAL AND ETHICAL.' With these words Musatti sketched his ideal, an ideal that is all the more striking today when competition has become more fierce and bitter and the corporate image grows ever more important.

I Behaviour

A general discussion of the term 'corporate identity' implies an investigation into various types of human behaviour that define the image or identity of an individual in relation to his environment. Although this question may appear to be an open door through which we continually come and go each day – after all, everyone has his own style of behaviour, whatever that may be – nevertheless, some of the many answers to this question may help to clarify the concept of corporate identity.

Human behaviour can be seen in terms of the group, the institution or the company – that is, in terms of a collection of people who represent certain intellectual, idealistic or economic interests. However, a company can also be seen as an individual, a personality having both weak and strong points. A museum director once defended his position with the words, 'AFTER ALL, A MUSEUM IS ONLY HUMAN', alluding to the fact that his museum wanted to distinguish itself from other museums. Every individual projects an image, either abstract or concrete, both visible and invisible, and together this produces a certain 'style'. The root of this word 'style' is the Latin 'stilus', a writing instrument, hence the word came to indicate the way in which someone wrote. In the same manner we could use the word 'signature'. And as we can recognize the way that a friend writes, so we also term his use of words and way of constructing sentences, his 'style'. This style is individual, and an expert can recognize, for example, a painting – or even a detail – as being by a certain artist. Consciously or unconsciously, visibly or invisibly, one person differs from the next, despite ideologies that propagate the contrary.

The different species of flora and fauna have their individual characteristics (internal and external) that distinguish them from each other and enable them to survive within a complex whole. The species 'man' has two tasks: he has to survive as an individual within a group and he must also support the group to which he belongs, and protect it against other groups. In his book THE NAKED APE, Desmond Morris describes the aggressive behaviour that the human animal exhibits to establish his position in the social hierarchy (this is me and which of us is the stronger); to establish territorial rights within the group (this is my house) or of the group as opposed to other groups (this is our land). Personal (family) territory should be distinguished from that of others – it is an individual spot with individual characteristics. This has become virtually impossible with high-rise flats but here too we find interiors vary, albeit usually within accepted norms. For the behaviour of the individual is dictated by the group norms (for us often prescribed by the market) even when maintaining or improving a position within the social hierarchy. Any deviation, any rebellion, is immediately viewed with grave suspicion, debated and if necessary punished.

There are written and unwritten laws aimed to preserve the status quo within a group and make life as bearable as possible, to survive or to maintain control and possibly to increase it. Although our society has become extremely complicated, although the population of our cities exceeds many millionst, we still live in tiny tribes. And in these our behaviour, be it that of the individual or of the group, is scarcely different from that of our earliest ancestors, even though the rules are continually adapted to new situations, as where urban living space is steadily decreasing.

What is true for the individual is equally valid for groups of people with mutual interests. One group has more power than the next, power, that is, in the sense of potential as well as prosperity, wealth and economic means. Groups that form a threat are attacked and wiped out. Power requires a unifying style, a code of conduct and appearance; what in religions is

expressed through ritual and the objects and gestures with which the ritual is celebrated. In political power groups it is the military (the coloured plumes and peacock screech) that is called in to quell any opposition. Here too we find the ritual of the military march, the procession, the protocol, the uniform (with decorations) – all these are manifestations of power. Elias Canetti, in his book CROWDS AND POWER, shows how particular patterns of behaviour are linked with the culture of a particular country. Thus he describes the culture of a country in terms of 'national crowd symbols': for Germany, he says, the crowd symbol was the marching forest; for Britain it is the sea, which, says Canetti 'IS THERE TO BE RULED'; the Dutch, also a seafaring nation, have as their crowd symbol the dyke. These hackneyed symbols belong to the crowd and still hold true. They are the abstract flags, the recognizable and predictable, the reliable signs, that with the passage of time have become permanent symbols.

The culture of a group, be it large or small, is maintained and nurtured because that is precisely what determines the identity of the group. At the same time, a culture can be manipulated by the media. Trend-setting cult papers like ROLLING STONE or INTERVIEW may dictate or promulgate a certain life style, which they create and nourish.

The behaviour of individuals or of crowds – which includes nations – that wish to be noticed or seek territorial expansion is connected with the urge to survive and thereby with the fear of death. Territorial expansion may no longer literally play so great a part, but in the ideological realm and, at the moment, this means production. In the epilogue of his book, Canetti writes: 'IF THERE IS NOW ONE FAITH, IT IS FAITH IN PRODUCTION, THE MODERN FRENZY OF INCREASE; AND ALL THE PEOPLES OF THE WORLD ARE SUCCUMBING TO IT ONE AFTER THE OTHER. ONE OF THE CONSEQUENCES OF THIS INCREASE IN PRODUCTION IS THAT MORE AND MORE PEOPLE ARE WANTED. THE MORE GOODS WE PRODUCE, THE MORE CONSUMERS WE NEED. THE POINT OF BUSINESS IS THE WINNING OF AS MANY CUSTOMERS AS POSSIBLE; AND IDEALLY EVERYONE. IN THIS RESPECT IT RESEMBLES, IF ONLY SUPERFICIALLY, THOSE UNIVERSAL RELIGIONS WHICH LAY CLAIM TO EVERY SINGLE SOUL. IT LOOKS FORWARD TO AN EQUALITY OF WILLING AND SOLVENT BUYERS. BUT EVEN THAT WOULD NOT REALLY BE ENOUGH, FOR ALL POTENTIAL CUSTOMERS MIGHT HAVE BEEN INDUCED TO BUY AND STILL PRODUCTION WOULD SEEK TO INCREASE. THUS WHAT IT REALLY WANTS IS MORE MEN. THROUGH THE MULTIPLICATION OF GOODS IT FINDS ITS WAY BACK TO THE ORIGINAL SENSE OF INCREASE, THE INCREASE OF MAN HIMSELF...'

Confronted by the picture Canetti offers of a de-railed world we can only hope that economic growth, so sacred today, will come to feel as menacing as the present arms pile-up and will be halted in time. It now looks as if the first brake will be supplied by environmental considerations, and possibly contribute to restoring the equilibrium.

The concept of a corporate image has a lot to do with this picture. After all, it is concerned with the image that clients and consumers have of the company, and which keeps employees loyal to a firm –both are vital for a company to flourish in the

de olympiade onder dictatuur
tentoonstelling:
sport, kunst, wetenschap, documenten

amsterdam
augustus
1936
gebouw
de geelvinck
singel 530

de olympiade onder dictatuur

marketplace and develop confidently. Such an image may be compared with that of an ideology or a religion, with Christianity, Islam, Marxism or National Socialism, all of which have acquired huge followings. Such businesses have their manuals: the Bible, the Koran, Mao's Red Book. Some companies may be found to have a strongly idealistic culture. In Japan, for example, a factory worker becomes part of the factory family, and behaves as such. Were he to go and work somewhere else, he would be deserting his family and seen as a dissident. He would become a deserter and traitor.

Such family ties are also to be found in Western companies, though they are usually less pronounced. Formerly, the director of a (small) company would be the first on the site, ready to greet his employees and wish them a pleasant day. One fairly exceptional example today is the McDonald company, with its Hamburger University where the company religion is preached to present and future employees. Once initiated, they belong to the Hamburger Community and will have a hard time switching over to the Chicken University. Aldous Huxley's book, BRAVE NEW WORLD, written in the 1930s, offers a daunting description of a world dominated by an all-encompassing corporate identity. Everyone is pre-programmed and grouped into types, easily distinguished by uniform, only at ease with their own sort.

These are the thoughts that arise from pondering on the concept of corporate identity. The examples I have given of crowd cultures and ideologies all propagate the illusion of ultimate salvation, of the promised land, which apparently has sufficient power to rouse millions to action. Although every company would like to see its market share increase, it is unlikely that a manufacturer's corporate identity would be able to make many thousands dependent on it. The consumer is still critical enough to make his own choices, and most average workers in a (Western) company still lay down their tools at five o'clock, promptly forget their work, and enter their own world.

II The image in the arts

Human behaviour is a never-ceasing source of inspiration for representation – be it in music, in literature, or in the visual arts. All these art forms, you might say, deal with the image: how people, how groups, how nations and how businesses think, feel and behave. They show the ordinary, unusual, and sometimes extraordinary events, based on life and death, on the dramatic happening, on good and ill fortune, on human characteristics. They show the image of friend or foe, of the agent or the victim, of the victor or the conquered. They deal with good and evil, with the spiritual and the physical, struggling together in a delicate balance in order to prevent total chaos.

Every culture has its descriptions of this struggle, presented as a warning and a (sometimes amusing) lesson. These stories and pictures are an attempt to grasp the ungraspable, to explain the inexplicable, to create order out of the chaotic complexity of life and history. An image that inspires confidence, through word or picture, produces some order and thereby quietude. In Homer's ILIAD, for example, we find the description of the Trojan War, and historic events are placed in

a certain perspective. In the stories of Odysseus' adventures Homer presents a heroic figure who travels through the world enduring many trials and tribulations until at length he safely reaches home only to find all is not a happy haven. And Dante in his DIVINE COMEDY introduces a multitude of illustrious figures from the shadowy past to show what has become of them and what remains of their earthly reputation now they are in the kingdom of the dead.

It may seem out of place to introduce the work of these famous writers in an introduction to a book on corporate image. In essence, however, this present book deals with the body and the soul of a company, the identity expressing the corporate mentality – elements that in our age are increasingly interpreted in materialistic terms. The allegorical value of classical literature has no contemporary equivalent, but possibly the common denominator is to be found in life itself, that, let us hope, still recognizes the human values that were respected centuries ago, albeit in a different form. Certainly, such concepts as good and evil (adapted and very differently interpreted) do still exist, and life still ends in death.

Nowadays parallels can be drawn with earlier periods in history. At the moment many companies vie with each other to amass art collections or commission artists to decorate build-ings. We see here a continuation of a past tradition practised by the nobility and the wealthy, of collecting items that inter-ested them. Individuals have often made way for committees or groups who delegate the responsibility for composing art collections to experts. The art acquisition policy should harmo-nize with the company's corporate identity. Art work, and par-ticularly the quality component, should reflect the corporate image.

The war lords of Europe competed not only on the battlefield, but also in the artist's studio. This accounts for the superb art collections that we now find in Europe's national museums, in the Prado in Madrid, glory of the Habsburgs, or the Uffizi of the Florentine Medici. Indeed, the image of the city of Florence is dominated by the arts: when in the early 15th century the duke of Milan, backed by a well-equipped army, attempted to extend his territory, the city state of Florence was his formidable opponent, who resisted not only with the sword but also with the spirit. During those years Florence commissioned artists, architects and writers to present an image of their city wholly distinct from that of the savage and uncivilized Milan. Florence was seen as the new Athens, guardian of spiritual values, bastion of the intellect. In the architecture of Filippo Brunel-leschi or the sculpture of Donatello and Nanni di Banco we find the rebirth of classical Greek and Roman art. This was to prove the beginning of the European Renaissance, that later spread northwards. This explicit corporate policy of the city of Flor-ence demonstrated that, for her, spiritual values weighed above material ones. It was a clear statement of corporate culture.

When in contemporary architecture we find examples of classi-cal work, in various forms, this return and reference to styles of long ago is not a response to an enemy threat, but arises rather because this language of shape apparently raises the status of the architect or the commissioner. It is nothing but a formal,

artistic trend, with no deeper significance. It seems to be a reaction to functionalism in architecture, a style that opposed any form of decoration and any reference to earlier periods. Functionalism, which was historically rooted in a period of belt-tightening and after 1946 of rapid building methods (prefab housing), had its own language of shape that dealt purely in the basic geometrical forms. From the 1980s on functionalism was shelved in favour of more decorative architecture. This tendency towards outward decoration, known as postmodernism, is reflected in the current practice of purchasing art works to beautify offices and factory buildings. These trends bear direct reference to the image of a company, to corporate style and corporate culture.

But the manipulation of the corporate image has its backlash too in the form of a negative image with the public. It has led to the image of the clever salesman, never at a loss for words, even though these may not always smack of the truth and nothing but. Although every company eschews the idea of malpractice, it is a daily reality in our complex world, whose very complexity assists its propagation. It is increasingly difficult to distinguish clearly between the reliable and unreliable and it is increasingly easy to bamboozle the public. A company speedily resorts to seeking advice from outside consultants when confronted with large organizational or financial problems; but the satisfactory solutions, presented in swiftly drawn-up reports, are not guaranteed.

Corporate malpractices have produced some scintillating literature. A fine example of the above is sketched in the story by the Flemish writer Willem Elsschot, entitled LIJMEN (literally meaning 'gluing together'). In this story we encounter a certain Mr Boorman, director of a newspaper with the imposing title of GENERAL WORLDNEWS FOR FINANCE, TRADE, INDUSTRY, ART AND SCIENCE – founded in 1846. By means of insinuating talk, this newspaper director persuades people to sign contracts and in this way manages to dispose of ten thousand copies per month of his GENERAL WORLDNEWS. This 32-page paper contains photographs, articles, and stories specially written for its clients – which on closer study appear to be virtually the same. Thus, with quantities of bravado and an overblown image, Boorman contrives to rake in sizeable profits. In his stately home there are many – all empty – rooms, for the editorial board, the administration, the directors and one for financial affairs. The few visitors are above all impressed by the Museum of National and Foreign Products, which contains among other things a marble bust of Leopold II, patron of Trade and Industry. In fact, Boorman is head of a one-man enterprise, but enlists an assistant whom he involves in his conspiracy and instructs in his methods, which are based on certain human characteristics: 'IT IS ALL THE RESULT OF VANITY ... EVERYONE WANTS TO BE NUMBER ONE, OR AT LEAST HAVE THE REPUTATION OF BEING NUMBER ONE. MOST PEOPLE PREFER TO BE A LEADER THAN THAT THEY REALLY WANT TO BE WHO THEY ARE ...'
Elsschot's book is almost a manual on how to acquire the image of overblown vanity.

III The picture, the ornament as image

A corporate image is determined in the first place by its visual characteristics, the logotype, the colours and the lettertype.

By means of this abstract iconography one company distinguishes itself from another, in the same way that throughout history individuals, groups and nations have used visual means to distinguish themselves from others. Such expressions form the basis of archaeological and historical studies. The way in which a shard is decorated can give a fairly precise dating of the pottery and suggest the country and even place of origin. It can also tell us something about cultural history. The development of styles in the art forms of all the major cultures has always been closely connected with the social and political history of that group or nation, and with the position of the ruler and religious leaders.

This applied, roughly speaking, until the mid-19th century when there came a burst of new styles in both art and design, succeeding each other in ever-accelerating tempo and paralleled by a continuous stream of new industrial products. Because there was a shortage of wealthy patrons, artists retired to their attics and worked for themselves, studying the possibilities and lack of constraints that had so far been achieved in the realm of autonomous free art. This opened the doors to new forms in the free arts, which in their turn affected product design, thus drawing the arts and crafts closer together.

We can find examples of distinctive signatures – corporate designs – among autonomous modern artists. Simple symbols (mark) and elements that are connected not so much with the world of art as with that of advertising make the artist or his work and setting instantly recognizable. The work of the French artist Daniel Buren has since 1965 born the personal trademark of a simple theme (supported by an underlying theory): on canvas or printed on paper, he alternates vertical, alternate white and coloured stripes, used in paintings, posters and objects. Any self-respecting modern art museum has at least one of his works in its collection. No-one else could use his design without infringement of copyright.

Far more complex is the work of the famous American artist Andy Warhol. He produced paintings, graphic work, photographs, films and publications, and his 'factory' – it could hardly be called an artist's studio – reflected the glamorous world of advertising in which stars, with Warhol as midwife, were born. Here, with a subtle mixture of irony and seriousness, products were presented, with the vehicles of promotion and publicity – a combination of art and advertising. Today Warhol's work has great market value and is a good investment.

Throughout the long history of visual expression (in lettering/graphics, in decoration, in the arts and architecture) a central concern has been to establish and eternalize the good name, the image, of the patron – be that a lord spiritual or temporal. What is therefore remarkable is that in the development of art and design in the West, the culture of Greece and the once so mighty Roman empire have been a permanent source of inspiration – as the art historian Abby Warburg expressed it, 'DAS NACHLEBEN DER ANTIKE' (the continuation of the classical). We saw this at the beginning of the Italian Renaissance in Florence and see it again in certain buildings of our generation. But it is an inspiration that has been drawn on since the decline of the Roman empire. Early Christian and Byzantine art is based

on classical models. Christ enthroned reminds us strongly of a Roman emperor, the evangelists are reminiscent of the Romans' consuls. Under Charlemagne, whose empire was almost as vast as that of the Romans, and throughout the period that Romanesque architecture flourished, the spirit of the eternal city was never far away. Even the Abbot Suger still used Graeco-Roman elements in the elaborate architecture of St Denis Abbey in Paris (1140), the spiritual heart of France, which first saw the holy light of Gothic.

In the later Renaissance there came a conscious re-creation of the classical world, not only of the outward forms but also – and especially – in the new awareness of man's intellectual and individual potential, an awareness that became increasingly evident with the centuries that followed. The style that appears most advantageous to him is dictated by the lord spiritual or temporal.

The developing stylistic characteristics of 17th and 18th century France we have labelled after the monarch of the day: Louis XIV, Louis XV, Louis XVI, and so on. But whether the work is restrained or excessively baroque, the Graeco-Roman shadow is always there, both before and after the French Revolution. Under Napoleon, in the French empire, classical motifs were combined with shapes such as the Sphinx from ancient Egypt, a country in which the emperor had also been victorious. The clearest example of the ever-present influence of the Roman empire is to be found in our handwritten and printed word. Gothic lettering survived only a brief period although it is still to be found in German-speaking countries, reminiscing on bygone days.

The unceasing presence of the classical may serve as an example of a corporate image still identified with power. It is not surprising that Mussolini and Hitler clad their buildings with a classical – albeit modern and stylized – mantle, which can be seen today in the work of architects such as Bofill.

IV Heraldry

Heraldry is also used to distinguish between individuals, cities, institutions, countries and groups. It is an area, in fact, very close to that of the modern trademark, being purely pictorial. Formerly, the coats of arms on flags, clothing and objects proclaimed the lord and told of his house and lineage. Usually the coat of arms would be accompanied by a short motto, often lauding the virtues of the prince. Such heraldic devices were extremely important in time of war, were it only that they served to distinguish friend from foe. They also became revered, and after battle the banners – often stained and scarred – would be hung reverently in the local church, in remembrance of victory.

The visual heraldic components might be plants – the lily, rose or thistle; creatures – lion or unicorn, eagle, dragon or serpent; or perhaps geometric shapes – square, diamond, cross, stripe. These forms in their turn arose from the culture and history of those they described. The cross, for example, was a symbol of Christianity, while the swastika (borrowed from the culture of China and Japan) originally stood for eternity. The fasces, or bundle of rods, arouses less strong connotations than does the swastika, although our word 'fascism' comes from it. The 'fasces' was borne in ancient times in procession before a Roman

magistrate, as a symbol of his authority and power.

The importance of a lord and his position in the social hierarchy could be read from his heraldic arms. The same was true of a person's clothing, which labelled people until well into the 19th century, so that you knew with whom you were dealing. This was important in many social contexts. Its traces are still to be found in the uniforms of today: in the army, with its ranks and rigid corporate style; in the robes and headgear of the law, the priest and the professor.

Many groups differentiate themselves with their clothing, hairstyles and general outward appearance (think of crowds of football supporters). Among younger people in particular, styles of dress carry instant statements and these differences are gratefully exploited by the rag trade. There are many unofficial uniforms (such as that of the businessman) worn by people to show their religious affiliation, or brass band – all projecting their chosen image, their corporate identity – via their clothing, minimalizing and obscuring individual characteristics. Dress is part of the style, of the ritual that supports the image of institutions, be they church, state or business.

In this context the flag always plays an important part and today we see more and more flags flying, proclaiming the presence of the business they represent. Small businesses in particular, throughout the ages, have developed their 'housestyle' and advertised themselves, often in the form of signs in the street marking their presence. Nowadays we have more sophisticated advertising through window dressing, newspaper announcements and door–to–door pamphlets, but in essence little has changed. Businesses, whatever their size, adorn themselves, dress themselves up to lure the client and show what they have to offer.

V The birth of the company image

A new age began with the French Revolution. In retrospect, this revolution would appear to be closely connected with the beginnings of the Industrial Revolution, which brought change not from the side of the nobles, but of the bourgeoisie. In the period of the Enlightenment, rational thought became the premise of a new age in which the natural sciences and technology laid the foundations of an industrial economy. The industrial revolution began in the second half of the 18th century, with discoveries in physics and chemistry and the development of industrial techniques. In 1770, for example, the first calculator, able to multiply, was produced by Hahn. In the final quarter of the 18th century the composition of certain chemical elements and liquids was discovered: sulphuric acid, hydrochloric acid, chlorine, (the gas) ammonia, and sodium. The year 1785 saw the first Channel crossing in a hot-air balloon, the first steam ship dates from 1787 and in 1797, lithography – which was to prove a major breakthrough for the 19th-century newspaper – was developed by Senefelder. In about 1811 the Krupp factories were set up in Essen.

Throughout the 19th century production techniques were continually improved and there was a constant stream of technological inventions all aimed at improving the speed and efficiency of the production process. These inventions, protected by patents, aimed to increase production and thereby lower the price of articles, thus making them more widely available.

A pillar'd shade
High over-arch'd, and echoing walks between
MILTON

Hand-made work was replaced more and more by machine production, that was soon able to reproduce all the existing and fashionable shapes. Elkington's discovery of electrolysis in 1840 meant that objects could be cast in an inexpensive metal and then coated with a layer of silver and this was the beginning of the mass production of goods that looked attractive and expensive, resembled hand-made articles, but clearly were not the same quality as the work of a silversmith. Now middle-class folk could vie with the wealthier members of society and exclaim with amazement about all that modern machines could perform and admire the ingenuity of new technological know-how. At last people could acquire a product in the shape they wanted. It was the triumph of bourgeois liberalism over the feudal past – though it should be added that the first motor car looked suspiciously like its forefather the horse-drawn carriage: a total break with the past was too painful.

The first World Exhibition, held in London in 1851, demonstrated all these modern wonders in its pompous and almost surrealistic exhibition spaces of which the Crystal Palace was the most arresting. All these economic and industrial developments found reactions in for example the writing of (romantic) idealists like the philosopher Thomas Carlyle, whose 'superman morality and mystical hero-worship' have been compared by the art-sociologist Arnold Hauser with the ideas of Hitler. Such writers were opposed to what they saw as the belittling of people, to people being seen as merely 'homo economicus'. In Britain, birthplace of the Industrial Revolution, a social crisis developed after 1832, in which the idealists held fast their romantic and idealized conceptions of history. They rigidly opposed change and new ideas. This attitude was presented more positively by William Morris in the Arts and Crafts Movement, an amalgam of the Middle Ages and Utopia, which foreswore the industrial product and hallowed the hand-made.

It is understandable that these idealists rejected the style of the Enlightenment that was based on rational, industrial thought. They were fervent supporters of Gothic architecture and pre-Raphaelite painting and most admired the period before the European Renaissance. As they saw it, art and design were not private, but rather public matters, in which the state should be closely involved. The artist needed to re-create his position in the society which it was his task primarily to serve. This was the beginning of what we have seen grow in our time into an accepted aspect of society in many countries: art in the city, art in public buildings, art in the factory. What the artists made, for example in the case of Amsterdam's stock exchange building, Berlage's Beurs, was something that emphasized the function of the building and also educated public taste. With the passage of time it became a type of status symbol and thus a component of corporate identity.

The theories of William Morris – the idea of art as a public matter, says Hauser, were primarily intended to propagate his socialist ideas; he was not particularly interested in the production of good art. But in Morris' own work and writings he appears to seek to combine a number of ideals. In his **A FACTORY AS IT MIGHT BE** (1884) he describes the ideal of a factory set in beautiful parkland (the owner's property) where

the worker labours with delight for a few hours each day: 'WELL, IT FOLLOWS IN THIS GARDEN BUSINESS THAT OUR FACTORY MUST MAKE NO SORDID LITTER, BEFOUL NO WATER, NOR POISON THE AIR WITH SMOKE ... NEXT, AS TO THE BUILDINGS THEMSELVES ... THERE WOULD BE NO SERIOUS DIFFICULTY IN MAKING THEM BEAUTIFUL ... SO IT IS NOT DIFFICULT TO THINK OF OUR FACTORY BUILDINGS, SHOWING ON THEIR OUTSIDES WHAT THEY ARE FOR, REASONABLE AND LIGHT WORK, CHEERED AT EVERY STEP BY HOPE AND PLEASURE ... IT WILL NEED A DINING-HALL, LIBRARY, SCHOOL, PLACES FOR STUDY OF VARIOUS KINDS, AND OTHER SUCH STRUCTURES ...' ON ALL SIDES WE SEE WRETCHEDLY UGLY FACTORY BUILDINGS, AND 'THIS UGLINESS IS ... A PART OF THE BESTIAL WASTE OF THE WHOLE SYSTEM OF PROFIT-MONGERING, WHICH REFUSES CULTIVATION AND REFINEMENT TO THE WORKERS AND, THEREFORE, CAN HAVE NO ART, NOT EVEN FOR ALL ITS MONEY ...' Beside the educational and medical facilities, the ideal factory also has the means to present musical and dramatic productions and – a new idea in those days, Morris claimed – the workers would have the opportunity to develop their appreciation of beauty so that they would be encouraged in the creative talents which they undoubtedly possessed. The most important thing, when all was said and done, was artistic creation, 'THE SATISFACTION OF WHICH IS OF ALL PLEASURE THE GREATEST'.

Even in Morris's day such ideas were naive; but in a completely different manner, and certainly with an eye to the interest of the factory itself, several of his suggestions have been incorporated, both then and now, into company life. Very likely influenced by Morris, the Lever brothers built their factory set in a parkland and with the buildings shaped in a circle. At the centre was the factory, surrounded by the homes of the personnel.

The sunlight and the fresh air were to provide a healthy work climate which would have a beneficial effect on the general atmosphere and thus on production. We still have this product – Sunlight soap, the reminder of an idyllic factory site.

There were comparable experiments in living, in other countries –for example the Dutch city of Delft, where in about 1900 houses were built for the workers near the Gist and Spiritus factory. In our time we see canteens, sport facilities and opportunities for further education, all provided in factories as a result of laws and regulations, no longer rooted in ideal notions. At the moment artistic creation seems to be the prerogative of the product designers; by the by, it is often as ugly as the mass-produced articles of Victorian England.

It should be said that Morris did not totally despise the machine, but felt it should be the servant of the worker, and should lighten his labours. It should not be thought of as a means to greater production, but as a helpmeet for the worker, who would thereby have more time for real craftsmanship.

The ideas of the Arts and Crafts Movement, of William Morris and Walter Crane, had a wide influence, but despite fears that handwork and craft skills would disappear, most architects and designers tended to choose in the end good use of the machine as an aid in the production of an artist-designed object. Architect and artist Henry van de Velde, one-time director of the Kunstgewerbeschule (College of Art) in Weimar, a precursor of

the Bauhaus movement, in 1908 spoke out in favour of
machine production of objects that formerly would have been
hand-made by craftsman. He was, incidentally, one of the first
architects to work with pre-cast concrete units.
Times changed and brought with them the rejection of the 'neo'
styles (neoclassical, neo-Gothic, neo-Renaissance). A great
need was felt for a contemporary style, and that generally
meant one that was connected with an individual artist.
Despite great outward disparity there was nevertheless
something in the world of art and design that could be seen as
a common style - hence the expressions 'Art Nouveau' and
'Jugendstil'. What is noticeable is that this style makes particular use of natural shapes (especially plants) and not of
machine forms. From this we could deduce the dialectic that
was to continue for many years, between matter and spirit,
between art and technique. But at that stage the machine was
still largely seen as a threat which explains why the advertisements of that period rarely show part of the production process. The product is enveloped in beautiful wrappings or subtly
recommended by seductive ladies, in the same manner as
today. Much can be said about style in advertising, as it bears
on the image of a company. What this boils down to is the
developments that took place qua content and form in the
history of the poster and the media.

VI The image of the Machine Age

The fin-de-siècle mood continued until the outbreak of the
First World War. Although there were some remarkable movements in early 20th-century art, such as cubism and expres-
sionism, they were largely restricted to the visual arts. Futurism
also had its beginnings before 1914 and within this movement
the machine – for many reasons, including aggressive ones –
had its place. In Russia, constructivism arose during and after
the Russian Revolution, and, like contemporary movements
such as De Stijl in Holland and Bauhaus in Germany, it saw the
machine and industrial processes as ways of lightening the
burden of the working man.
Artists connected with these movements designed products
that made specific use of industrial materials such as chrome
steel, or similar metals. There was a search for the elementary
and above all functional, in which the decorative, so beloved of
the 19th century and Art Nouveau, no longer had any place.
The ideas about art and design were intimately linked with
society and with creating a new and better world. This explains
why architects and artists who held such ideas were given
commissions by the business world.
In Holland a factory was built in Rotterdam (1926-1930) for the
Van Nelle firm. It was designed by Brinkman and Van der Vlugt
and is one of the best-known examples of this new functionalism and socially-orientated architecture. The company, import-
ers of tea, coffee and tobacco, also spent considerable
thought in the 1920s on the packaging of their goods and on
advertising. Jac Jongert, who worked as designer for Van
Nelle, said in 1923 that the 'INDUSTRIALIST MUST ACQUIRE
CONFIDENCE IN THE ARTIST, BUT THE ARTIST MUST REALIZE
THAT MANY OF THE DEMANDS MADE ON INDUSTRY BY DAILY
LIFE, ARE QUITE REASONABLE'. In these words Jongert tried to
unite his ideals with the everyday reality of industry. The fusion
of ideal and reality.

4 aders worden tot een kabel geslagen.

1 2 3 4

de papierkabel op de trekschijf.

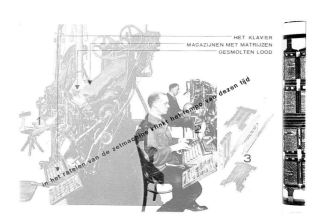

We could mention many companies that during those years spent time on producing a modern image. Designers and artists made this easier by uniting and jointly exerting their influence over the business world. These progressive designers' graphic press, which Herbert Spencer called 'Pioneers of modern typography', were particularly – and internationally – active during the 1920s. It was through them that the Dutch 'typotekt' Piet Zwart (1885-1977) gained international fame with his functional typography. He wrote of this in the 1920s: 'THE TASK OF FUNCTIONAL TYPOGRAPHY IS TO CREATE THE TYPOGRAPHICALLY DEFINED IMAGE OF OUR TIME, AS FAR AS IS POSSIBLE AND DESIRABLE, UNTRAMMELLED BY TRADITION. IT SHOULD TRANSLATE THE IMAGE OF OUR AGE INTO A TYPOGRAPHICAL IDIOM; IT SHOULD DEVELOP CLEAR, ORDERLY MEANS OF EXPRESSION; IT SHOULD DETERMINE THE SHAPE OF NEW TYPOGRAPHICAL WORK ...' And elsewhere he writes: 'TYPOGRAPHY HAS ALWAYS DEFINED THE IMAGE OF A PERIOD. IS THERE NOT LURKING AMONG THE FEW WHOM I HAVE INDICATED A REBEL, WHO WILL HELP DETERMINE THE COLLECTIVE EXPRESSION OF TOMORROW? THINK ABOUT THIS QUESTION, AND REALIZE THAT A BEAUTIFUL CREATION MADE FOR AESTHETIC REASONS WILL HAVE NO SOCIAL SIGNIFICANCE TOMORROW; IT WILL SEEM A FUTILE SELF-GRATIFICATION ...'

The major exhibition Trends of the 1920s, held in Berlin in 1977, provided an almost complete retrospective of international art and design from that period, in which the constructive went hand in hand with the destructive and pessimistic, as in the Dada movement. This exhibition also showed the cooperation between designers and industry in the field of industrial and graphic design. In Germany the Bauhaus was the first to marry art and industry but this forward-looking institute was banned by Hitler in 1933.
During the 1930s, the severe, functional design that hallmarked both architecture and mass-produced goods became more florid and aesthetic. The stark, functionalist creations formed a firm foil to the movement that reintroduced individualism and decoration in art, even bursting occasionally into baroque shapes, comparable with what is taking place today. Perhaps such innovations were also a result of the fading ideals of a better world, for the impending catastrophe seemed ever more imminent. And having survived the catastrophe of the Second World War, it was not until the end of the 1950s that a new design movement arose that embraced the two distinct factions of the constructive and the decorative formed in the 1920s and 30s. A change in this situation came in the 1960s, which finally resulted in three main channels: stern, functional design; a freer movement, sometimes with provocative use of typography and the pictorial; and third, as reaction, the 'pure typography' that seemed to reinstate the letter in its unadulterated form.
Although we have seen many variations on these three themes over the past decade, on the whole graphic design shows a levelling tendency. Nothing looks new. Despite desperate attempts by designers to be original, there is little really revolutionary design work being produced at present. It is as if everything has been done before, as if there is nothing else to discover. This is why well-known schools of graphic design are

being re-examined and re-interpreted. The same is true in art and architecture. The last quarter of the 19th century is being repeated – which suggests there is indeed hope of innovation from an unsuspected quarter.

The term 'corporate identity' was first used in the period of reconstruction that followed the Second World War, and became increasingly popular as companies expanded. The term evolved during the first half of this century, though the germ may be found in the 19th century. In about 1850 several British railway companies, spurred on by keen competition, sought uniformity and identity, not only in the architecture of the railway stations but also in the interior furnishings of the trains and in certain graphic manifestations. Like the airline companies, who vied tooth and claw from 1950 on, the railways, both in Europe and America, tried to make travel enjoyable. The traveller entering a railway station should feel as if he were entering a royal palace.

The earliest example in the 20th century of a company commissioning a single designer to compile a cohesive design was the AEG. In 1907 they asked Peter Behrens to develop a well-designed corporate identity for them that would be recognized in their buildings, products and advertising. What is extraordinary is that this was not immediately taken up by other firms; presumably its significance was not yet appreciated. Although the logo of AEG has been adjusted over the years, this symbol is still valid, as is the trademark of Philips that has remained unaltered from the company's earliest days.

The same goes for the box of matches so familiar in Holland, with the flying swallow symbol, that still shows in the trademark the medals it has won in design competitions. It looks like a 19th-century design, but in fact dates from 1922.

This loyalty to a particular logo is very strong, although many companies are happy to re-vamp their identity and so demonstrate how progressive they are. The question is, whether or not this is always advantageous – and there is no hard and fast answer. The famous alphabet designed by Edward Johnston in the 1920s for London Transport is as clear and effective as it was seventy years ago. A logo, or trademark, is a relatively small but very important component of corporate identity and it is interesting to consider the marks that have preserved their power from the past. In his book, LA LINGUISTIQUE STURCTURALE (Paris, 1968) Lepschy demonstrated that the words most frequently used are those which are short, old, and have the simplest form as well as an elasticity of meaning – that is, not only one limited interpretation. The same can probably be said of a logo: powerful, striking, symbolic, almost a cliché, somewhat like the heraldic devices of the Middle Ages.

One of the oldest examples of 'curly' handwritten lettering is the Coca-Cola logo from 1887. It has only been slightly modified over the years, for example by adding the flourish under the words, literally and figuratively emphasizing the name. This undulating line has been likened to the ribbon in the beak of the eagle on the great seal of the USA.

Some cars have trademarks that have not changed since they were first produced, such as Ford or MG while others have marks that have only slightly been altered, such as Renault and Citroën.

AEG AEG

There are symbols and initials that have long since lost their original meaning. An example is the Dutch PTT, which stands for Post, Telegraph and Telephone although in 1990 it consists of two and not three companies – Post and Telecom. And the Dutch ANWB, which stands for General Dutch Cyclists Association, is now almost totally composed of car-owners and has abandoned its bicycles.

The keen competition between airline companies that was mentioned above led in about 1950 to their developing the first corporate identities, which penetrated every level of the company. The identities of the airlines KLM and BEA were both developed by the British designer Henrion (see elsewhere in this book). Henrion produced a clear and consistent image, although adjustments –some slight, some far-reaching – have been made over the years. These modifications relate to developments in art and design (which, especially in the 1960s and 70s, were affected by social upheavals) and to trends in marketing and advertising. In order to maintain a strong market position constant adjustment and updating has been necessary, as it will be in the future. This leads to a demand for superficial snappiness, something diametrically opposed to the idea of corporate identity.
It is to resolve such contradictions that we need more information on the subject of corporate identity, although it would be impossible to write a recipe book on this subject because this would restrict the growth and change element so essential for a company. The so-called production style concentrates on fast change and a consumer society. The other approach to corporate identity is connected with durability, and a clear, informative attitude to the public and particularly with creating a familiar face. That face, however, must not be dogmatic, but flexible, with features that all add up to a cohesive whole.

The fact that this book is appearing now, in 1990, illustrates how corporate identity has lost nothing of its immediacy – indeed, it has gained in interest. Certainly, as far as we can ascertain, it is an invaluable tool in company life.
We are greatly influenced by the media and, in every publication dealing with advertising, marketing, graphic design, architecture and suchlike, we come across vividly illustrated examples of corporate identity. We apprehend our world visually and the myriad inputs received each minute on our retinas may numb our response. We are forced to select if we are not to be overwhelmed by what we see and hear.
The art of a company is to penetrate that selection barrier with its corporate image, even if it only succeeds with a small percentage of the public. This book offers many examples of the strict discipline required of a company to implement its identity. There will be constant problems in balancing strict adherence to the corporate identity programme with the inevitable desire for freedom among employees involved with the company image. It is not too difficult to draw up firm rules and take stern measures against their infringement. The question is, whether such strictness creates a good working atmosphere in a company. Furthermore, a company with a more tolerant outlook will certainly be more able to put things into perspective. Within the context of design they will be able to come up

with unexpected products, striking company publications, or annual reports of exceptional design, or unusual gifts for clients. It is a matter of striking a balance between the cliché and the demands of the marketplace, and on the other hand of achieving something exceptional that is a ladder to other worlds beyond that of marketing – the worlds of art, design or literature.

As for designing a corporate identity, we can 'manipulate' the permanent image and the free variations on it by means of design management. Within the corporate identity programme we can itemize which visual expressions of a company should be uniform (permanently or for a limited period) and which may be freely interpreted by the designer.
Thus the image of a company is seen as representing a complex challenge, never to be perfectly realized.
Bad examples of a corporate image serve to enliven the debate about which methods and principles are best adopted in compiling a new corporate identity. It has become clear from the history of the corporate image that the three essential elements are design, organization and behaviour, which includes responsibility. These are things that through the years continually shift in meaning and implication.

Paul Hefting

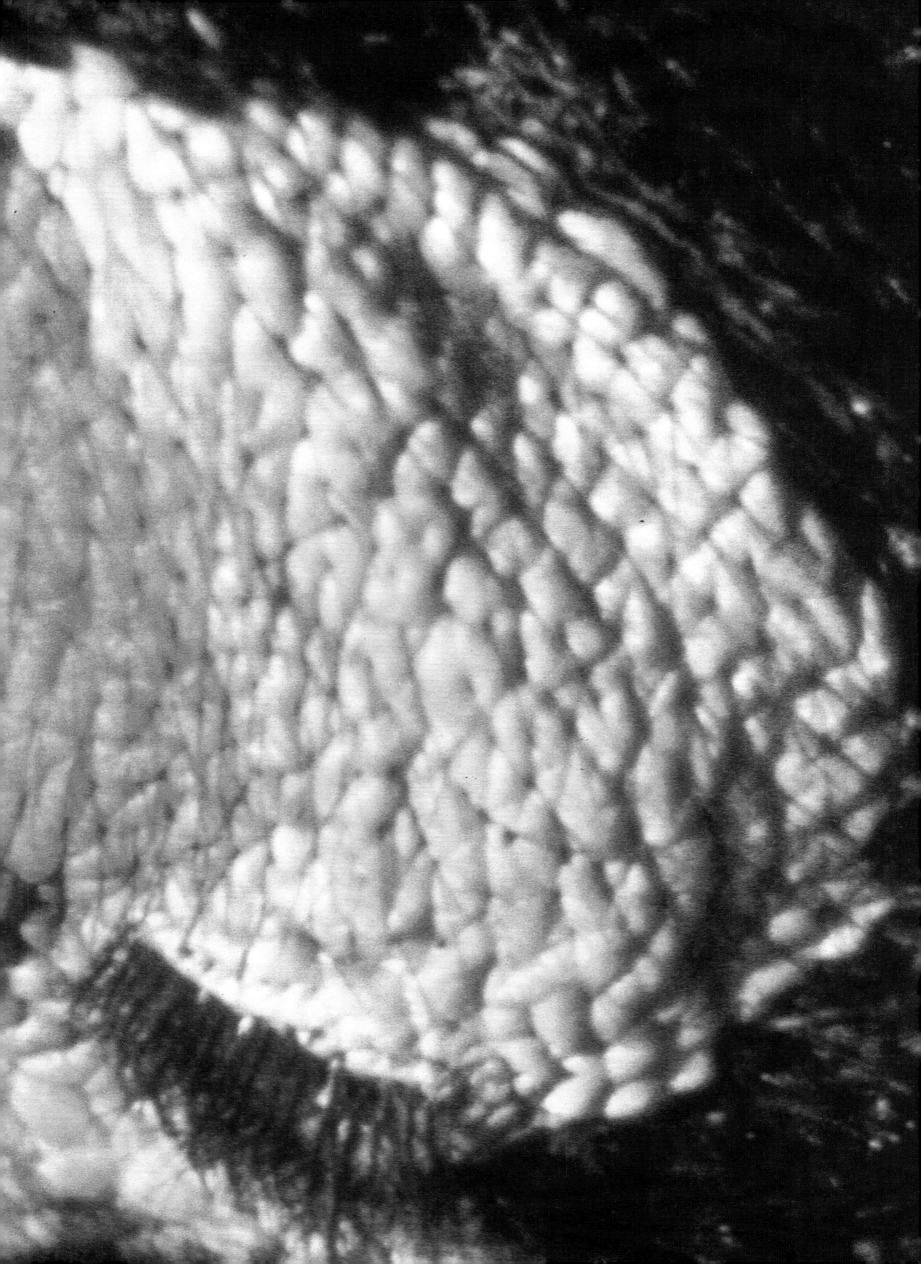

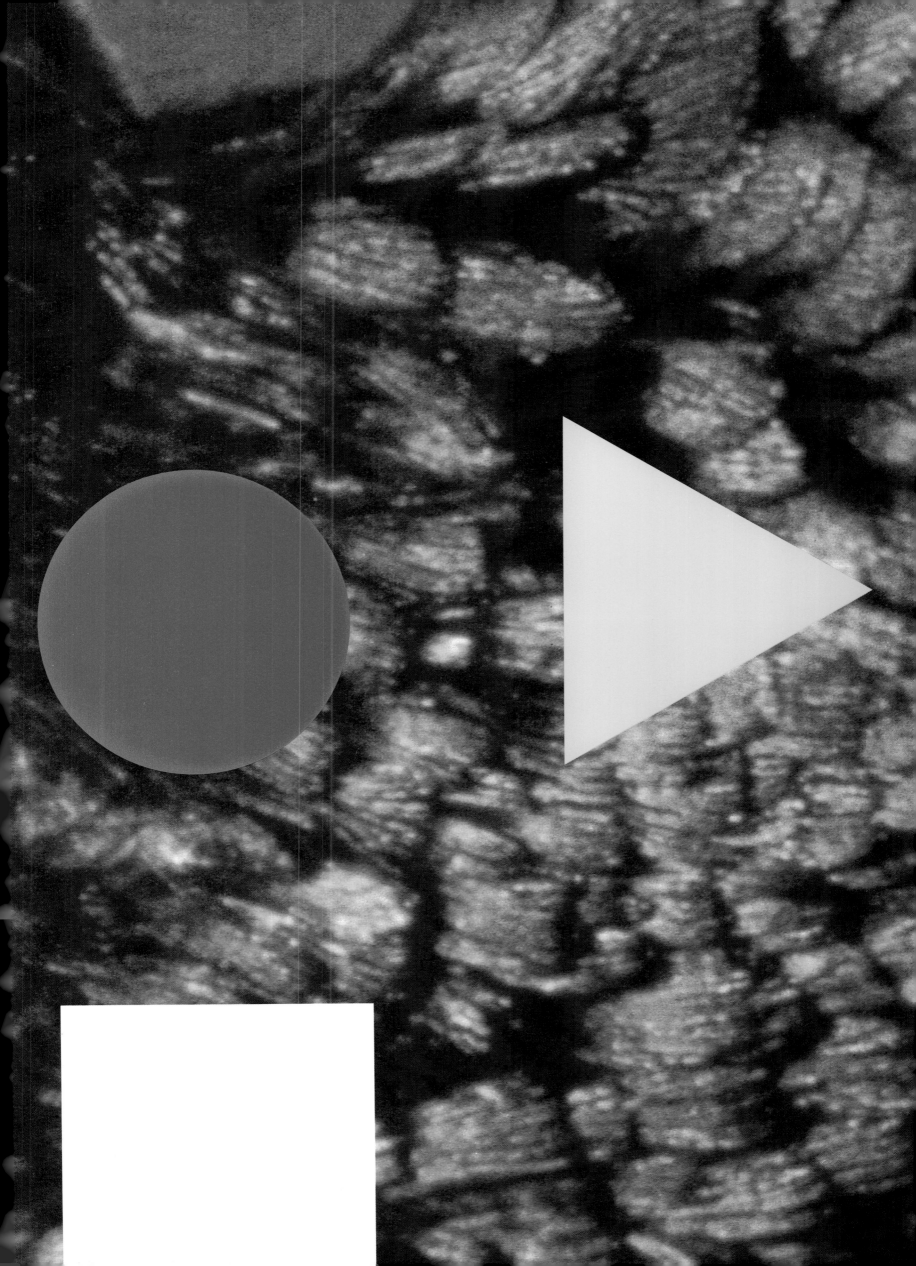

The image of a company

In the early 1950s, my office had many clients and design areas: symbols and logotypes, publications and printing, art direction and typography, exhibitions and displays, plus product design and packaging. In fact the office worked on any conceivable design assignment.

At this point I discussed with my associates whether it would not be of greater interest and challenge to work for fewer clients but be responsible for all their activities in a visual sense. The aim would be to achieve a cohesive appearance of a corporation by coordinating all its visuals along the lines pioneered by AEG and Olivetti. These two companies had embarked on such an all-encompassing design policy even before the First World War, with the result that their products, their advertising and promotions, the design of their factories and administrative buildings, as well as their showrooms, were each exemplary in their field, yet visibly unified – not superficially from without, but originating from a well-thought-out, long-term policy from within.

This policy was based on an underlying corporate philosophy initiated by architect/designer Peter Behrens (1860–1940) and Adriano Olivetti (1901–1960), who founded the social movement **MOVIMENTO COMMUNITÁ** in 1948. Manufacturers and industrialists should not only be concerned with increasing turnover and profit, but also be aware of a social responsibility to employees, customers and society at large. The impact of the application of such a philosophy was felt after the war and quite a few of my colleagues and myself felt highly inspired by this phenomenon.

Back in our studios we felt and hoped that if some of our clients could be convinced about embracing such corporate design policies, their contribution would go well beyond making profits, by adding to the quality of life and by improving – if only in a more orderly sense – the environment. We were extremely lucky in finding and convincing some of our clients that such a policy was worth pursuing.

The first international company was KLM in 1955, obviously a big assignment, complex and wide-spread internationally, requiring an enormous range of design items, including planes, ground transport, timetables, advertising, displays, on-board equipment, signs and insignia, to mention a few. We called it the KLM Housestyle as the term Corporate Identity was unknown at that time – at least in Europe. I still like this description today, as it says what it means and is easily understood.

In 1968 when Alan Parkin, one of my associates, and I wrote what is probably the first book on the subject, we called it **'DESIGN COORDINATION'**, this being the essence of a housestyle. Yet the American publisher insisted that the words 'and Corporate Identity' should be added, as by then this was how it was identified in the USA.

Recently the design office which I started 40 years ago – via Henrion Design Associates, HDA International and now Henrion Ludlow and Schmidt – organized a design forum on, amongst other aspects, the definition of Corporate Identity. Here are some quotes from different experts:

'CORPORATE IDENTITY IS A VEHICLE THAT PROJECTS AN ORGANIZATION COHERENTLY AND COHESIVELY . . . UNAMBIGUOUS VISUAL COMMUNICATION.'

'CI IS A REFLECTION OF EVERYTHING THAT IT SAYS AND DOES, WHAT IT IS AND WHAT IT DOES.'

'CI IS THE EMOTIONAL GLUE WHICH HOLDS A COMPANY TOGETHER . . . IT IS A MIX OF STYLE AND STRUCTURE. IT AFFECTS WHAT YOU DO, WHERE YOU DO IT AND HOW YOU EXPLAIN WHAT YOU DO.' 'EVERYTHING A COMPANY HAS, MAKES, DOES AND SAYS IS AN EXPRESSION OF CI.'

"CI IS NOT LOGOS AND SYMBOLS. THIS IS AN OVERSTATEMENT OF THE ROLE OF DESIGN. THEY ARE ONLY VISUAL ELASTOPLASTS.'

There is a noticeable and sharp distinction between those who refer to the visual and those who stress the cultural, strategic and organizational aspects, often excluding reference to visual end results entirely. Going back to terms, another area of confusion is that which surrounds the words 'design', 'identity', 'image', 'strategy' and 'communications', which are used indiscriminately to describe anything vaguely to do with outward appearances.

Today, based on long experience – which after all is only the sum of one's mistakes from which one has learned – we have refined our definitions to help us understand better the problems and situations we encounter, and also to communicate more clearly to our clients.

Corporate Design CD) consists solely of the *visual* communication of an organization – from logotype and typographic style to sign systems and environmental design. Corporate Identity (CI) or corporate image, on the other hand, includes both visual manifestations and non-visual expressions – ways of behaviour in relation to social, business and political matters, which can be shown, for example, in the behaviour of staff, in a style of writing in publications or in the way in which suppliers are treated. Corporate strategy is the policy of deploying a corporate image in terms of employee and customer relations, of PR, promotion, product development, packaging publications and, of course, marketing. Corporate Communications (CC) are the means of conveying this strategy to the respective target groups. Corporate identity, corporate strategy and corporate communications are interdependent: each influences the other.
After the war, the USA and UK multinationals – now called transnationals – like IBM, Ford, General Motors and Westinghouse, along with many leading banks, oil companies and

airlines, all primarily national organizations, also felt the need to embark on CC programmes.
This new field became an important concern of top management. Most, if not all, of the corporations mentioned have a vice-president in charge of CC. In the UK there was a similar development, again with the multinationals in the lead.

On the one hand, as a result of the Second World War, multinationals in Continental Europe were slower off the mark than Anglo-Saxon countries to realize the importance of CC as a management tool. It could be said that in Continental Europe CD is better understood than CI and CC. In the Anglo-Saxon countries the communication and marketing strategies which differentiate CD from CC and CI are better understood and therefore better developed. Seen from London, with equal interest across the Atlantic towards the US and across the Channel towards the rest of Europe, we have perhaps a clearer understanding of the need of CI and CC to control CD. Aesthetic design exercises are no longer enough. In fact, unless there is a clear CC strategy, CD can become a beautiful failure. To sit on our island sometimes helps to combine the right elements of USA know-how with European requirements.

Problem situations, however, have much in common. To illustrate this I am listing twelve situations which might confront a corporation. Each of these is a clear indication of the need to call in outside expertise in the areas of CD, CI and CC.

Situations in which Corporate Communication can become an urgent problem

1 A new corporation comes into being. Only in exceptional situations does this happen; even when it does, corporate planning, CI and CC are influenced by pre-existing parameters, namely by pre-existing manifestations of the competitors in the field.

2 A corporation has merged with another, or others, or is taken over by another, or takes over other companies. This creates the situation where a number of existing images come together, each with recognition value or a goodwill of their own, yet with different histories. They have to be integrated into an existing image, or, alternatively, a new image has to be found which clearly represents the new situation after the merger or takeover.

3 A corporation diversifies its product range. This makes it necessary to adjust the old image to represent the new situation or to create a new image more appropriate to current policies and activities.

4 A corporation has a growing awareness that its existing housestyle is no longer relevant to a company which is developing, modernizing and updating itself. This malaise becomes more acute when competitors have just undergone a visible and impressive rejuvenation of their image.

5 A corporation offers almost indistinguishable services and products at almost identical prices to those offered by competing companies. This is particularly relevant for airlines, petrol companies, banks and insurance companies.
Most airlines offer travel in identical planes, in identical conditions to identical destinations at usually identical prices. Likewise, the services, products, conditions and prices of petrol companies, insurance companies and banks are almost identical. The only differentiating factor is the CI of each company.
It is not unusual for airlines to change and update their CI every 10–12 years, suggesting change and progress by a new housestyle rather than by changing their fleet of planes.

6 A corporation's products are known worldwide but the holding company is practically unknown. In this situation it can become important that the corporation is clearly visible behind the products.

7 A corporation has a new chairman or managing director who starts a new regime with new concepts and strategies and wishes to manifest these changes. CI assignments can often be carried out more efficiently and economically in such circumstances as less time is usually lost over decision-making.

8 A corporation is identified with too many elements which fragment what should be a bold and integrated impact. In such cases, word reference must usually take precedence over the visual.

9 A corporation calls in management consultants to advise on reorganization. It is symptomatic that in the case of at least five of our major clients we were consulted after a firm of management consultants had been called in to give advice on reorganization and to investigate how historic evolution and present requirements could be reconciled.
In most instances, it resulted in a new concept of corporate organization, strategies and communications, all projected in a new corporate identity.

10 The subsidiaries of a holding corporation are well known, but not the holding corporation itself. If the corporation's objectives include that the holding company should be recognized, then a strong corporate identity would solve this problem.

11 A holding company has an identity which is so powerful and therefore restrictive that the individual subsidiaries are unable to develop an identity of their own which they need to satisfy specific market conditions.

12 A corporation has many subdivisions which need to be individually identified – yet each must be seen to belong to the others. The part and the whole must be seen in their interrelationship, each for its relative importance.

These twelve situations could, of course, overlap in any one case – or a corporation could have one, two, three or more of the problems simultaneously and to different degrees. For corporation you could read government department, institution, hospital, ministry, town or city.

But, once the problem is recognized (or *a* problem is recognized, there may be others) the need is to decide how to tackle the problem – whether to call in outside help or when to use in-house resources.

Generally speaking, an outside consultant is in a better position to identify problem areas and to formulate a plan or proposal to tackle the problems. The consultant has the important asset of being able to put himself/herself in the position of the customer or the man in the street. A corporation's image is often assessed according to internal values, by senior management with unique special knowledge of, and loyalty to, the history of the corporation. The public often welcomes a change which shocks the board of directors. It is the outside consultant's job to represent the public viewpoint to management. Another advantage of the consultant outside the normal hierarchy of the corporation is that he/she is able to discuss and recommend at top levels.

The best consultant is aware of future trends in the visual world: this is an essential part of the job. He/she must anticipate what is likely to be visually valid tomorrow. It is often difficult to accept today what will be valid tomorrow. The 'conventional wisdom' described by Galbraith in 'THE AFFLUENT SOCIETY' affects design as much as any other field. It is up to the consultant to earn the confidence of his/her client, while remaining an informed outsider, so that his/her judgement will be trusted and acted upon. Most clients ask for something new, which by definition has not been done before. At the same time, they would like to be reassured that what is new is a proven success, by precedent. Market tests can sometimes, but by no means always, help. In the end, only informed judgement can make the right decision.

Often before the consultant is called in, a great deal of heart-searching and argument takes place as to the necessity or desirability of a corporate identity exercise. Unless the initiative comes from the top, the person or department raising the issue finds the first task is to convince the board. This is exactly the point at which the consultant's participation can be most useful. Given all the necessary background information, he can work out a complete outline plan including costings and schedules. He can provide arguments, drawn from similar experiences with other organizations, on why it may be necessary to embark on a project. He can help with verbal and visual communication between the individual or department concerned and the board.

Every job is different and has its own peculiar problems. But every job must follow a certain sequence of stages. These can vary in order, but from our own experience we would state the stages as:
- Analysis
- Briefing
- Concept
- Development
- Design guidelines
- Motivation
- Implementation
I shall explain each of these stages in more detail.

Analysis
The object of the analysis is to arrive at a position where both consultant and client are aware of the existing situation and of all the factors which will influence the design solution, and can thus write an accurate design brief. Many points should be covered in the analysis, for example:
- historic development of the corporation
- the corporate philosophy
- the organization and legal structure
- the market position in relation to competitors
- the marketing organization and strategies (present and future)
- the attitude of personnel
- the attitude of customers and the public
- the attitude of suppliers.

The historic development of a corporation usually requires special consideration for the corporate identity concept.

The corporate philosophy will probably provide indications for solutions in most areas of the corporate identity project and is crystallized to some extent in the organizational and legal structure. The corporate philosophy will probably also describe the company's socio-political and environmental attitudes and will contribute to establishing design criteria which relate specifically to the corporation.

The organizational and legal structures will provide important criteria for the identity concept and for the working procedures and implementation. The organizational structure also provides indications as to where, through design, coordination and rationalization, possibilities exist.

To contribute to an adequate marketing image and to define the identity in relation to competitors, it is essential to know the market position of the corporation and to have an overall view of the corporate identities of competitors.

One of the most important requirements of a corporate identity concept is to provide assistance in marketing. The marketing strategies and product concepts must be known in order for them to be taken properly into account when developing the corporate identity concept.

The attitude of all personnel concerned is important for the acceptance of the new corporate identity and its implementation: their interests and problems must be understood and the corporate identity concept should, if possible, take these interests into account.
The corporate identity should, through its various media, positively influence the attitude of suppliers, customers and the public to the corporation. The knowledge of existing attitudes is a prerequisite.

A survey of all obtainable visual manifestations of the corporation must be carried out. A certain degree of evaluation of the status quo can be done at the analysis stage as some of the objectives for the project will already be clear. Even when this is not so, the results of the evaluation will be useful in any case. General points to be considered might include:
- Does the style project an appropriate image?
- Has the nature of your business changed since you last considered your image?
- Does it communicate the true nature of your business?
- Is the style distinguishable from that of competitors?
- Have you defined your audience, both present and future?
- Do you have corporate communications objectives?
- Does everything seem to come from the same source?
- How do the items relate to each other?
- Are the existing elements used consistently?
All possible areas of application for the proposed corporate identity should be investigated with the aid of a comprehensive checklist supplied by the consultants.

Another important consideration at this stage is to investigate the availability and quality of any in-house design or implementation facilities whose activities may have to be taken into account.

There are various ways in which information for the analysis can be obtained including interviews with relevant personnel, visits by consultants, questionnaires, documentation supplied by the client and research by specialists, for example market research and attitude surveys.

It is vital that staff are brought into the process at this stage for two main reasons. Firstly, they can provide first-hand, relevant information in critical areas. Secondly, if they feel themselves to have been taken into account during the decision-making process, they will be much more enthusiastic to apply the results of those decisions when the implementation stage is reached.

Briefing

The second stage of the project, briefing, is always carried out in very close collaboration between client and consultant.

The brief contains the objectives and criteria of the project – to enable non-subjective judgement of the eventual proposals to be made – and a precise definition of the amount of work involved.

The objectives must be carefully listed in order of priority. This is important because some may be mutually exclusive and it may be considered necessary to exclude one objective to the advantage of another. The sum total of the objectives defines what should be achieved by the new CI programme. Obviously, every corporation has a different philosophy but there are usually common denominators of desired results including progressiveness, retention of tradition (at least its positive aspects), dynamism, social consciousness, readiness for innovation, emphasis on research, reliability, clearer and more positive communications – internally and externally – and a better platform for marketing, promotion and PR.

Constraints and parameters must also be listed. They define the design areas which cannot be trespassed on.

Constraints refer to the internal, integral limitations of a project (or design item which forms part of a corporate identity programme), whilst parameters refer to its environment, its specific conditions and the people choosing and using it.
Constraints and parameters control every design item relevant to a corporate identity programme, whether it is a product, a pack, a stationery range, a sign system or a building. Let me explain:

Constraints

Parameters

PRODUCT

materials, mechanics, manufacturing process, performance, etc.

the buyer, the user, the market, competitive products, production time, available budget, etc.

ILLUMINATED SIGN

method of lighting, materials to be used, size, luminosity, numbers required, etc.

legal restrictions in street, town or country, competitive signs, target publics, financial budget, production time, etc.

PACK

contents, materials, physical make-up, production processes, texts and information to be shown, illustrations, etc.

the store, the self, competitive products, the market, buyer and user, etc.

This useful division between constraints and parameters is of great help in analysis, evaluation and concept.

Objectives and parameters form a checklist of conditions which should be constantly referred to during the creation of a concept. The criteria makeup another checklist of conditions which the concept, once developed, has to fulfil.

Criteria are the yardstick against which a proposed solution can be objectively measured. If the yardstick fits the solution – even an intuitive one – it can be rationally proved to be correct, rather than exposed to subjective prejudice called taste, where the odds are that the highest person in a hierarchy will impose his or her own subjectivity. There are two categories of criteria:
A client-specific, which apply only to the CC programme of the particular company
B general, which apply to all CC programmes.

General criteria are, for instance, that the CI system must be open-ended, flexible and economic in application in all media and methods of reproduction, in two and three dimensions in all relevant materials, sizes and colour combinations, valid for a long time and therefore not fashionable, legally registerable, etc.

Objectives, parameters and criteria form the basis of the brief which has to be agreed between client and consultant. They form an objective basis for developing design proposals and for judging them.

Concept

Within the matrix of the brief, appropriate concepts, design elements such as symbols, logotypes and colours, can now be created. This is the beginning of the concept stage.

The application of the design elements to representative examples in various media can

demonstrate that the proposals satisfy all criteria and are likely to achieve the selected objectives.

Presentation of these examples will hopefully find an objective and rational approval. However, if conditions and requirements have changed since the original briefing, adjustments will be necessary and the original concept must be revised. In a dynamic company this happens quite frequently and the possibility of making necessary adjustments must be anticipated. Presentation of the final proposals should include recommendations on the sequence and rate of application, and on design management in the corporation.

Development
It is now possible to develop the concept to form a coherent system. Every possible aspect of corporate design and communications must be anticipated and proved to fit into the overall system. Very often rationalization becomes necessary in order to simplify ranges of products, packaging and stationery which have grown out of control.

A design coordination programme is often a good opportunity for a corporation to review its paperwork from an organizational and methods standpoint. The system design and flow of paperwork in a corporation is often as haphazard as the visual design of the forms themselves. A rational study of the paperwork as a whole can almost always demonstrate major savings in reducing errors, reducing time taken to enter and extract information and time taken to file and retrieve, as well as economizing in stationery, inventory and production.

Guidelines
It is always necessary to produce guidelines to cover foreseeable applications in as much detail as possible. These guidelines often take the form of a manual, which is usually a hefty bound volume – the corporation's 'visible Bible'. Design elements are shown in all their possible versions. The house colours are specified and samples included by different printing methods on different paper stock and on enamels for vehicles and metal containers. The guidelines can specify in detail, and by example, the appearance of all stationery items. The layout of publications is also dealt with. Working drawings give the size and position of design elements on vehicles. General standards for design of forms, packaging, uniforms and product identification and for internal and external sign systems are usually included. In addition to these general requirements, common to most corporations, there are usually areas specific to particular corporations.

Motivation
I have already mentioned the necessity of involving staff in the early stages of the project, in order to motivate them in accepting new ideas.

In addition to this, it is increasingly considered necessary to include a special information or motivational stage in a corporate identity project. The actual means of doing this might vary from a printed brochure to a complex audiovisual presentation. The effort might be directed to typists or to directors, but the aim is the same – to persuade staff that their cooperation is needed in order that the project should succeed and that ultimately they themselves benefit from the new CI.

Implementation
Introducing and implementing a corporate identity is always a long and complex process. Work will proceed along the lines in the plan agreed between client and consultant and according to the rules contained in the corporate identity guidelines. But even so there will be unforeseen problems and complications which must be dealt with on a day-to-day basis. Here the continuing help of the consultant is necessary to ensure that implementation is being carried out correctly and that ad-hoc problems are solved in accordance with the spirit of the identity.

We have seen, on too many occasions, identities which have fallen apart because of hasty implementation, usually caused by the client forging ahead without reference to the consultant. The manual can go only so far: there are always nuances of meaning whereby misunderstanding can arise, or unforeseen contingencies requiring individual decisions.

Nor does the vigilance stop there. There is always a large amount of mainly administrative work in the daily management and maintenance of design policy. In many cases there is enough work for the corporation to employ a full-time design manager to work in cooperation with the design consultant.

Design management is the name given to the activities of controlling and coordinating visual design for a corporation – initiating special projects, commissioning and briefing designers, testing and approving the results, all within the context of the overall policy. A design manager must understand visual design, but he need not necessarily be a designer himself.

A person with the right balance of experience and ability is hard to find. The balance required may be different from one case to another. If a design manager is allocated a place in the normal hierarchy, it may be too low to give him the authority he needs on some matters, and yet high enough to cause serious personnel difficulties within the corporation.

The authority for design management must ultimately come from the top management of the corporation, and in come cases a satisfactory solution has been a design manager working as part of the managing director's or president's office. In any case, some form of direct access to top management is essential.

Now we have listed all the stages of the project, let's remind ourselves of some of the benefits to be expected from an effective corporate communications strategy:
- increased recognizability
- increased memorability
- increased employee confidence
- greater attraction for potential employees
- cost savings through standardization
- a stronger presence in the marketplace
- more confidence among sources of finance
- increased public awareness
- in short, a more appropriate image.

In the last year, it seems as though an ever increasing number of corporations are in need of new, modified and updated identities, what with mergers, takeovers, buy-outs, diversification and break-up of companies as listed daily in the financial pages of our newspapers.

Corporate image programmes have become part of every design college curriculum. It is being taught to and learned by most design students. The increased need has created a bandwagon effect: art students become design consultants on leaving college. Rarely have they been acquainted with the interface of design, marketing, communication and management techniques. They enthusiastically design symbols, logos and colour schemes – but there is a lot more to it than that: there is an essential body of knowledge, based on experience and research which deals with the complex mix of design, marketing, psychology, sociology, information and communication theories, which together form the basis of decision-making. No sooner does a bank or a High-Street chainstore commission a designer than their competitors follow suit. They cannot afford not to do so. This trend has resulted in design's accelerated shift from 'form to formula'. Often designs are commissioned by clients who do not understand it, from designers who lack experience, for a public that does not know any better. The result is that all three parties are happy and the man-made environment impoverished. More designers are needed to satisfy this snowballing demand, many of whom, however, lack experience, competence, intelligence and professional conscience.

Exteriors, interiors, logos and corporate identities proliferate, all inevitably conformist and mediocre – like summer hats, mass–produced for the High Street. One season after they have been launched they need to be replaced, passé before they have really been used.

They fail to achieve the aimed-for distinction as they are made up of commonplace, interchangable elements, lacking originality in the first place. Lifestyle is confused with quality of life, form gets in the way of content as the medium becomes the message. The bond between signifier and signified no longer exists. Yet design in every field must be a goal-related activity. Once you lose your goals you lose your way.

There is still a considerable body of designers who can produce relevant, original and good designs, whose intelligence, experience and undoubted talent is monitored by a social conscience: professionals who have ideals and aspirations beyond the money nexus to enrich our environment and in some measure add to our culture and enjoyment. Alas, unlike a corporation's balance sheet, these results are more difficult to quantify, yet this does not make them less important.

It is my sincere hope that this book will add to a wider understanding of the width and depths of corporate identity problems so that all, industrialists, designers, students, as well as members of the general public, will benefit.

F.H.K. Henrion

Company images

Company images

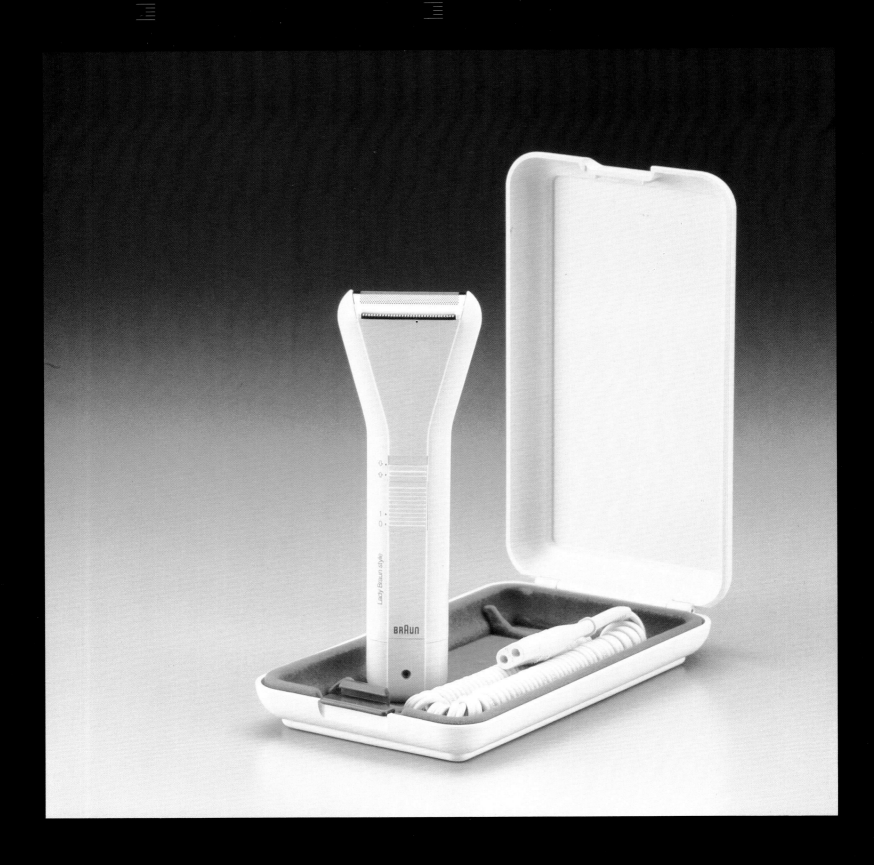

BRAUN

Braun
Partners with the consumer

(opposite, above)
Lady Braun Style
ladyshaver, 1988.
(below) Variations
on a theme: the
logo from 1932,
1938, 1950 and
1970.

Stereoviewer from
the 1950s.

A photographer friend showed me a curious stereoviewer from the 1950s. It consisted of a smallish metal box with semi-circular sides which came in a plastic case. It was a rather flat model, greyish-green in colour. Underneath to the right there was an aluminium button. A few simple operations released the metal bellows which sprang up with their adjustable lenses, and the turn of a knob set in motion a celluloid film with 33 stereo images, 32 in black and white and one in colour.

The 'film' opens with an extensive tour of the various departments of the former Braun factory, taking in the executive quarters, the drawing offices, the delivery department, the company canteen and various production departments. The employees are all simply but neatly groomed and it is as if the company's activities are performed by the same special type of person. They work in sober, orderly rooms where everything, or virtually every thing, seems to be functional, and where there are none of the usual signs of either job satisfaction or discontent: the walls are free of postcards, pin-ups, calenders and posters; instead, employees can glance up at the large clock positioned at some central point in most working areas. Their working surfaces are provided with natural light as far as possible and where necessary, so that the strip lighting fitted throughout the building only has a back-up function. The floors are spotless; products and components are arranged in rows on tables, shelves and racks.

Then a number of products are shown in context. For example, an electric razor – highly advanced in its day – is demonstrated plugged into the dashboard of a car.

Finally the colour frame depicts a friendly-looking lady in a modern raincoat showing the viewer a camera with a flashlight. Her stylized personality harmonizes with the character of the equipment she is presenting. More precisely, she seems to be a charming and contemporary personification of Functionalism, the philosophy propagated in the Netherlands and Germany in prewar days, which Ludwig Mies van der Rohe described as 'A NEW WAY OF LIVING WHICH, THOUGH SIMPLE TO THE EXTREME, IS HEALTHY, HONEST AND FULL OF PROMISE'.

The images are of an unusually high quality. One could imagine snapping one's fingers and the workers coming to life. Their speechlessness is reinforced by the orderly silence that pervades the working areas and the canteen, where the only decoration is a mistletoe wreath and a portrait of Max Braun, the founder of the factory. The photographs were apparently taken just before Christmas 1956.

It is not at all clear what the purpose of this stereo viewer was; presumably the photographs served to illustrate the representative's sales talk. What is clear, however, is that both the photographs and the design of the stereo

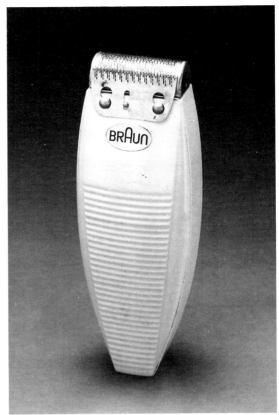

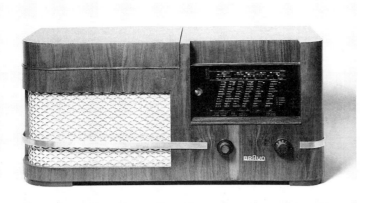

(left) Phonosuper radio-cum-record player, 1935. (right) S 50 shaving appliance, 1950.

viewer itself reveal the essence of the Braun philosophy. The stark, streamlined working areas are inspired by the same spirit as the geometric, super-rational, aesthetic products they produced. They all have the same Braun 'feel' about them. Though the design and model of the stereo viewer are now dated, it is still an eloquent statement of the strong new underlying sense of life and optimism about the future.

In 1921 Max Braun started out with a small factory making a machine of his own invention for joining drive belts, but a few years later he went over to producing parts for the up-and-coming radio industry. It was not long before he was producing complete radios and record players. In 1932 he was the first in Europe to manufacture a model that combined the two machines. His design demonstrated that technical innovation and product design should be approached jointly. It is not known whether Braun had connections at this time with Bauhaus and the Werkbund, both of which were working on this same theme.

He designed his first razor, the S 50, in 1938 but it was not presented at the Frankfurt trade fair until 1950. This product illustrates the general transition that was to take place in the use of materials, as the dark-coloured bakelite used for the body of the S 50 was replaced by plastic in subsequent models. There was a far greater range of applications for synthetics after 1945. Also, synthetics became available in lighter colours and these were in great demand during the optimistic postwar reconstruction years.

The S 50 was not the only product to be introduced in 1950; Braun also brought out its

'Multimix', the first of its domestic appliances. It was rather late in doing so, considering that similar products had been mass-produced in the United States for some time already. Raymond Loewy's 'Coldspot' freezebox was brought out in 1934, its advertisements urging the public to 'study his beauty'.

Once every home had been linked up with the electricity network in the 1920s, the way lay open for the introduction of household electrical appliances. This marks the start of a long evolutionary period for domestic appliances, the prototypes of most having been developed around 1900. As yet, design as such played no part, since technology and ergonomics were still in their infancy.

Contrary to the United States, most housewives in Europe were wary of these newfangled inventions. In 1946 the number of appliances in circulation was approximately the same as at the outbreak of the First World War. Although there had been a slight increase around 1930, the trend only really continued after 1950.

Nevertheless, in the 1930s a small group of women had expressed the wish to cut down on housework. The extension of the electricity network brought excellent opportunities to realize this. Modern kitchens such as those conceived by Grete Schutle-Lihtsky (1926), Bauhaus' Weimar kitchen (1927) and the Bruynzeel kitchen (1938) by Piet Zwart, were basics for the 'intelligent housewife'. This offered Braun almost unlimited possibilities for developing different ways of utilizing them, and his inventions were not to stop at the modern kitchen.

Braun Multipress automatic MP 80

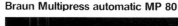

- Voor vers sap uit groente en fruit
- Automatische pulpafvoer
- Makkelijk afneembare pulpcontainer
- Deksel dient tevens als praktisch werkplateau
- Sapcontainer met schuimafscheider

BRAUN

Braun Multipress automatic MP 80

Snel en eenvoudig vers sap uit groente en fruit

BRAUN

After the death of Max Braun in 1951, management was taken over by his two sons, Artur and Erwin. One of the first, seemingly minor, though in fact essential, changes they commissioned was the restyling of the company logo. The basic design – undoubtedly conceived by their father – had first appeared on a radio made in 1935. It clearly bore the stamp of constructivism and had certainly been influenced by typographical notions such as Bauhaus propounded. Although there were a number of variants they all had in common a tall arched A in the middle.

Wolfgang Schmittel altered the logo in 1952 to its present form and drew up a basic formula. This consisted of a square grid and the 2:1 height-to-width ratio of the letters, except in the case of the tall middle A, where it is 3:1; the roundings of the letters were formed by quarter circles. Compared with options provided by contemporary graphic techniques and insights into perception, Schmittel's concept was extremely simple, but at that time it satisfied the need for a standard and standardization as the range of products became increasingly diversified.

The rejuvenated logo was the first indication of the modified company strategies implemented by the two brothers, which were to form the basis for the company's present corporate identity. The fact that today – almost 40 years later – this logo has never been adjusted or updated, not only attests to Schmittel's professionalism, but stresses the validity of the Bauhaus notion underlying the logo, namely, that good typography is based on 'CLARITY, ECONOMY AND PRECISION'.

Artur and Erwin Braun are known to have kept abreast of the developments in industrial design. They were anxious that their company should set the pace. To this end they decided to appoint Dr Fritz Eichler one of the directors and make him responsible for Braun's entire product design and presentation.

The advent of Eichler was of major significance. He was instrumental in establishing an exchange between Braun and staff and students of the Hochschule für Gestaltung in Ulm. This Ulm design college was meant considerably to influence the design of all Braun's products. In Ulm young designers were trained along the Bauhaus principles, which provided them with good grounding for translating the new postwar attitudes. Sober postwar Europe felt a strong need to formulate a new lifestyle. This need was reinforced by the propaganda for 'good' homes, i.e. homes that were modern and efficient, and that should be 'airy, light and spacious' according to a popular slogan. Erwin Braun was also the main figure behind the agreements made with the Knoll, Rosenthal and WMF factories to make a conscious contribution to the new lifestyle.

Other contacts were made too, among others with Otl Aicher, Herbert Hirche, Wilhelm Wagenfeld and Hans Gugelot. The latter set up a small, extremely engaging design department together with Dieter Rams. The two were responsible for the new look of Braun's products, and hence of the whole company. Gugelot's contribution consisted in integrating the aesthetic principles and technical discipline on which he lectured at the Hochschule, into the whole production process.

Both the march of time and new technological advances led to the first Multipress of 1952 (left) being entirely redesigned in 1988 (right).

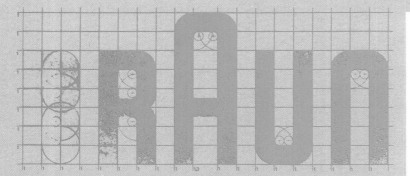

Huishoudelijke apparaten
1989

Braun quartz wekkers

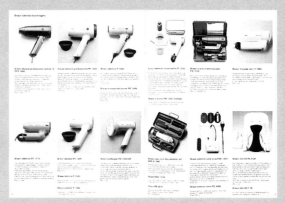

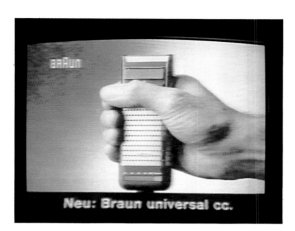

Het mooiste geluid is geen geluid.

Dat je de Braun Silencio haardroger helemaal niet hoort, is overdreven. Dat je hem aanzienlijk minder hoort, staat vast. Maar te zien valt er des te meer. Zijn drie standen: één voor elk type haar. Zijn koelstand om je haar langer in model te houden. Zijn slimme anti-slip nopjes. En uw perfekte kapsel, natuurlijk. Maar dat is niet van ons. **Braun. De volmaakte eenvoud.**

Rams was appointed head designer in 1955. Shortly after, together with Jurgen Greubel, Dieter Lubs and Hartwig Kahlcke, he managed completely to transform the production line. In 1958 the Museum of Modern Art in New York devoted an exhibition to the products that had resulted from their collaboration. Some of the exhibits were bought by the museum six years later.

'LESS DESIGN IS MORE DESIGN' was Rams' credo, adapting Mies van der Rohe's famous words 'Less is more' to the field of design. Mies van der Rohe founded the Bauhaus training on this belief when he became Principal during the institution's difficult closing years, overshadowed as they were by upsurging fascism. Another of Rams' statements shows a trace of this: 'I CONSIDER IT AN IMPORTANT TASK AND THE RESPONSIBILITY OF THE DESIGNER TO HELP BRING ORDER INTO THE CHAOS IN WHICH WE LIVE.'

Braun's designers, now as in the past, have always allowed their design ideas to be coloured by contemporary currents. Their attitudes were influenced by the fast-growing German industry and by the debates on form and function which escalated, particularly in the Werkbund, into a schismatic conflict between factions defending different schools of thought.

The Werkbund was an association of designers and manufacturers, founded in 1905 to further the manufacture of quality products by fusing aesthetics and functionalism. Hermann Muthesius, co-founder, architect and writer, greatly determined the prevailing views in the Werkbund. He believed 'industrial beauty' could only be achieved with the aid of technical descriptions and prescribed standards; vague speculations and subjective projections about 'good designs' could only be countered with convincing logic.

His view was the subject of a heated discussion at the Werkbund's 1914 annual conference, when his main antagonist was Art Nouveau designer Henry van de Velde, who spoke in defence of the artist's freedom. The debate on the designer's role in industry is one that keeps cropping up. Man is always seeking a balance between beauty and functionality, a balance which ever-changing factors make it seemingly impossible to strike.
Such discussions were not exclusive to the Bauhaus, but were also to be heard at the Hochschule in Ulm that succeeded it. The idea of this design college was conceived by Otl Aicher in 1949, and though founded in 1953, it did not really get off the ground until 1955, when it moved into a building designed by Max Bill. Here it was hoped the Bauhaus concepts could be revived and disseminated anew. Bill, who was appointed principal of the college some time later, drew up a modern version of these concepts. But they differed substantially from those of Aicher's, and the controversy they caused eventually led to Bill's departure.

His successor, Tomas Maldonado, believed that the Bauhaus principles could only be put into practice by not hanging on to them. He felt new concepts and methods ought to be developed. These should allow future designers sufficient flexibility to cope with the technological and industrial problems they faced. Also, if they had an insight into the workings of society, they would be perfectly capable of supervising the whole production process. In short, Maldonado wanted to train product designers 'WHOSE TASK IT IS TO CONSIDER THE WEAKER SIDE OF OUR INDUSTRIAL CULTURE'.

Thus students were offered the opportunity of combining training with practice at a high level. Thanks to Eichler's overtures, mentioned earlier, Braun and the Hochschule came to a collaborative arrangement that would later prove a milestone in the history of product design and corporate identity.

(opposite, top to bottom, from left) working drawing for the logo that was adapted to its present form by Wolfgang Schmittel in 1952; a leaf from the Use the logo instruction manual; various pages from the Household Appliances catalogue, 1989; the Braun design team.

(left) Still from the German commercial for the Universal shaver, 1988. (right) Dutch Silencio Professional hairdryer advertisement, 1989.

(above)
Multipractic food
processor, 1988;
(below) two stills
from a food mixer
commercial, 1989.

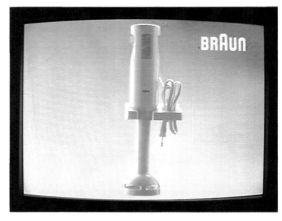

(Above left to right) Coffee maker, 1972; Control Sensor toaster, 1989; Citromatic fruit press, 1989; (below) Braun shavers from 1950 to present.

Dr Traugott Malzan, head of the communications division for Braun in the 1960s, once said: 'A COMPANY THAT ONLY MAKES HALF-HEARTED ATTEMPTS AT GOOD DESIGN, WITHOUT THE FULL SUPPORT OF TOP MANAGEMENT, MIGHT WELL LOSE ITS SHIRT.' His statement is a confirmation of the clear course along which the company was cruising.

Erwin Braun formulated his views as follows: 'OUR APPLIANCES MUST BE SILENT, UNOBTRUSIVE SERVANTS. THEY GO ABOUT THEIR BUSINESS QUIETLY, ALWAYS THERE WHEN YOU NEED THEN, BUT OTHERWISE DISCREETLY UNNOTICED.' This management interpretation offered sufficient leeway for Rams' concept 'Less design is more design' to evolve into a powerful design strategy.

The unusual nature of the Braun philosophy is reflected in the way the logo was used, which was modest and functional. The logo determined the style of photography and presentation. Packaging and advertisements, showrooms and stands at fairs, are all in the same vein.

Three journalists hired as copywriters were responsible for writing the texts that accompanied the products, in the same lucid, informative style. The idea was to attune communications so finely to the products that they functioned as one. In this way, communications, design and product design are the pillars on which Braun's corporate identity is built. Success has its cultural as well as its commercial aspect. Over the years Braun's products and packagings have received awards and prizes, including the Compasso d'Oro, Gute Form, Eurostar and the Interplas Design Preis. They have been featured at many exhibitions, at the Centre Georges Pompidou in Paris and Amsterdam's Stedelijk Museum, for instance, apart from the Museum of Modern Art already mentioned.

Some time ago an exhibition in Berlin was devoted to Braun's 1960s' products, underlining once more the significance of the designs for that period. Today they are examples of an industrial culture that almost everyone found new and exciting.

The artistic nature of industrial design has since substantially changed: it is now less rational and its decorative possibilities are being strongly exploited, sometimes at the expense of the way the product functions – a drawback that manufacturer and consumer alike are frequently prepared to put up with. A good example here is the Alessi kettle.

Today's designs combine an increasing number of different materials and colours. Traces of this trend can be found in Braun's wares, though they affect only minor details: a coloured knob, a metre, a switch or clock hand. Braun does not seek to reinforce its image by shadowing design trends, but rather by re-affirming the proven strength of the character of its products, which are allowed to be no more than 'silent servants'.

In 1954 Braun signed a licensing agreement with Ronson in the United States, mainly so that they could exploit the technical know-how and production facilities on the two sides of the Atlantic. Thirteen years later, Braun was taken over by the Gillette Company of Boston, which had succeeded in acquiring a majority share. Company strategies remained unaltered.

Early in the 1980s, for reasons of efficiency, the company decided to cut down drastically on its range of products. They had had three product groups until then – photographic equipment, hi-fi, and domestic appliances. If they wished to retain their share in the market, they would need a separate sales operation for each group. To keep service up to the standards the public had been used to, the company sold its manufacturing and sales rights for its photographic products to Bosch, and the hi-fi went to ADS, a German corporation like Bosch. Braun's product assortment now consists exclusively of domestic and personal grooming appliances.

With its reduced assortment, Braun remains true to a tradition that has proved successful for more than 35 years. Over the decades Braun has succeeded in developing a corporate identity that still reflects its subtle reinterpretation of the Functionalist ideal of 'A NEW WAY OF LIFE WHICH, THOUGH SIMPLE TO THE EXTREME, IS HEALTHY, HONEST AND FULL OF PROMISE'.

Jaap Lieverse, Ronald de Nijs

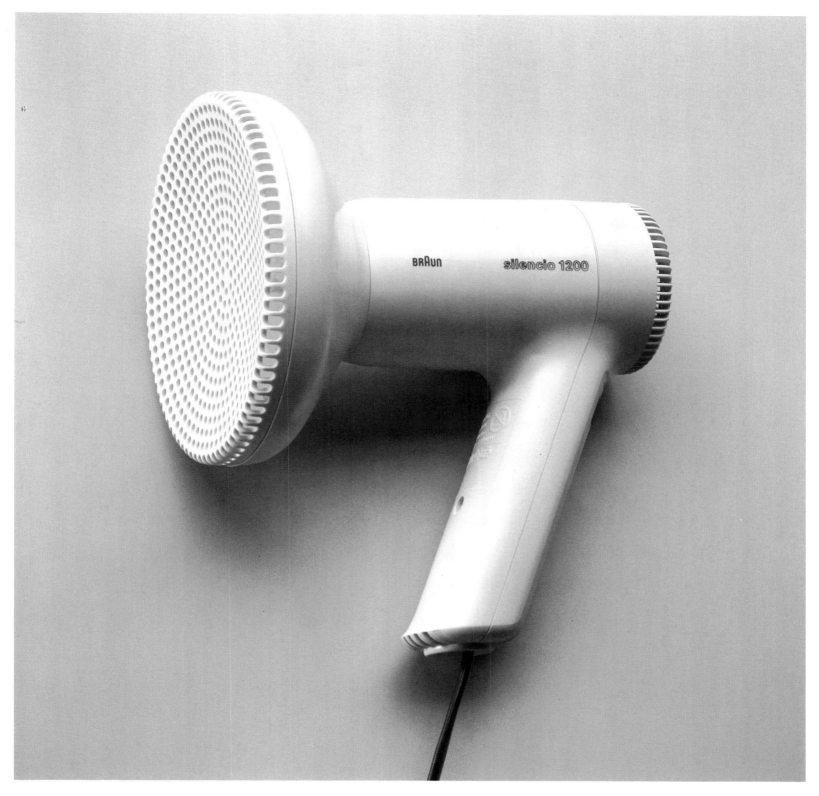

(above) Softstyler
hairdryer, 1989;
(below left)
Aromaster coffee
maker, 1984;
(right) Reflex
control alarm
clock, 1988.

ptt

Tradition in a new form
The Royal PTT Netherlands

(opposite) Jacket
for manual of PTT
housestyle, 1989,
design by Studio
Dumbar.

(below) The Post
Office in Utrecht,
designed by
J. Crouwel Jr and
dating from 1924,
badly needed
renovating in
1981. Architect
René van Raalte
managed to update
the post office to
meet modern
demands while
leaving its
original character
intact.

Probably the first government organization in the world to adopt a policy of good design embracing all its visual manifestations was the Dutch PTT, the mail, telegraph and telephone company. That was in 1920, but the origins of that policy go back to the late 19th century when Dutch designers and architects sought a social application for art and design. They were inspired by the ideas of William Morris and Walter Crane, which had become accessible with the appearance of Dutch translations of their writings around the turn of the century.

The views of William Morris and Walter Crane profoundly affected the work of members of the Dutch Society for Crafts and Industrial Art, founded in 1904 to bring about the 'HARMONIOUS UNION OF THE ARTISTIC CRAFTSMANSHIP AND MACHINE TECHNOLOGY'. This preoccupation can be clearly seen in the work of such artists as H.P. Berlage and K.P.C. de Bazel, who besides being architects also designed consumer articles. Their aim was to elevate the aesthetic tone of everyday objects, believing that this would benefit the spiritual well-being of the user.

Similarly, in the words of J.F. van Royen (1878–1942), PTT felt that good design was the only way to ensure 'PTT PRODUCTS WERE APPROPRIATE AND MERITORIOUS AND WOULD HELP DETERMINE THE QUALITY OF ITS SERVICE TO SOCIETY'. Van Royen was the driving force behind the first 'PTT COMPANY STYLE', as it was then called. This singularly gifted and erudite man, himself a designer, typographer and printer, not only spread his ideas on art and design within PTT, but gave inspiring leadership and invaluable service to every sector of contemporary art in the Netherlands.

In his work for PTT, Van Royen soon set about tackling matters of graphic and industrial design, a task later taken up by the company's special Department of Aesthetic Design created in 1945. Van Royen's interest in art and design reflects the ideas of 'community art', the name given to art with a social application. He believed that contemporary art should appeal to laypeople and held that art 'BATHED THE WORLD IN ETERNAL LIGHT' AND 'WAS NEITHER AN AMUSEMENT, NOR A PASTIME, NOR A BUSINESS, NOR A REFUGE FOR IDLE HANDS'.

PTT was able to take full advantage of Van Royen's connections with artists and designers, since he contracted them to design stamps, furniture, advertising and other typographical manifestations, such as forms and signs on buildings and vehicles, having first overcome a considerable amount of prejudice within the company. He also concerned himself with the art in post offices and inside or on the outside of PTT's office buildings. He felt that the fact that the company devoted a good deal of attention to visual presentation would show the company cared about the quality of its services and would be a way of winning the confidence of the general public.

This strategy, set out by Van Royen, was further shaped by the PTT Department of Aesthetic Design, which was responsible for 'ALL ACTIVITIES UNDERTAKEN BY OR ON BEHALF OF THE COMPANY THAT INVOLVES PRESENTING THE COMPANY TO THE PUBLIC. THE DESIGN AND IMPLEMENTATION OF SUCH ACTIVITIES SHOULD BE CARRIED OUT IN CONSULTATION WITH THE AESTHETIC ADVISOR. ... IN THIS CONTEXT THE TERM 'ACTIVITIES' REFERS TO ANY INTERNAL AND EXTERNAL COMPANY MANIFESTATION INVOLVING DESIGN. THIS INCLUDES – AND THE LIST IS BY NO MEANS EXHAUSTIVE – BUILDINGS, INTERIORS OF BUILDINGS, ROOMS, ETC., WALL ORNAMENTS AND DECORATIONS, PRINTED MATTER, EXHIBITIONS, POSTAGE STAMPS, SIGNS, STAMPS, POST-BOXES, BOOK BINDINGS, PHOTOGRAPHS, FILMS ...'

This list provided a basis for the work of this department, which today is closely connected with PTT's corporate identity. The Department of Art and Design, as it has been known since privatization on 1 January 1989, is also responsible for purchasing the art works for the offices of PTT staff and all the visual applications on PTT buildings. These include the PTT Post's twelve large regional sorting centres which were built in the 1970s following a reorganization of this subsidiary and the introduction of a new infrastructure. The Department also supervises all PTT's graphic and industrial design manifestations, such as postage stamps, annual reports, diaries, telephone boxes, posting boxes and viewphones.

After KLM and the Dutch Railways had acquired memorable corporate identities, in 1969 PTT recognized the need to develop a distinctive visual style of its own. At that time visual communication was not seen as an essential component of their corporate strategy, and design in general was considered something of a decorative afterthought. The immense growth of the PTT concern and hence its increasing complexity meant more

Postal sorting office, Den Bosch.

and more design activity went unchecked and uncoordinated. This trend had to be replaced by a well-defined visual identity, one which would convey the corporate statement, an image which was both familiar and would inspire confidence in a company providing communication services on a mass scale. Fortunately, PTT offered the conditions for an integrated approach to all its design activities, partly because of its own aesthetic traditions.

In 1976, the Aesthetic Advisor commented that a situation had been created within PTT, 'WHICH ALLOWS YOU TO TALK ABOUT THE SIGNIFICANCE OF THE SHAPE OF A LETTER, ABOUT FORM OF LETTERING AND TYPOGRAPHY IN RELATION TO CONTENT OF THE PRINTED WORD, ABOUT THE APPEARANCE OF OBJECTS, ABOUT THE QUALITY OF THE WORKING ENVIRONMENT AS COMPONENTS OF CORPORATE POLICY. THIS IS BASED ON THE UNDERSTANDING THAT PROCESSES OF CHANGE IN OUR CULTURE BOTH SPRING FROM AND EFFECT OUR SOCIETY AND SHOULD FIND VISIBLE EXPRESSION THERE AND NOT JUST IN MUSEUMS.'

PTT conducted an inquiry into the image that the public and personnel had of PTT, and in 1970 its initial findings were incorporated into its general criteria and design brief for the new corporate image. It was clear then that a new corporate design would have to be paralleled by a revision of the service mix and even rejuvenated services.

The new image would have to evoke new associations of a versatile, vigorous, generous and courteous company while retaining the existing image of honesty and reliability. It should present the PTT concern as unique, modern, and socially and technologically progressive, and as a company responsive to the needs and wishes of every Dutchman.

To translate these abstract ideas into a corporate design or 'housestyle', PTT called in the expertise of two leading design offices – Total Design and Tel Design – both of which had a good deal of experience in the field of corporate identity. Total Design, an Amsterdam agency, had already compiled the earlier report on various corporate design aspects of the PTT concern as it was then and as envisaged in the future. Tel Design from The Hague was later replaced by Studio Dumbar. Working independently, the two consultants presented separate detailed proposals in March 1972, but it was not until 1978 that these led to a final joint concept.

Research was carried out from every feasible angle – into the readability of forms, the corporate symbol, into the typography and colours and that could best be used – and covered every imaginable PTT design item scheduled for a new look. Three years later, in 1981, the PTT corporate identity was officially implemented.

(opposite) Various postage- and commemorative stamps issued over the years by the PTT. (bottom) The cover and inside layout of the Dutch Postage Stamps Annual 1982, design by Anthon Beeke.

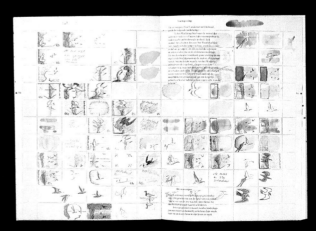

A new alphabet was designed for the first PTT corporate design for the logotype, headings in advertisements, and the lettering on buildings and vehicles, but the letter was eventually rejected as unsuitable in favour of Univers (types 55 and 65), an existing sanserif that was legible even at a distance and which every typesetter would stock. Moreover the business-like appearance of this typeface effectively expressed the neutrality appropriate for a modern state-owned company.

It was felt the Univers would make up into a good logotype, and the simplest form was chosen of the three lowercase letters ptt (post, telephone, telegraph). Although this existing logo did not entirely describe the concern, it was retained because it was so wellknown. A longer, more accurate alternative might have been associated with a completely different company.

As to the colours, red was an obvious choice. The Dutch Mail service had used bottle green at some stage in the 19th century, but it soon followed the example of British Royal Mail and switched to red. The blue of the Post Office Giro and National Savings Bank was retained, as it had been used extensively in advertising ('Giro blue is for you') and was well entrenched with the general public.

A new colour, light green, was introduced for Telecommunications. Light green was chosen in preference to orange, a fashionable colour at the time, because green has greater luminosity. This was important since Telecommunications vehicles are often parked at dangerous spots and therefore need to be conspicuous. Yellow, the most noticeable colour, was ruled out, as it was reserved for the Ministry of Transport, the Dutch Railways, and the Dutch Automobile and Touring Association. Moreover, research showed green to be a utility colour, being clearly visible yet unobtrusive, and as such ideal for a nationalized company.

A fourth colour, brown, was chosen for PTT Headquarters and the services they provided. Brown was considered restful and much warmer than the notorious grey PTT used just about everywhere.

An extensive corporate identity manual was produced containing detailed guidelines especially on typographical applications, such as stationery and forms. Certain types of representative printed matter for external consumption and important consumer-orientated items were more or less excluded from the corporate identity. The main exception was postage stamps, which had traditionally always been designed by the best designers, but other items included telephone directories, diaries, annual reports, uniforms, and the interiors of old post offices, some of which are now listed buildings.

In other words, though a PTT corporate iden-

tity had been developed, it was not to be applied dogmatically and unimaginatively and it allowed for exceptions, provided these items were designed to the highest standards by professionals. Quality remained the chief objective and as a rule this meant attending to detail and making sure the individual components added up to a cohesive whole. It is this quality aspect that partly determines the image of the company.

The same flexibility formed the basis for PTT's second corporate identity – the third, counting design of the 1920s and 1930s – which became effective on 1 January 1989, when PTT was privatized, now known as The Royal PTT Netherlands. PTT's new status as a private company – although for the time being all the shares remain in the hands of the government – demanded a new corporate image. In many respects this would have to mirror the old, for the new company's Board of Management felt, 'THE OLD CORPORATE IDENTITY HAD LOST NONE OF ITS ORIGINAL CLARITY, FORCE OR CHARACTER'. The old image simply needed adjusting to clarify the difference between the old and the new corporation.

However a different corporate image was created which embraced a number of the basic elements of the earlier version. A new ruling insisted that the corporate identity was applied consistently throughout PTT and that its application in the years to come should be monitored more carefully than had been the case with the previous programme.

PTT has lost its monopoly position in some areas. General scaling-up and progressive quantitative growth in all areas of society resulting in keener competition, mean that the new PTT will have to be more immediately recognizable, operate faster, and be better tailored to the needs of the market. Good design tends to be undervalued in such situations – if not in theory certainly in practice-since people are inclined to resort to slick

(opposite)
Overview of company housestyle elements, 1989.
(below)
Fleetmarking detail.

Telephone directory 1981, design by Total Design.

Intriguing wall
design by
P. Struycken for
the Utrecht PTT,
1985.
Aspects of PTT
buildings: by
Ilse Mater,
P. Struycken and
André Volten.

advertising consultants. For a company seeking to win custom by putting across its identity and a quality image, it is absolutely essential that its visual and non-visual manifestations are well-designed. What is more, a company will need to adjust to a changing society and its corporate identity will therefore need to be flexible within the confines of its basic matrix.

The board decision to introduce a new PTT corporate identity was only taken in April 1988 although it had to be ready for implementation by 1 January 1989. A highly efficient organization was therefore necessary to guarantee the success of the operation. Hundreds of people from Headquarters, PTT Post and PTT Telecom, the districts throughout the country, as well as external suppliers joined forces to ensure the exercise was completed on time.

Everything had to be changed: the lettering on larger buildings, the logos on rolling stock, cars and vans, the signs, all the promotional material and advertising, thousands of different forms, all the stationery, stickers, crockery, business gifts, office equipment, sugar and salt sachets, uniforms and sportswear, in-house magazines and publications by the different company divisions, everywhere all over the Netherlands, and information for business clients and the general public had to be adapted.

Studio Dumbar was chosen for this mammoth design task. The brief specified that each major company division had to be identifiable in the corporate symbol to avoid the prolifera-

tion of logos which had resulted from their need to distinguish their own identity within the PTT concern.

Several basic features of the former PTT identity were retained – the Univers typeface (the letter was specially restored and perfected for the logo), and the colours red and green. In the early 1980s the Post Office Giro and National Savings Bank services had been made an independent company named Postbank. With them went the colour blue – albeit a somewhat lighter shade than the 'giro blue' of its PTT days. This gave PTT the opportunity of replacing the brown used by Headquarters with dark blue for the new parent company. A second typeface, Plantin, was introduced alongside Univers as an alternative for longer texts.

The PTT logo with all its variants for the subsidiaries, was more intricate than the one it replaced. The coloured field and little coloured squares (red, green or blue) ensured easy identification of each company division even at a distance. In monochrome or black-and-white representations the squares are shown as lines, their set position within the symbol indicating which division they represent.

Lines, dots and squares derived from the basic symbol form the main components of the corporate design and are readily recognized as PTT logotypes. PTT crockery, for instance, does not feature the corporate logo as such, but its pattern of coloured dots and lines is immediately identified with PTT. The same goes for many other PTT items. This is a novel develop-

Cover and inside
of a book on the
history of the PTT,
1989, design by
René van Raalte
Assoc./SDU
Publishers.

ment in the history of corporate identity.

In the lettering on larger buildings, the designers have adapted the logotype to the building's specific architectural features. This has produced a variety of logotypes though they are all bear the same unmistakable PTT stamp. This caused some confusion within the company and led to a design management programme being drawn up, which laid down the design liberties for various categories of PTT expressions. The degree of freedom varies from strict adherence to the prescribed principles to considerable freedom allowing variations provided they are designed by professionals.

The programme aims at maintaining the basic corporate identity framework, but there are ways of evading the design dogma. This does not make applying a design policy any easier, but it does provide a challenge and makes the work more interesting, particularly – at least, if the job is well done – since it ensures the corporate identity is kept intact.

A manual is an essential and vital instrument of design management and, contrary to common practice, it must be easy to understand for everyone who uses it. Several smaller company publications were compiled in the course of 1989 providing the first practical guidelines on specific aspects. Thanks to these booklets, it is not always necessary to consult the hefty corporate identity manual on every matter. As with the previous identity, a number of explicit exceptions are made,

mainly for manifestations of a representative nature such as postage stamps and annual reports.

PTT was wise in adopting an undogmatic approach. A company that is changing so rapidly, one that must respond to the signals of society, cannot do with a dogmatic image; but it can draw attention to itself, with a dash of audacity and flair even, provided of course it has high-grade products and services to offer.

It is too soon to judge the success of the new PTT corporate identity and its underlying principles. No doubt many adjustments will have to be made in the years to come and the design policy will need to be outlined anew in order to maintain the overall identity. To safeguard the quality of the image, a number of measures has been taken for monitoring application of the identity, correcting excessive deviations, announcing new developments and providing guidelines, some as amendments to the manual.

The Board of Management directors will need to confer regularly with the corporate identity teams. Ultimately the overall responsibility for the image of the company rests with the Chairman of the Board. After all, if the image of a company is to be anyone's concern, it must be that of the senior management.

Paul Hefting

(above) Facsimile
(1985) of the PTT
book, published in
1934, written,
compiled and
designed by Piet
Zwart who,
together with Dick
Elffers, was
responsible for
the illustrations.

(following pages)
The covers of
PTT's four-part
housestyle
manual, 1989
(above), and
various random
pages from it
(below and facing
page).

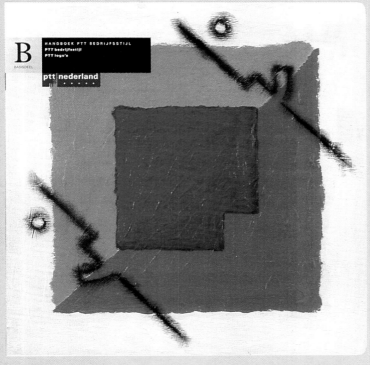

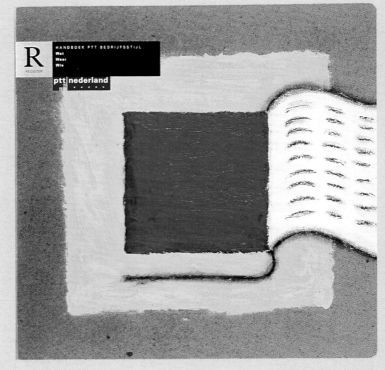

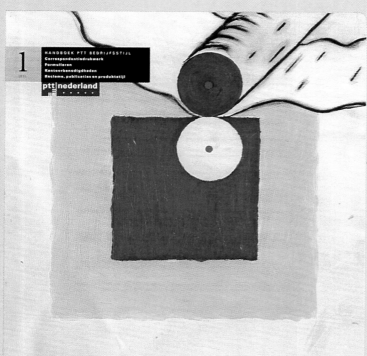

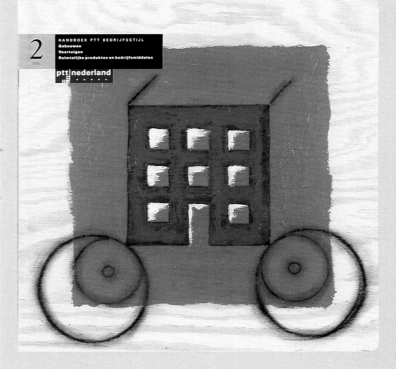

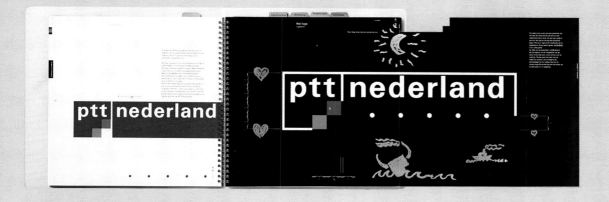

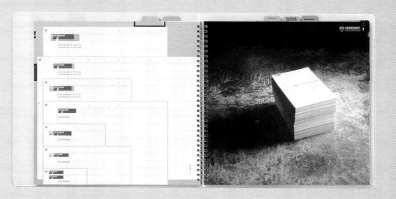

London Underground
A study of roots

Overseas visitors may stare in amazement at it, but for the Londoner daily entering Arnos Grove to take the westbound platform of the Piccadilly Line the image of the London Underground has long ceased to create a stir. The, at the time, controversial architecture of Charles Holden is no longer the gateway to a pulsating city, but more the portals to the tunnel of hell. Trains are sometimes on time, sometimes late. The euphoria created by their uncompromising modernity has long given way to exasperation at the packed carriages – you hang on grimly to one of the oscillating 'straps' poking out of the ceiling, all the time reading the paper to avoid having to look at anyone. Then at destination South Ken, it is an obstacle race through the masses, tunnel in, tunnel out, up a wobbling escalator, through the turnstiles and reaching fresh air as quickly as possible. The Underground is still a fast means of transport, providing the trains are not delayed, there is a power failure, or the staff are striking. Nevertheless, you surface with grime under the fingernails even if you didn't actually touch anything.

A transport system which was once a marvel of revolutionary design and a blueprint for many other societies has come up against the dialectics of progress. What was good, doesn't necessarily remain so. In the early 1930s, while Joseph Stalin was conferring an Order of Merit on the chief executive of London Transport, the Moscow Underground was already much more advanced in many aspects than its illustrious London prototype. In her book **BRITISH DESIGN, IMAGE AND IDENTITY,** published in 1989, art historian Frederique Huygen somewhat cynically recalls the terrible fire at King's Cross station a year before. Since then smoking has been forbidden on all Underground stations, yet King's Cross was only one of a series of accidents and disasters on the Underground – a situation that a smoking ban, let alone a company housestyle, can hardly keep up with. Huygen writes that the criticism of London Underground has never died down and it can do nothing more than point out: 'THE LACK OF CONSISTENT POLICY TOWARDS URBAN PUBLIC TRANSPORT BY THE POLITICIANS, THE LACK OF AN INTEGRATED LONDON TRANSPORT/ BRITISH RAIL STRATEGY AND THE CONTINUED USE AND DISGUISED SUBSIDY OF THE PRIVATE CAR'.

Among the rare exceptions to this sad stock-taking, Huygen counts the work of Misha Black, who in the late 1960s designed new carriages for the Underground. Perhaps there is also a redeeming ray of hope in the appointment of a new design manager for London Regional Transport, a post which remained unfilled until 1985.

Nevertheless, the Underground is justifiably recognized as having one of the earliest and most influential examples of a corporate image, developed at a time when the term was not on everyone's lips during board meetings.

(opposite, below)
Piccadilly Circus
station, 1929.
(right) Interior
Piccadilly stock,
1925.

(below) New
automatic ticket
machines now
installed
throughout the
Underground.

The London Passenger Transport Board (LPTB), officially set up in 1933 after a full-blown merger, slowly evolved by the first half of the century out of a confusing conglomerate of transport companies. All these companies, privately or publicly owned, had previously run the occasional underground line, operated buses in designated areas of the city, sent forth trams and maintained their own railway networks.

Frank Pick (1878–1941), the man who eventually gave London Transport its whole look, came to London on one of these networks in 1906. A young lawyer, he arrived via Underground Electric Railways which controlled part of the underground network. The company was not exactly flourishing, and American banks had to step in finally and save it from bankruptcy. From America, too, came Albert Stanley, who as new director had the duty to keep a watchful eye on the investments and with whom Frank Pick would remain working until his very last day with LPTB. In the course of the years, Stanley acquired th title of Lord Ashfield. Pick remained who he was – a man with very pronounced views on management policy and the recognizability of services which his company offered. He was a jack-of-all-trades in British design history, not only because of his innovative involvement with tube and bus, but also because of his role with the Design and Industries Association (DIA). This was established in 1915, following the example of the German Werkbund, and for a time Pick was chairman of the institute, where they particularly concerned themselves with the 'in appropriateness' of goods from trades and industry. No manual can ignore his exceptional role. In her **DESIGN SOURCE BOOK** Penny Spark writes: 'THE DRIVING FORCE BEHIND THIS INNOVATIVE PROGRAMME [of the London Underground: GS] WAS FRANK PICK, CHIEF LONDON TRANSPORT DESIGNER, WHOSE INSIGHT REGARDING THE ROLE OF DESIGN IN CONTEMPORARY CULTURE WAS VERY ADVANCED. HIS VIEWS HAD MUCH IN COMMON WITH THOSE FLOURISHING IN GERMANY AND FROM THE DIA HE WAS THE ONLY ONE WHO TRIED TO BRING BRITAIN IN CONTACT WITH THE MODERN DESIGN IDEAS OF THE EUROPEAN MAINLAND.' And Stephen Bayley writes in the **CONRAN DIRECTORY OF DESIGN**: 'when he WAS COMMERCIAL MANAGER OF LONDON TRANSPORT IN THE 1920S, HE INSTITUTIONALIZED ONE OF THE MOST THOROUGH CORPORATE IDENTITY PROGRAMMES IN HISTORY BY APPOINTING THE ARCHITECT CHARLES HOLDEN AND THE TYPOGRAPHER EDWARD JOHNSTON TO CREATE UNIFORMITY IN THE COMPANY'S APPEARANCE. IT BECAME A TYPICALLY BRITISH INTERPRETATION OF THE STANDARDIZATION THEORY ADVANCED TWO DECADES EARLIER BY HERMAN MUTHESIUS.' For this achievement Pick, on his death in 1941, was compared in the **ARCHITECTURAL REVIEW** with Lorenzo de Medici, the Italian statesman and first patron of Michelangelo.

The housestyle, however, for London public transport was not born out of a sort of artistic patronage. Pick the lawyer was too deeply entrenched in cool figuring for that. When Stanley appointed him in 1909 as head of Traffic, Development and Advertising and later as commercial manager of Underground Electric Railways, it was not for his cultural enthusiasm or aesthetic idealism. Stanley wanted to make busybody Pick responsible for that part of the company he was continually attacking. The set-up succeeded. Pick made sure that his company's posters were more eye-catching than those of other advertisers on the tube's station walls. At the time it was not done out of any aesthetic sense, but simply to achieve results. More people should use the trains, especially more people should use the trains of Underground Electric Railways outside the rush hour.

On Frank Pick fell the onus of making the invisible network of connections more visible. He did this by naming his first poster 'Underground to Anywhere!' and then in an uninterrupted flow of new posters by continually drawing attention to an attraction above ground. This could be the countryside on the edge of the city, the architecture of London, or the annual sales and all were aimed at travelling the tube outside the rush hour. His posters were recordings of his own visual image of the city and their influence as advertisements gave the capital a particular flavour. They said something about the many aspects of this great city, arguably one of the most interesting in the world. The late 1960s proved just how strong this projection was. The logo of London Transport in a tourist folder was enough for tourists to conjure up the image of a pulsating international city, the heart of a youth movement which perhaps only by accident called itself the 'Underground.' The British Museum or trendy Carnaby Street? — everything within easy reach when you travelled the modern and efficient tube. London and all that that implied came to a halt with the last stop of the Underground.

In Pick's heyday, this image was much closer to reality than the grime encrusted Under-

ground of the swinging sixties, but it proves all the more the powerfulness of an image Pick was able to conjure up. The historian, Adrian Forty, goes even further by linking the design policy of London public transport with the manner in which Londoners have come to experience their city. He maintains that all too often the importance of design in a company's survival is underestimated. 'MANY PEOPLE DON'T REALISE HOW GREAT THE INFLUENCE COULD HAVE BEEN ON THE WAY LONDONERS REGARDED LONDON TRANSPORT, AND THAT THIS COULD HAVE INFLUENCED IDEAS CONCERNING THE SIZE, FORM AND CHARACTER OF THE CITY.'

It is indisputable that Pick cherished this view-point. In his plans to expand the underground network he looked in depth at the conglomerations being built on the outskirts of the city, and where possible when building new tube stations tried to influence the surrounding urban development. He saw public transport as 'THE FRAMEWORK UPON WHICH THE TOWN IS BUILT.' Abroad, in countries like Sweden, Germany and the Netherlands, he familiarized himself with comparable situations and the solutions architects had found for solving the problems of the modern city.

Before he got around to the building of completely new stations, his involvement with modern design had been largely limited to graphic projects. To design the posters – initially from the hands of commercial artists – during the First World War he increasingly commissioned artists, including Charles Paine. They were asked to come up with advertisements for a particular destination, not the actual getting there. In this way, in 1916, Pick challenged the young American artist, Edward McKnight, to paint some landscapes. Kauffer, who with his use of pure colours and simple composition was regarded as a modernist of the first order, surprised him with four views of Surrey which were made into posters.
By choosing a variety of styles and predominately modern artists, the poster series on the Underground became an art gallery for average folk, and that at a time when modern art in England was hardly understood. It was never

Frank Pick's intention to produce a collection of art. For him, posters had first of all to 'attract'. Nevertheless, Forty concludes that these posters were made in artistic styles seldom seen outside the galleries of Bond Street. They were advertisements extolling the pleasure of travelling on an efficient and orderly means of transport. The steady growth in their quality must have convinced Pick that the posters were 'THE MOST ELECTRIC FORM OF ART.'

At about the same time as the appearance of McKnight Kauffer's posters, Frank Pick finally got to see the definite result of his 1913 commission to the typographer, Edward Johnston (and initially his pupil Eric Gill), whose work championed a return to classic lettering, to design a new type for the Underground.

The brief was to design an open, readable and masculine alphabet that would be noticeably distinguishable from that used by other advertisers. Travellers casting a quick glance at the posters had to be able to see immediately by the lettering that it was an announcement from the Underground.

Pick wanted an unmistakably 20th-century type which at the same time had the convincing simplicity of classic lettering, and Johnston was of a similar mind. The metro-man was in fact already giving concrete form to a vision of the Underground which was to take off during the 1930s: uncompromisingly modern, yet in harmony with the best of the past. Johnston's sanserif type perfectly conformed. It was designed totally for readability and within the shortest possible time became the prototype for the typography of the entire company, including the lettering for station names, maps, posters, carriages and ticket machines. The type singled the company out and identified its holdings, including those of the bus company it had recently taken over. Far more than the elongated and fashionable Art Nouveau lettering of the Paris Métro, Johnston's type set a timeless standard, a universally acceptable design according to the principles of the German

(left) Poster by Dame Laura Knight, 1921; (centre) The first schematic plan, designed by Harry Beck in 1913, was only officially used twenty years later. (right) Edward Johnston's alphabet, 1916.

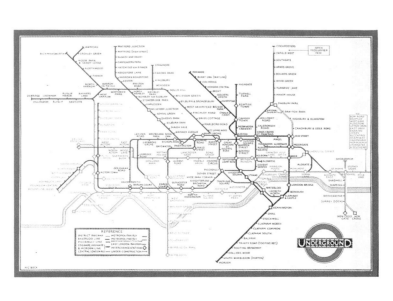

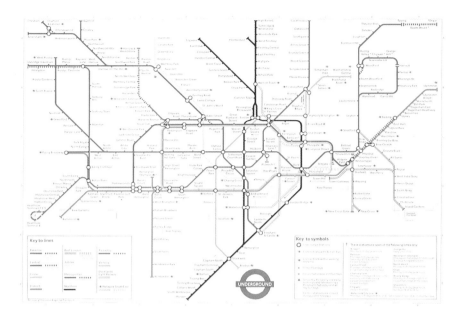

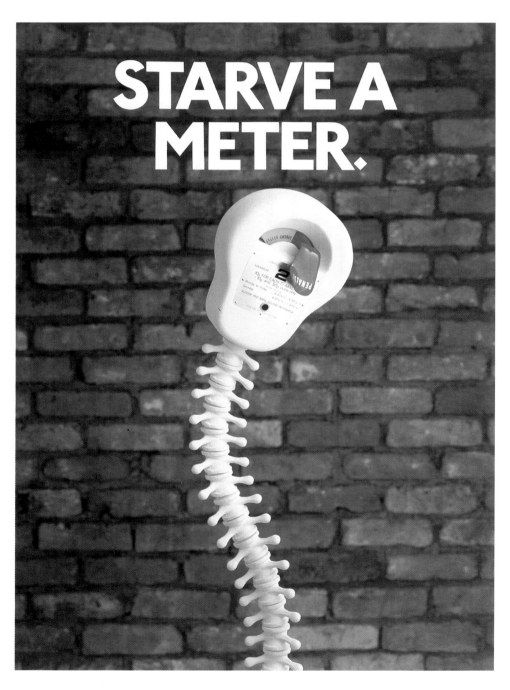

(above) the
present plan of the
Underground;
(left) the poster
for the 'Starve a
Meter' campaign,
made by Foote
Coone & Belding
Ltd, gained the
Design & Art
Directors award in
1988 for best
poster category.

Werkbund. The designer himself was hardly impressed by the 'blessings' of the modern age: 'THE GREAT MODERN WORLD OF MONEY, MOTORS AND MACHINES IS OPPOSED TO US,' was his firm conviction. The industrial application of his lettering never stirred his imagination; he was too knee-deep in the traditional conventions of the Art and Crafts movement for that.

During a period of mergers and expansion, the so-called bull's eye, a red circle and a blue band which still does service as London Transport's logo (as does Johnston's typography), began to come into its own. It was increasingly seen on buses and trains and from 1933 it was carried by the entire London public transport service. At that point the British transport minister decided that every public transport company within London had to be absorbed into the newly created London Passenger Transport Board, later shortened to London Transport. Frank Pick, working under Lord Ashfield, became its chief executive. Even so the black and red emblem was not as yet regarded as a component of a housestyle. It was seen more as a traffic sign, a signal to travellers that they had reached their destination.

London Transport was an amalgamation of no fewer than 165 companies, each with its own history and appearance. Therefore it was imperative to achieve unity within the new conglomerate as quickly as possible. By giving everyone the same wages for the same job and centrally regulating the terms and conditions of employment, any tensions in the initial transitional phase were curbed and possible strikes avoided. Design, too, played an important role in the power of convincing.
London Transport had to show a recognizable face to the outside world. The 'corporate identity' which had hesitatingly come into being in the previous years now had to do duty as the instrument of management policy. Particularly people who still did not use the

Restored 1863 platform on the world's first underground railway, Baker Street.

Underground and bus had to be convinced by the 'message' given by London Transport's buildings, trains, buses and even bus stops and refuse bins. They were designed to be sober, efficient and coherent, to reflect a forward thinking and well-coordinated transport company. Even for the seat covering of the new city RT doubledeckers (1939), the pride of London Transport, special avant-garde designers were commissioned.
The message was clear – this company leaves nothing to chance. Down to the doorknobs and screws the best crafts people had bowed their heads.
It was precisely this impression Frank Pick wanted to drive home to his travellers. For him, the smooth operation of a ticket machine was just as important as the nightly inspection through the tunnels looking for signs of wear and tear. Designers were there to keep a watchful eye on the comfort and safety of passengers: simplicity coupled with quality was his devout aim.

In this sense Johnston's typography was tailor-made for a mentality which not until the 1930s did London Transport begin to make typically its own. The new lettering met the objective of being readable, yet had a classical quality to it. Or as Pick put it during a lecture in 1933: 'AN OBJECT IS ONLY SUITABLE FOR ITS PURPOSE IF IT IS NOT ONLY PURELY PRACTICAL, BUT ALSO CONFORMS TO A MORAL, SPIRITUAL ORDER.'

While it is not known to what extent Frank Pick was involved with its design, the map of the Underground has to be seen as the embodiment of this credo. Only it wasn't immediately recognized as such. Its originator Harry Beck was a totally unknown 29-year-old draughtsman in the Establishment Section of the London Underground when he submitted his preliminary sketch for the map to the publicity department. At that time he had been temporarily sent home and had used his spare moments to simplify the tortuous map then in use. He drew only horizontal, vertical and diagonal lines to connect the stations, ignored precise geographical locations and instead used only a schematic interpretation of the Thames to indicate the real world above ground. Moreover, on the map Beck enlarged central London so that all its stations and lines could be clearly reproduced, while greatly reducing the area outside.

The unsolicited design was brushed aside in 1931 and it was only after a second attempt that the management agreed to use it for a trial period. Beck had written in by hand all the names of the stations on the map using Johnston's lettering: 2400 capital letters, well-spaced and so placed as to avoid their competing with one another. Shortly afterwards Beck replaced the small circles of the original with a small horizontal line to indicate stations. Its circulation was a great success and by the end of 1933 the map hung in all stations.

Its success can almost certainly be explained by the concordance between the unreality of travelling under the ground and the abstract interpretation Beck's map gave of the experience. In the tunnels a sense of direction is not the main concern, but the counting of the stations – still three to go before you're above ground at Covent Garden. There reality begins once more, and that is where a map has to be geographically accurate.

Until 1959 numerous new improved versions of the Underground map appeared under Beck's name. His life's work received better colours, better indications for where to change trains and so on, until in 1960 a newly appointed Underground chief attempted to produce a map of his own. Shortly afterwards, the Underground reverted back again to the spirit of Beck's design and even today the world-famous diagram is still largely Beck's work. He never received much public recognition for it. In Frank Pick's official biography his name does not even appear! He was not paid much either. The man who in his free time tried to refine his map of the capital to a universal matrix of London did not consider it worth the trouble to present London Transport with a bill. Nevertheless, there is hardly a transport network established anywhere in the world that did not use his sophisticated diagram as a reference work.

The exact relationship between Harry Beck and his boss Frank Pick remains unclear. However, it was wellknown that Pick greatly valued having a personal contact with the professionals with whom he worked. Perhaps Charles Holden, among all these, was the man closest to his heart. His arrival as architect for London Transport was performed almost secretly. During the construction of Westminster station the self-willed commercial manager had allowed Holden to build simply a side entrance so that the 'house' architects of London Transport would not feel they had been overlooked, and which would also give him a leg up to bigger commissions. These came quickly. First the designing of Clapham South followed by the construction of Piccadilly Circus.

Charles Holden's task was to build stations for the future of the Underground: open, light and dynamic. Piccadilly Circus, which in 20 years had seen the annual number of travellers grow from 1.5 to 25 million, desperately needed expanding and Pick wanted to make a statement. Together with Holden he worked on a circular shaped hall with eight entrances and encircled by shops. In its centre was the pride and glory of the redesigned station – a new type of automated ticket machine. By inserting coins the traveller received the appropriate ticket plus the necessary change. The dispenser was both smaller and quicker than the old model and enabled the traveller to look over the top of the row of machines.
Piccadilly Circus, completed in 1928, heralded a period of meticulous orchestration between

architecture and design. A little earlier, London Transport had taken delivery of new trains in which there were more seats, improved lighting, less noise and each carriage had four large sliding doors to speed up passenger traffic and reduce delays between stations. The same verve for efficiency marks Holden's design for the new London Transport headquarters (1929), whereby he was commissioned to produce a building, cost what it may, which in no way symbolically expressed the social power of the company. The solid utilitarianism of the design failed initially to reap much praise with the public, although the design critics were enthusiastic, in the same way they were to rave about Holden's new stations of the 1930s. The art historian Nikolaus Pevsner described Sudbury Town station as 'A LANDMARK...ITS COMPLETION MARKS THE BEGINNING OF A CLASSICAL PERIOD IN THE ARCHITECTURE OF THE UNDERGROUND', while Pick proclaimed at the same time that 'NOTHING WILL BE CONSTRUCTED UNLESS IT IS SPECIALLY DESIGNED IN ACCORDANCE WITH THE TOTAL ARCHITECTURAL SCHEME.'

He was supported in his view by the example of Charles Rennie Mackintosh, the Scottish architect, who was not content to design just an empty house but also specified its interior down to the last detail. Total attunement was the most dominant feature of London Transport until Pick's enforced retirement from the company in 1939. In other words, all the components – from bus tickets and litter bins to maps and station buildings – were recognizable as visible expressions of one and the same company.

Charles Holden had in no mean way contributed to this, especially with the stations and the northern expansion of the Piccadilly Line. These designs followed a trip abroad, including to the Netherlands where Pick and his travel companion were impressed by the modern designs in brick of Willem Dudok. When the stations including Wood Green, Arnos Grove and Southgate were completed in autumn 1933, the two men had been collaborating for ten years. Ten years in which, according to Christian Barman: 'A SERIES OF STATIONS WERE CONSTRUCTED IN WIDELY SPREAD AREAS OF LONDON, EACH A LITTLE DIFFERENT FROM THE OTHER, EACH CAREFULLY ADAPTED TO SUIT ITS SURROUNDINGS, BUT ALL AIMED AT A CONSISTENTLY RECOGNIZABLE STYLE OF AN EXCEPTIONAL LEVEL.'

Even nowadays it is still possible, notes Adrian Forty, that commuters amid the decay, repair work and demoralized personnel, which have all seriously eroded the power of Pick's vision, can, on the outer reaches of the Piccadilly Line, still catch a glimpse of a once revolutionary style, consistently applied, which created an organization of which every employee was proud to be a part.

Gert Staal

(opposite, above) Speeding into the future: the new rolling stock for the Central Line due for delivery in 1992.
(below) Cover and inside layout for Shaping up for the future, a publication describing the history and development of the London Underground's corporate identity, 1987.

Shaping up

for the

future

Fifty years and more of London Transport

London's great bus and Underground system developed from the operations of a series of individual companies over a hundred years ago.

Around the turn of the century, the nature of these operations changed dramatically with the impact of new technology.

The Victorian steam underground railways were electrified and a network of new deep-level electric tube lines was opened. On the roads, horse-drawn vehicles gave way to motor buses and electric trams running over much longer routes. Most of the private companies running the buses and tubes became part of a large parent company known as the Underground Group, which included the London General Omnibus Company.

As London grew in the 1920s the network of bus routes and Underground lines expanded with it to serve the new suburbs.

The Underground Group's road and rail services set the pace in this development. Good design played a key role in underlining the purpose and function of the company's operations, both to passengers and staff.

A special type-face was introduced for signs and publicity. Striking pictorial posters were used to promote services. A carefully devised architectural house-style was applied to new stations and other buildings.

Most noticeable of all, the bullseye or roundel made its appearance as the organisation's symbol.

Full realisation of London's bus and Underground systems came in 1933 with the creation of the London Passenger Transport Board.

This public corporation, soon generally known as London Transport, was responsible for all bus, tram, trolleybus and Underground services in the capital.

The strong, co-ordinated identity that was already the hallmark of the Underground group was now extended to cover all London Transport's operations. Its design elements – the Underground map, the bright red buses and the bullseye symbol on stations and bus stops – became familiar parts of London's life, attracting both admiration and imitation around the world.

Even though the war interrupted the rapid growth of London Transport, the passenger services continued, and Underground stations were frequently used in air-raid shelters.

The most significant Underground developments of the post-war period were the opening of the Victoria Line – with a completely integrated new design – the Jubilee Line, and the Piccadilly Line extensions to Heathrow. The buses too changed, with the famous London Routemasters being progressively replaced by more modern, specially-designed one-man-operated buses.

Throughout its history that instantly recognisable London Transport "look" was maintained as the system grew and adapted to the changing operating conditions of more than fifty years.

The New Identity

To reflect the nature of the various elements of the organisation, and to help people understand the new structure, a new identity has been adopted.

The key objectives of this identity are to:

– Distinguish the overall planning and service-procurement role of LRT from the roles of London Transport and the transport operating businesses the name embraces

– Highlight London Underground and London Buses as separate subsidiary businesses.

– Provide a link between each of the transport-related activities, as well as separating them from the other businesses.

LRT is different from London Transport. To mark this difference and make its role clear:

– LRT will not use the roundel, because that is synonymous with the transport operations embraced under the "London Transport" name. To help make this distinction LRT has created a new mark and house style of its own.

– The initials "LRT", and not the words, will always be used for London Regional Transport itself, to avoid confusion with the more specific London Transport operational businesses.

– In most cases "LRT" will be accompanied by a qualifying phrase "Organising transport for London" – to explain its role. The exception is when "LRT" is being used as an endorsement to signify its ownership of a business.

London Transport, London Underground, London Buses and the Roundel

The main transport and transport-related businesses will continue to use the roundel in one of a number of approved forms.

– London Transport: the collective trading name for the transport network – will use the red roundel which will appear on tickets, bus stops, posters, in fact anything that is not specific to one transport operation.

– London Underground will continue to use its familiar red and blue roundel.

– London Buses will use a red and yellow roundel incorporating its name on the coloured bar.

– The London Transport Museum, London Transport Advertising, London Transport International and London Transport Lost Property will also use the red roundel.

Adidas
The sporting look

Take the Bormio. It is a mid-calf Italian hiking-style boot suitable for winter sports holidays. Made in suede, it has a removable insole, and a thermoplastic rubber sole with special long-distance tread and studs. Or what about the Boast, an aerated shoe which comes in a combination of nylon and suede. It has a removable jersey-covered insole and a rubber sole with two-tone squash tread. Then there is the Samba Special II. This shoe is particularly suited to very hard, frozen ground, snow or ice. The inlay sole roy-air sansole, thanks to the different layers of material, has high sweat absorption effectiveness thus offering high wear comfort; furthermore because the components are treated the inlay sole is not affected by typical odours.

The three models are as different as day from night. All they have in common is their tripartite adidas symbol: on the Samba three stripes fading into black; on the Boast they are black and orange; the Bormio, which is multi-coloured and has no room for added ornament, sports a trefoiled emblem instead. Three stripes or trefoil – both have stood for adidas for years.

Today adidas produces nearly as many shoes as there are sports and wearers, and it is hard to believe that this footwear emporium has grown out of the company that set out making simple plimsolls in 1920. Seventy years later their assortment is too big to itemize.
For many years now it has been extended to include products other than the footwear designed to improve sporting achievements of both men and women and reduce the risk of injury. Sport has become synonymous with leisure so that adidas now also deals in leisure wear, ski equipment, various ball sports, sports bags, tennis rackets and rainwear.
In just over fifty years, the dividing lines between sportswear, leisure wear and working attire have become blurred. This is nothing new; garments have often found alternative uses. The sports jacket associated with smart day wear began life as a tennis or cricket garment. And where will the track suit end up? As a trendy uniform for road sweepers or as the new bank clerk's two-piece suit?

Adidas is Adi Dassler's brainchild. He welded his Christian name and surname, wrapped them in stripes and topped them with an Indian crown, the three-leaved insignia.
The West German sportsman and inventor, who became director of his own company, was way ahead of his time. Long before the notion of leisure had been popularized, let alone subjected to research in the western world, Dassler was endeavouring to develop ideal footwear for sportsmen.

What did sportspeople wear on their feet before 1920? Did they go barefooted or wear heavy brown brogues? For the answer we have to go back to the Greek amphora and plates, which show us athletes wearing sandals or with nothing on their feet. Nineteenth-century

(opposite) Bormio
sports shoes,
1989.

(below) Adidas
headquarters in
Herzogenaurach,
West Germany.

Designing for the
sports business of
tomorrow:
optimum
presentation of
sports- and
leisure wear with
the help of a
'shop-in' shop
concept (above
and below).

prints portray the occasional young lady
clutching a tennis racket, dressed in an evening gown of sorts and trotting about in laced
bootees. There is little actual evidence, but one
cannot resist the suspicion that such footwear
prevented her from getting many balls back. In
fact one might venture to conclude that it was
not until Dassler's plimsolls were invented that
the sport itself was actually discovered.

Sport must have been a lot simpler in 1920
with only wrestling, athletics, boxing, football,
tennis and skating. There was hardly any
skiing let alone table tennis, ice hockey, aerobics or squash. The world – and the world of
sport too – has become more complex since
then. There seem to be sports tailored to the
needs of every individual, with a choice of
specializations within each branch for sportspeople to prove their own particular worth.
The long-distance runner today is faced with
the task of deciding between a shoe with an air
pad under the instep guaranteeing extra
bounce, one with a low or high heel protector,
a third with a cushioned inner sole, and an
assortment with different treads for use on
different running surfaces.

It is the old story of the wood and the trees,
especially when you realize that sports baron
adidas once had the land all to itself.
The leisure and sportswear sector has become
a busy junction, with increasing traffic from
the West (Nike, Brooks and Reebok), a thin,
but by no means negligible, supply trickling
down the northern route (Karhu), and an inex-
haustible stream from the East (generally
copied, dump makes and occasional brands).
The congestion is partly due to the capricious
behaviour of the young consumer whose
tastes are group-determined. Sport to them is
a way of distinguishing themselves, a status
symbol or sign of good taste, a protest symbol
or something to identify with.

Adidas has had its share of fickle adolescent
behaviour. The brand was suddenly dropped
by youthful consumers in certain western
European countries when Nike became the
new sports idol until they too were rejected for
the cult of Reebok. Adidas had one important
advantage over its competitors, however – it
was there before all the others and had been
able to build up a reputation solid enough to
found sports careers on today.

In this respect the West German company has
utilized its fall from grace to advantage.
Its sportswear range is promoted in an intelligent and highly efficient manner and sportspeople are invited to test and try out their
merchandise or alternatively map out their
sports careers at adidas' expense. The company's business card is peopled by a sporting
corps d'élite – tennis players Steffi Graf and
Stefan Edberg, swimmer Matt Biondi and the
Dutch national football team, victor of the
1988 European cup, and its opponent, the
Kaiser of West German football, Franz Becken-
bauer, who has sworn by adidas for years.

Asked why West Germany's other pride and
joy, Boris Becker, was not involved, the com-
pany's promotor and sponsor expert offered a
simple explanation: 'YOU SHOULD AVOID
OVERLOADING YOUR PLATE WITH CAVIAR,
LOBSTER AND FOIE GRAS. LADY DI MIGHT
FEASIBLY MAKE A BETTER ADVOCATE OF
ADIDAS THAN ANOTHER SPORTS STAR.'

(opposite) Cover
and inside layout
of adidas'
housestyle
manual, 1989.

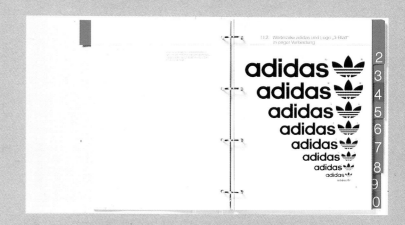

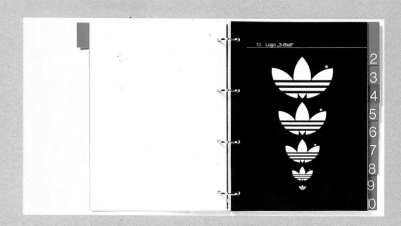

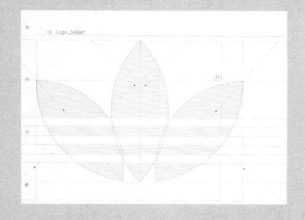

Top sportspeople have a second function besides being human hoardings. They are adidas' designers. They test the shoes, give advice, and help determine the design before the product is turned over to the anonymous design team for finalization. Close collaboration of this kind with the German national team produced the football boot with replaceable studs in the 1950s.

Adidas conceived its trade name in 1948 and adopted its three stripes as its corporate symbol in 1949, at a time when the leisure industry was still in its infancy and well before the branch was giving any thought to such things as corporate identity. Dassler was the first to give a specialized retail product a broader context, supplying with it a distribution network and an efficient production line. This bold move was remarkable considering that the 1940–1945 war years had stunted the firm's development. Forced by the postwar shortage of raw and other materials, Dassler produced a shoe made of canvas from army tents and rubber taken from discarded petrol tanks. They were the first postwar sports shoes, the first in a series of products to supersede each other in their revolutionary use of materials.

The move had been set in motion before the Second World War. Dassler Sportschuh-fabriken had presented itself quite as a matter of course at the 1936 Berlin Olympics. Jesse Owens, the star of the Games, ran for gold, adidas-shod in what seems today a touchingly simple, fad-free shoe that gave the athlete sufficient footing for new records. Long before these Olympics, Dassler had set himself the task of engineering a shoe that would protect the user from injury, one that was solid and would hold out well. For an athletic shoe it was

important to develop spikes that would guarantee stability during the run. He also studied the different requirements of shoes for short and long-distance runs, for use at track events or on marathon runs.

Born in Herzogenaurach near Nuremberg in 1900, Dassler grew up with sport, which was the only real form of recreation during the First World War, and it was his own personal experience that alerted him to the shortcomings of the equipment available. His maxim from the outset was 'YOU NEED THE RIGHT TOOLS TO DO A GOOD JOB'. He studied at a special shoe college in Pirmasens to learn the ins and outs of the trade, but the practical world proved his main training ground. In 1938 he could be seen launching himself off a slope not far from his native village using a table top as a ski jump, gaped at and emulated by the local youth. It was his way of researching a problem and promoting sport. Where his own empirical experience was lacking he consulted athletes, trainers, orthopedists and medical experts, as well as the organizers of sporting events.

Dassler realized that his ideas could only succeed if they were confirmed by athletes, and preferably at global events where they would be witnessed by others. There is no doubt that the hausse in sports equipment, particularly in the 1960s, would not have been possible without the media, which channelled into people's homes crystal-clear close-ups of athletic feats, including passing shots of the brand names of the athletes' trappings. Three stripes would flash across the television screen and viewers would appear at a sports shop asking for adidas sport shoes the next day. They might have seen Ard Schenk win the tournament in a body-hugging adidas skating suit or Gerd Muller complete his hat-trick in

(below left) Inside pages and cover from an adidas brochure, 1989. (right) Join the game! adidas brochure, 1989.

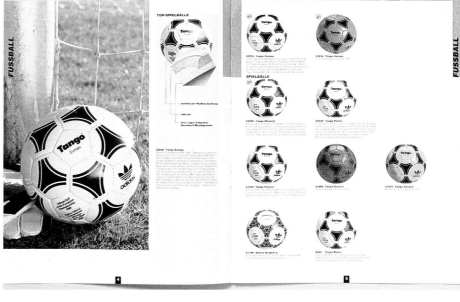

adidas boots. (Cast in gold, these are on display at the special shoe museum – showcase of past glory – at the Herzogenaurach headquarters.)

Adidas and the Olympics are on these accounts almost inseparable. The firm mentions proudly the number of athletes that have used their products – 75 per cent in Rome (1960), 80 per cent in Moscow (1980), and which innovations they have marketed commercially – an ultra lightweight shoe in Tokyo (1964), the Azteca shoe specially designed for Mexico's hard synthetic athletic tracks (1968). The close relationship between adidas and the Olympic movement, in particular the friendship between the current President of the IOC, Juan Antonio Samaranch, and Adi's son, the late Horst Dassler, has been questioned by some. Personal friendships, similar aims – to promote sport throughout the world–and, let us be clear, the need to make some money out of sport–meant that the IOC and the adidas group have done much together. But it is wrong to think that the three stripes rule the five rings.

Dressing the Olympic teams tends to create obligations and certainly does not leave the Olympic Committee entirely free in its choice of a location for the Games. Adidas has, for instance, fitted out the Eastern European teams since 1972 and in so doing they have proved a generous sponsor, courting the prospect of an attractive market. It is no secret that Dassler Jr came to an understanding with Samaranch – the preparatory talks were conducted when Samaranch was still the Spanish ambassador in Moscow – to allow the 1988 Games to go to Seoul so as to prepare the Asiatic market for Adidas as a sequel to its Eastern European overtures. China was bound

to be the first to sign on for the Seoul Games and Dassler was well aware of the effect of his Russian sponsoring: the younger generation in Russia had been converted to Adidas. The allegations made in the press are not entirely unfounded – three stripes do rule the five rings.

But that is something the sports world will have to learn to live with. Over the past few decades adidas has constructed a commercial network comparable to that of Coca-Cola. It has penetrated to the sporting hearth and is not very likely to give up its warm nest without a fight. Sport has always been governed by *citius, altius, fortius* (faster, higher and stronger), and it is impossible for an industry so dependent on sport to stand aloof of this drive.

A blue lower-case logotype is the binding agent throughout the company. So consistently is it applied that the name adidas always appears in texts in lower case. The blue is described as K+E Novaboard blue No. 203936, and the type is a sanserif – highly modern in 1949 – and describes a perfect circle. It was Dassler himself who conceived the logotype and the trademark with the three stripes.

The trefoil symbol was the invention of Hans Fick, a freelance designer from Nuremberg. The company wanted to stress their fashion line and the three stripes had shown themselves ill-suited to this. On a track suit they were either lost or so dominating that they left the designer little room to play with.

The introduction of the trefoil logo emphasized the new course Adidas was steering in the direction of the leisure sector. At the close of the 1960s Dassler realized that sport was a

'I want, I can', autumn 1989 advertising campaign.

narrow field, particularly top sport, and he anticipated the arrival of occasional sports – jogging, aerobics and the fitness craze. The leaf symbol settled on a new segment that sometimes had little to do with sport.

Today the consumer can go to adidas for a raincoat or a sweater. The company has even opened several of its own fashion stores. The fashion component is gaining ground alongside the quality, durability and comfort which govern the sportswear range. Adidas presents a new collection every season in the tradition of the great fashion houses, stressing individuality of dress.

Sport is far less a question of teamwork than it used to be. Today the sportsman or woman can opt between jackets made up in a variety of patterned fabrics ranging from dots and geometrics to futuristic motifs. The influence of ski fashions has clearly left its mark. Aero-dynamic second-skin suits have become stand-ard for skating, cycling and athletics too these days. The collection offers a pageant of colour to the roving eye.

It is conspicuous how the diversity of sports has banished uniformity. The track suit is virtually non-existent in its original form, avail-able today in a host of variations – in tight and shiny polyamide, salopettes, sweater-'n-pants sets, or garments bearing closer resemblance to party wear. For its fashion line, adidas relies partly on its in-house designers and partly – particularly for its fabric designs – on independent designers.

Amid the dazzling assortment, the trefoil that catches our eye on the heel of a shoe, on the strings of a racket, acts as leitmotif. The three stripes are enough to conjure up associations with the sportswear manufacturer.
This symbol is not meant to put across a crea-tive or audacious image – that would only detract from the German solidity of the product the company claims. Shoes which you can fall back on, fashions that do not shock, surprise or outrage.

Adidas is a family business. Besides Dassler, its founder, who died in 1978, his wife Kathe Dassler was the driving force behind the enter-prise until her death in 1984. After that, their son Horst Dassler took over the management until his premature death in 1987. Initially it was Dassler who conceived and tested all the products. Nowadays the company is a con-glomerate of staff design teams. Sport is a field where it is customary for the consumer rather than the designer to go off with the glory. And even if the designer were to claim a fairer share, as the maker of a mass product he would no doubt be doomed to anonymity.

Adidas has registered 700 patents varying from the unscrewable stud under a football boot to the use of ceramics in the same inven-tion. All their innovations serve the same goal of making things as functional, light and comfortable as possible for the sportsperson. Where they succeed, adidas' three stripes serve to underline their achievements.

Jaap Huisman

(above) Waterproof watches. (opposite) Free 'n easy sportswear.

Coca-Cola
World's best-known logo

The story of Coca-Cola is the story of success. It was the dream of a 19th-century Atlanta chemist to produce a completely new flavour that would conquer the world. Shortly after inventing it he died. The nostalgic cellar where he brewed his wondrous concoction, stirring the mixture in his copper pan with a large spoon, has long since made way for a great many modern factories. His dream came true, though he himself did not live to see it.

After a vain attempt in 1914, in the 1950s, about sixty years after the drink was first made, Coca-Cola was introduced in the Netherlands on a large scale. It was one of the tokens of the new postwar era, which was frequently identified with the goods people bought. The first encounter with this modern soft drink in its special bottle was an experience many were unlikely to forget.

Mine was in the village I grew up in, in a room with a bar and a pool table – the makeshift canteen of the local youth club, which were legion in the Netherlands at the time. One evening two men came in dressed in green overalls with a red and white emblem on their sleeve and breast pocket. In each hand they were carrying a small crate containing 24 bottles of Coca-Cola, which we were astonished to be invited to drink free of charge. Free Coca-Cola, as much as you wanted! After that evening the crates were a familiar sight, only now we had to pay 25 guilder cents a bottle, but we thought it well worth it.

Not long after this, a Coca-Cola factory was erected on the outskirts of the village. The patch of land behind the shed where the rattling bottling machine was installed was suddenly doubly interesting. Besides being a football pitch, it was a place where you looked for the Coca-Cola crown caps that were dumped there with the broken bottles. If you were lucky, hidden under their thin layer of cork, you could find the letters you needed to spell the word Coca-Cola. Every complete word qualified you for a free bottle of Coca-Cola.

Our introduction to Coca-Cola back in the 1950s illustrates the public relations policy the company pursues to this day. The complimentary drinks you were first offered you paid for with all the Coca-Cola you drank later. By approaching the consumer directly Coca-Cola has introduced its product in every conceivable corner of the globe and this policy has been particularly instrumental in establishing the company's world market position. Their slogan 'THINK GLOBAL, ACT LOCAL' holds the key to Coca-Cola's international fame.

The success of Coca-Cola's methods is confirmed by the results of a survey, conducted in 1988 by the American research organization Landor Associates, into international awareness of world trademarks, which reported Coca-Cola the unrivalled champion. With

(opposite) One of the many soda fountains of the last century. In 1886 Coca-Cola made its debut in these popular drinking establishments, which were a unique cross between cafe, tearoom, chemists shop and confectioners.

Enamel advertisement from 1911.

the help of its idiosyncratic Atlanta bottle, the soft drink has become one of the icons of the 20th century along with such celebrities as Vincent van Gogh and Marilyn Monroe.

But to return to the United States towards the end of the 19th century. In 1869, at the age of 36, ex-major and chemist John Syth Pemberton moved to Atlanta, where he started a wholesale drug business. His true ambition as a chemist, however, was to create a new soft drink that would become the rage of the soda fountains, which were fashionable at the time. On 8 May 1886 Pemberton's notebook mentions that he had succeeded in creating a flavour to his liking by mixing a number of ingredients he had used before in less successful syrups and elixirs, with a solution of sugar and water. The new formula was based on a recipe called 'French Wine of Cola', which in turn was inspired by a popular soft drink known as 'Vin Mariana'. But it was the extra ingredients Pemberton added after the syrup had cooled that gave the drink its special flavour. To this day they still remain a well-guarded secret.

This open secret, perpetuated by the mysterious reference to these ingredients in the recipe as 'natural flavouring', has received a good deal of publicity, which was not always favorable. Coca-Cola has been subjected to various smear campaigns, some accusing the company of adding cocaine to the drink. Accusations have resorted to some absurd insinuations, like the charge that it was not a poisoned goblet that killed Socrates but a glass of Coca-Cola.

As on many other occasions, Coca-Cola succeeded in making a virtue of necessity. Without realizing it, the prosecutor had given the company a splendid idea for an advertising campaign – 'Things would have gone better with Coke', in which Coca-Cola 'rectifies' the outcome of world history events.

Robert Woodruff, president of the Coca-Cola Company from 1923, based his statement that 'COCA-COLA IS A RELIGION AS WELL AS A BUSINESS' on the belief that secrets are appealing and that a secret recipe is an important asset, for publicity purposes as well. For the secrecy can lead people into thinking they are buying something special.

Despite Coca-Cola's well-entrenched name and extensive advertising, design literature is conspicuously silent on the subject of Coca-Cola. The one exception is Herbert Leupin's poster, which is featured because of the poster design rather than the Coca-Cola bottle and logo. Perhaps this has something to do with the fact that neither the bottle nor the logo were designed by professionals. Their amateurish character has not exactly helped win them a place in the history of design. The idea of calling Pemberton's drink Coca-Cola came from his bookkeeper, Frank M. Robinson. It is a contraction of the names of main ingredients – the coca leaf and the kola nut. It was also Robinson's idea to change the K to a C. Aided by the engraver, Frank Ridge, Robinson designed the trademark, which shows distinct traces of Art Nouveau. Underneath, he added with simple logic the words 'Delicious and Refreshing' – the most concise and effective copy ever written.

A unique fountain sampling unit from the mid-1930s.

STANDARD COCA COLA COOLER

Cooler holds 72 bottles, 4 cases in reserve. Ice capacity 50 pounds. Size 31½" x 23½" x 40" high, 10½" deep inside. Packed knocked down in crate. Shipping weight 127 pounds.   Price $11.60

Manufactured (under license from The Coca Cola Company) by
GLASCOCK BROTHERS MFG. CO.
Muncie, Indiana

1927 MODEL IMPROVED *Icy-O*
BEVERAGE REFRIGERATOR AND DISPENSER

Note Simplicity of Operation.
Manufactured and Distributed by
THE ICY-O COMPANY, CHARLOTTE, N. C.

In his book **THE CORPORATE PERSONALITY**, Wally Olins only once mentions the name of Coca-Cola, when quoting Thom Wolfe criticizing abstract logos: '... **OR THE HAND-WRITTEN LOGOS OF COCA-COLA OR HERTZ – THEY STICK IN THE MIND AND PRODUCE INSTANT RECOGNITION. ABSTRACT LOGOS ARE A DEAD LOSS IN THAT RESPECT** ...' It is certainly true that Coca-Cola's hand-written logo lends itself well to publicity purposes. It also ensures instant recognition. From the viewpoint of design psychology these are two invaluable assets. The fact that the calligraphic logo has remained unchanged since 1890 is sufficient proof of its efficacy.

The corporate symbol as a whole, on the other hand, has undergone several drastic face-lifts. A thick white undulating line was added under the trademark, literally and figuratively under-lining Coca-Cola's dynamic character (discussed later). In 1970 the bright red can with the new logo was brought onto the market. Recently a second line was added, which narrows in the middle and varies in colour from country to country. In the Nether-lands the line is grey whereas dark brown was felt to be more appropriate for Belgium.

Coca-Cola owes its fame more to the epithet 'sexy bottle', coined in 1915, than to the design itself. In its early days the new soft drink was distributed through independent agents. One of them, Joseph A. Biederharn, ran a soda fountain. He was the first to sell Pemberton's drink in bottles so that customers could drink their Coca-Cola off the premises if they wished. Biederharn's move caused sales to soar. Other proprietors were quick to follow suit, and an assortment of bottles was used, most of which bore the Coca-Cola trademark. Motivated by the lack of homogeneity, Harold Hirsch, the company's lawyer, advocated developing a uniform bottle. 'WE NEED A NEW BOTTLE – A DISTINCTIVE PACKAGE THAT WILL HELP US FIGHT SUBSTITUTION. WE NEED A BOTTLE WHICH A PERSON WILL RECOGNIZE AS A COCA-COLA BOTTLE EVEN WHEN HE FEELS IT IN THE DARK. THE COCA-COLA BOTTLE SHOULD BE SHAPED SO THAT, EVEN IF BROKEN, A PERSON COULD TELL WHAT IT WAS.'

The first bottle was designed by Alexander Samuelson, an employee at the C.J. Root Glass Company. It was based on the shape of the cola leaf and the kola nut, and was the company's pampered child. However, the French designer Raymond Loewy, who had settled in the United States in 1919 and designed dispensers and a streamlined car for Coca-Cola, had misgivings about Samuelson's creation. He felt the shape was too explicitly feminine and out of tone with its commercial or consumer functions. But 'the queen of the soft drink bottles' was sacred to the manage-ment and the debate on its shape dragged on for a long time. Raymond Loewy's persever-ance was finally rewarded and he was commissioned to give the bottle a slimmer line. This bottle not only became one of the most famous packages but, as Loewy agreed, also one of the most perfect of the era.

Before the bottle was restyled there were several attempts at plagiarism, something which the company was repeatedly confront-ed with. To counteract this, the bottle was patented as early as 1916 and protected by copyright – a distinction few packages enjoy.

The introduction of the bottle prompted Coca-Cola to alter its advertising strategies. Previously, advertising had revolved round film stars of dazzling beauty posing with glasses of Coca-Cola; now it was the snappy little bottle itself that was the centre of attention, identi-fied with various forms of recreation tinged with somewhat aristocratic overtones.

(above left) The first bottles were straight sided, but were supplanted by the 'sexy' bottle in 1915, which has since undergone slight modifications.

(middle) Coca-Cola developed a cooler whereby drivers from 1929 onwards could get a chilled bottle of Coca-Cola at local petrol stations. (right) A more sophisticated model from 1927.

(opposite page, top to bottom, left to right) One of six posters which illustrator Norman Rockwell produced for Coca-Cola between 1928 and 1935; poster from the Second World War; 'The four seasons' - a window display screen from the turn of the century, almost two metres wide and a metre high. (bottom left) 1930s six-pack packaging. (right) wooden 24-bottle crates used in the 1920s.

Coca-Cola came to stand for dynamism, though this connotation is possibly stronger today than it ever was then. In the past, the glass had to be carefully cupped in two hands to ensure none of the precious nectar was spilled; now the most carefree, even one-handed, positions were allowed, making it ideally suited to work breaks or sporting occasions. Gradually the atmosphere in which Coca-Cola was drunk became the central theme of the company's advertising campaigns.

Throughout all these different campaigns, the product itself has always remained the hub of all the advertising. No doubt this is why the company rejected the idea of collaborating with the arts. Artists found the constraint of every expression having to serve the product too limiting. Any individuality of style or vision would detract from the product. For this reason a corporate architecture is only second on the priorities list. This may also explain why there is so little reference to Coca-Cola in design literature.

Coca-Cola is the symbol of The American Dream and it is understandably anxious to remain so. This is the product of publicity, which is aimed not at an élite audience but at all layers of society. As a senior executive once pointed out, 'BASICALLY, ANYBODY CAN MAKE A DRINK...THE REASON FOR OUR SUCCESS IS OUR ACCUMULATION OF ADVERTISING AND THE ATMOSPHERE OF FRIENDSHIP WE CREATE.' Everything revolves round our thirst not for liquid but for a care-free life. Thus Coca-Cola owes its success mainly to its publicity. Its corporate identity can be considered synonymous with the way its product is advertised.

Coca-Cola did not share Woodruff's belief that their licensed bottlers should be in touch with local cultural and social life, since they felt it would do the product no good to keep up with such trends. The response from artists to Coca-Cola's popular image, however, was staggering. By the 1960s, the bottle had become a symbol of the rapidly expanding American economy. Artists used the bottle to

make ironic comment on this economic power – Pop Artists and NOUVEAUX REALISTES in particular, such as Duane Hanson, Daniel Spoerri and Robert Rauschenburg, to name but three from the long list. The Coca-Cola phenomenon has been used on more than one occasion by such diverse artists as Salvador Dali and Dieter Roth, and his great predecessor Joseph Beuys.

The British Pop Artist Richard Hamilton pointed out that the characteristics identified with Pop Art – popularity, transience, expendability, low cost, mass-production, youth, sex appeal, gimmicks, glamour and big business – were no less valid for Coca-Cola. It was this inventory that inspired Andy Warhol to devise his perfect cycle of art–advertising–business–lifestyle–success–art. The most impressive art work connected with Coca-Cola is Edward Kienholz' 'The Portable War Memorial' (1968). This installation, built round a chrome-coloured Coca-Cola dispenser, offers an imposing impression of the 'imperialistic lifestyle' of American society at the time. Kienholz' monument is a top Pop Art piece which pretends to debate – within the four walls of the museum – the place of the consumer and advertising in art.

Coca-Cola has frequently and miraculously turned difficult situations to its own advantage, as in the case of the smear campaigns I mentioned earlier. They did this on a grand scale during the Second World War. Not that the company took unfair advantage of the troops, on the contrary. Within three weeks of the United States' entry into the war, Robert Woodruff had managed to convince the leaders of the armed forces that it was important for the troops on the other side of the ocean to be supplied with Coca-Cola, and gave orders 'TO SEE THAT EVERY MAN IN UNIFORM GETS A BOTTLE OF COCA-COLA FOR 5 DOLLAR CENTS WHEREVER HE IS AND WHATEVER IT COSTS THE COMPANY.'

(below left) 24-bottle wooden crate, 1950s. A 1963 can, which followed the first ones made in 1960. Seven years later the famous bright red can with the white, wavy line would make its debut around the world. (right) The 'sexy' bottle, 1915.

Two images from the famous 'Coke is it' campaign of the mid-1980s.

Forty-nine complete bottling plants were shipped out as 'strategic supplies', which was a good deal more efficient than forwarding filled bottles. Woodruff was not mistaken in his judgement. Numerous documents, such as General Dwight Eisenhower's urgent telegram for three million bottles of Coca-Cola, substantiate how important the presence of their national drink was for the morale of the American troops. One colourful comment is particularly telling: 'I HAVEN'T TOLD ANYONE YET, BUT IT WON'T BE LONG BEFORE I ORDER BAYONETS TO BE FITTED WITH BOTTLE OPENERS. I AM DAMMED IF I WILL STAND BACK AND WATCH THE MEN IN THE FRONT LINES SMASHING THE TOP OFF THEIR BOTTLES BECAUSE THEY HAVEN'T GOT A BOTTLE OPENER WITH THEM.'

The demand for Coca-Cola was so great that the army command asked if the factory could be exempted from sugar rationing. In the end, details of secret army manoeuvres were being communicated to Coca-Cola's export division to ensure supplies were on the spot when and where needed.

Advertising naturally kept close track of these developments. Despite the bitter pill of war, business had never been better for the soft drink manufacturer.

Their postwar distribution network was considerably extended with the sale of Coca-Cola at the petrol stations that were springing up everywhere. It was an intelligent move of the company. Then, as if by a law of nature, there came a setback in Coca-Cola's success story when turnover slumped between 1951 and 1959, chiefly as a result of the Cold War. The company made a magnificent recovery after these dark and daunting years, and in 1978 turnover was higher than ever. But they were increasingly disturbed by their dwindling lead over their number one competitor, Pepsi.

Headed by their new director, Roberto Goizueta, who had joined the company in 1981, Coca-Cola decided on a dramatic change of strategy to beat off their pursuer once and for all. At a press conference on Tuesday 23 April 1985, they announced their new Coca-Cola brand that was to change the world. Years of debate and costly research assured the company of the infallibility of their decision – or so they thought.

Reactions were overwhelming, violent, and chiefly negative. A society of 'Old Cola Drinkers' was even founded, which, backed by outsiders and the media, campaigned for the re-instatement of their old flavour. Several weeks after the introduction of the new flavour, turnover figures were showing a pronounced downward trend. Tension on the top floor of the company's Atlanta headquarters was stretched to breaking point.

Within two and a half months of the historic April press conference it was decided to hold a second press meeting, this time to announce the comeback of the old, familiar flavour, which was to be sold under the name of 'Classic'. Once again Coca-Cola had turned a precarious situation to its own advantage.

This whole operation gave rise to a great deal of speculation. Had Coca-Cola made a marketing mistake, or was the whole thing planned in advance. 'WE ARE NOT THAT STUPID AND WE ARE NOT THAT SMART' was the company's shrewd comment.

Their advertising programme includes a wide range of merchandise – mirrors, trays, suitcases, standard lamps, clothing, even helmets. The 3000 thousand members of the Coca-Cola fan club are fanatic collectors of these items and no less dedicated than stamp collectors or football fans. With the number of club and non-club collectors ever-increasing, trade is so brisk that a price catalogue is brought out each year. The record for the highest bid is held by a metal tray, which was sold for US$ 15,000.

With these accessories fetching the price of precious jewels, we may conclude that the dream of Coca-Cola's Atlanta chemist has been realized beyond even his wildest fantasies.

Jaap Lieverse, Ed Lute, Ronald de Nijs

In 1985 a special space can was designed for astronauts, making Coca-Cola the first soft drink able to be consumed in outer space. In July of that same year, Commander Gordon Fullerton tests the space can aboard the Challenger shuttle.

Esprit
The comprehensive outfitters

It would be hard not to notice the sign 'NO DETAIL IS TOO SMALL' at Esprit's head office in San Francisco. It glares down over the studio as if to impress on the staff each and every day what Esprit's trademark and strength is. For the lifestyle enterprise, the little things are as much their concern as the big. It wants to get across that clothes maketh man, though not exclusively. People dress to show which group they belong to, accentuating their status with carefully chosen accessories; their appearance is engineered to suggest even their mentality and social and political attitudes.

Doug Tompkins, Esprit's founding father, claims clothes are capable of expressing a person's whole personality and taste. He is out to create a comprehensive design, and believes this can only be achieved if it stems from a central concept. This concept of Tompkins' and Esprit's is formulated in rather vague terms, and it is probably more a feeling than an idea. It can best be described as the close harmony between a product, the organization behind it and the way it is marketed, which aims at the finest possible attunement of concept and realization, like two sheets of paper perfectly aligned one on top of the other.

Out of this there has developed a tradition of contextualized products. A product is only successful if it fits in with the range and the company culture. Esprit sees its products as the bricks, and its strict adherence to company concepts as the mortar that holds them together. This is how they have succeeded in building a solid fashion house in twenty years.

This first postmodern multinational is young, founded in 1969 by Susie and Doug Tompkins. Although strategies were changed in 1980 when a new logo and different alphabet were introduced, the ideas they set out with are still valid. The Tompkins endeavour to create a lifestyle product that harmonizes with the spirit of the times. Their concept is 'mix and match' and it implies that colours and patterns, shapes and styles complement or pleasantly contrast one another. Esprit caters for teenagers and young women up to the age of 35. Sunglasses, watches, shoes, bags and even umbrellas, like the clothing, all carry the Esprit label, and together convey what Esprit stands for: a bright outlook on life, sunniness straight from California. Esprit may be regarded as the successful commercial translation of the flower-power movement that thrived in California in the 1960s.

The concern is not afraid to experiment but it gallantly admits to burning its fingers on occasions. How do you design goods that will appeal to the people of Mongolia or inhabitants of Siberia? This was one of the questions the top management seriously asked themselves but they were unable to come up with an answer. Global outfitting is too ambitious

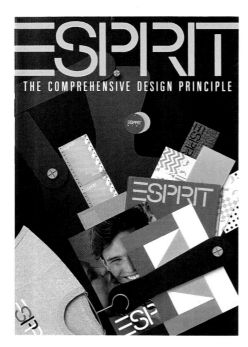

an ideal. Esprit has learnt by trial and error not to set itself too extreme a goal. It has found there is no market for products that are too extravagant.

Instead it concentrates on a clientele drawn to a consciously chosen, outspoken lifestyle. Outer appearances are explicitly coupled to inner attitudes. Esprit clothes and feeds the consumer. Caffe Esprit is not only where a happy purchase can be celebrated with a glass of wine, it is also the company's business card. The cafe interior and menu reflect the attitude of the concern. In San Francisco an adjoining garage was converted into a restaurant and done out in natural materials, in wood and metal. The menu is in the same vein. Caffe Esprit in California specializes in health foods and regional dishes ranging from tacos and hotpots to special pizzas. Europe was introduced to Californian cuisine in Esprit's Amsterdam branch.

Esprit thinks of everything, right down to the box that Americans use to take home their left-over food in – for the dog, of course. Instead of the usual tatty brown bag, customers are given a small transparent plastic box, rather like a lighted lantern, to show that the quality of the food is fit for scrutiny and need not be tucked out of sight.

The finishing touch is the concern's trademark. The 'to-go box' for left-overs is one of a whole range of surprising, ingenious and unusual packagings. Esprit's graphic designer Tamotsu Yagi tried to find a presentation formula in keeping with the clothing and was not afraid of using ordinary materials in novel

ways. He packaged clothes like supermarket articles: Esprit underwear appeared in tubs better known as yoghurt containers, and towels were packed in polythene bags used to pack bread. In this way Esprit turned everyday objects into something special.

Even the receipt was given special treatment. Esprit was not satisfied with a simple computer print-out; the customer is presented with a bill on marbled paper. Yagi tried to find something unusual to replace the ordinary plastic carrier bag the customer is sent off with in most shops. He explored the possibilities of cement bags, he even tried a bag that was radio-activity-proof. He finally came up with a solution closer to home – the potato bag. This is the bag in which Esprit customers take home their newly purchased jeans.

Bags are not bottom of the list for Esprit. On the contrary, the concern feels they make the best walking advertisements. Moreover Esprit dislikes disposables. This is not strange considering the company's Californian origins.

It was here, where people have a greater awareness of life, that the ecological movement first took root in the United States, colouring the way Californians live and do business. Concern for the natural environment is expressed in the biodegradable packagings they use.

The company also shows a predilection for natural materials in its interiors. When in the 1970s a fire destroyed Esprit's headquarters, designer Jim Sweeney put together a make-shift office from beams and bits and pieces of

(from left) Cover for Esprit, The Comprehensive Design Principle, 1989, various versions of the Esprit logo, the Esprit alphabet, Esprit Eyewear and Esprit packaging designs.

left-over timber. Sweeney, who had not started out as a designer, but who, like so many
others, had felt attracted to the Tompkins' idea
and had asked to join the 'club', inadvertently
created the style Esprit had been looking for.
Desks, tables and stockroom shelving were all
handmade from natural wood, and the style
was christened neo-Chippendale by the staff.

Tompkins describes his Esprit look as democratic, a qualification that suggests mediocrity
and the highest common denominator. Tompkins simply means that he makes what most
people like to wear. 'IT IS FASHION FOR PEOPLE
WHO ARE NOT REALLY INTERESTED IN
FASHION.'
The sharp edges have been planed down; the
Esprit cortege are not trendsetters or avant-
gardists, but trend followers. Tompkins is anxious to avoid the intimate, initiated character
of, say, the English street and college styles.

The models that promote Esprit are the
teenagers next door, the paperboy or the
butcher's daughter. In actual fact, it is the
Esprit staff themselves that people the posters
and advertisements, for who is better suited to
putting across the Esprit idea than the people
who sell Esprit wares day in, day out?

Esprit's corporate identity embraces a vast
area, including the staff itself. For the concern,
experience in the trade has taught that it is
crucial to find the right person with the right
skills for the right job. The employee's personality must match that of the company and its
culture. 'THE LONGER YOU WORK FOR ESPRIT,
THE MORE YOU BECOME ESPRIT,' explains one
of the company managers. It sounds as if the

subject is some benevolent sect. The idea is not new. For centuries organizations, institutions and industries have thrived on the commitment to an idea.

The Esprit concern started out as a wholesale manufacturer of children's and women's wear. Their customers were up-market department stores and shops all over the world. They set out to make a stylish collection that was casual and comfortable to wear. Their formula worked, and not only in the United States. Success took them so much by surprise that Tompkins soon decided to open Esprit shops. In 1984 a second design studio was built in Dusseldorf for the distribution in Europe.

Esprit means young in spirit, and its name leaves no doubt as to where the corporation wishes to stand. For many years the concern was known as Esprit de Corps, a reference to its free spirit, its liveliness and its team spirit. Architect Norman Foster believes that Tompkins really hit the mark in combining the best of two worlds, East and West. 'WHEN I FIRST VISITED JAPAN, I WAS IMPRESSED BY THE STRONG SENSE OF VISUAL STYLE WHICH I FOUND EVERYWHERE – IN DRESS, FOOD, PACKAGING AND GRAPHICS….IN MANY WAYS IT REMINDED ME OF ITALY, WHICH ALTHOUGH A WORLD APART, SHARED A SIMILAR INSTINCTIVE SENSE OF STYLE.' Esprit offers a mouth-watering taste of East-West interaction and fervently believes – to quote Charles Eamus – in the importance of taking one's pleasures seriously. 'THAT', Foster feels, 'SUMS UP THE SPIRIT OF ESPRIT'.

Foster overlooks the most important component – America, i.e. Tompkins. Tompkins is the commercial link and he ensures the organization keeps Esprit's parts firmly glued together. He appointed three people to assist him in this – Tamotsu Yagi from Japan, and Italians Oliviero Toscani and Roberto Carra.

Yagi is more than a graphic designer. As we have seen, he is also the originator of packaging ideas. Toscani is Esprit's photographer and more besides. He is an art director, an image-maker whose powerful photographs zoom in on the world of Esprit. Finally, Carra is the company's graphic designer. The three of them together, generally supervised by Tompkins, present a lifestyle product that adds up to more than just a coat or skirt. Japanese precision, Italian spontaneity and American efficiency are the pillars on which the concern solidly stands.

The corporate symbol, with its striking open E, was conceived by John Casido in 1978. The light airiness of the design – the letters are literally and figuratively open and clear – is synonymous with the image of pleasure and youthfulness that the company radiates. A variation on the logo features the letters overlapping one another in combination with the name of the branch's host city. The company uses capital Univers 59 as its corporate alphabet for designating categories or target groups – KIDS, JEANS, SHOES.

Casado's logo is bold in its unambiguous appeal to a single target audience and consciousness, exemplified in its images of laughing young people frolicking in the snow or on the beach. Toscani dares to go as far as abstracting the clothing: in the costly catalogues Esprit distributes (another product which sets the company apart from others), frequently he features merely a face or a single detail, a fabric swatch or zip fastening. For Esprit initiates, the message is perfectly clear straightaway: it is Esprit.

Esprit has branches in 30 countries, and although Tompkins streamlines its fashions, he diversifies in other areas. From the start the concern felt strongly that every national branch should have its own distinctive appearance and ambience, so long as the corporate ideology was not violated. Tompkins worked with the top architects of the 1980s. Shiro Kuramata was responsible for designing shops in the Far East, Norman Foster styled the London branch, Ettore Sottsass (of the Memphis design school) designed the many German and Swiss stores, and Antonio Citterio the shops in Amsterdam and Antwerp. In every country they called on the guidance of local architects.

It was the first opportunity for Memphis, the most talked-about design movement of the 1980s, to realize their architectural concepts on a large scale. Their shop-cum-showrooms in Cologne, Hamburg, Munich and Lugano were playfully dressed in true Memphis fashion with wild laminates in fancy wood grain or microbe motifs. Memphis carpeting was specially woven for some of the stores. At the other end of the scale are the interiors Kuramata and Citterio designed for Esprit's Oriental and northern European stores. These shops stand out for their stark, sober interiors made up in unadulterated materials, chiefly wood and metal, especially zinc. Esprit, keen to avoid a high-tech label: 'WE JUST CALL THEM NATURAL MATERIALS.'

The interiors are styled to tie in with the host environment. Hence the large Los Angeles showroom looks like a gigantic film studio and the store in Minnesota is reminiscent of a huge prairie house, complete with beams, trusses and wooden roof. The Singapore and Hong-Kong branches reflect the crisp, efficient style of the banks, stock exchange and sophisticated technological industry in its immediate vicinity.

Esprit is keenly geared to what adolescents think is important – the family, the group. They go along with the group and are careful not do to anything that might make them stand out, negatively or positively. Advertising centres wholly on the group idea. Esprit calls them 'THE REAL PEOPLE' and reinforces the image. 'WE TRY TO BE ONE STEP AHEAD OF THE CONSUMER AND CREATE OUR OWN DEMAND,' says Esprit, demonstrating its affinity with the market.

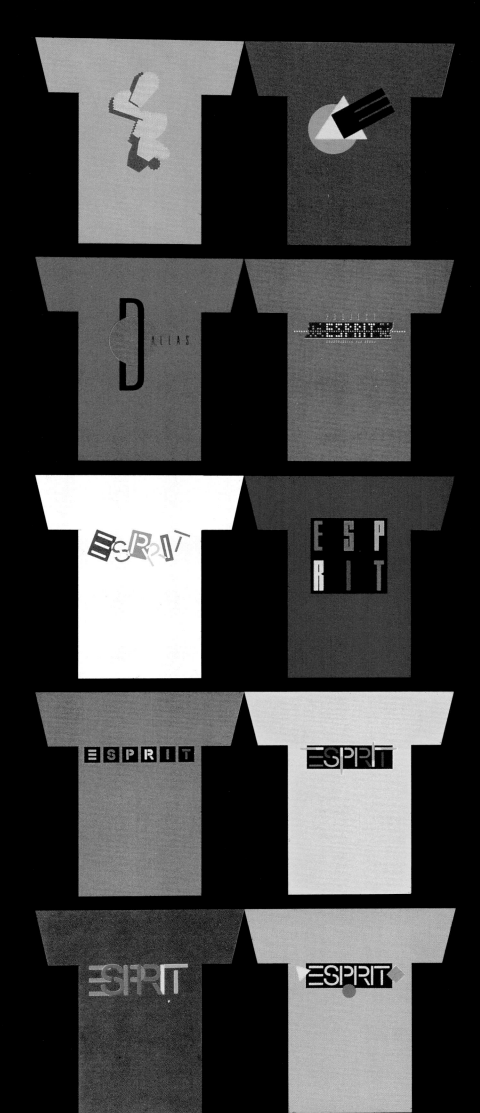

Kids for a Clean Earth.

Covers for the
biannual Esprit
magazine in which
the new
collections are
featured. (far left)
A spread from one
of the issues.

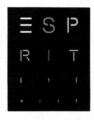

Cover and inside layout for the Esprit Eyewear brochure.

Their fashions are not revolutionary, and yet they are copied. Tompkins has no objections. On the contrary, the day you are no longer being copied is the time to worry. Ettore Sottsass says: 'ESPRIT MAKES CLOTHING. MOST EVERYONE KNOWS THAT THERE ARE MANY CLOTHING COMPANIES ALL OVER THE WORLD, LARGE AND SMALL, BUT FROM WHAT I CAN TELL, ESPRIT IS ABSOLUTELY UNIQUE. ESPRIT MAKES CLOTHES FOR A YOUNG AND NOT VERY YOUNG GENERATION; ALSO FOR A GENERATION THAT'S NOT YOUNG AT ALL. THIS LAST GENERATION, AFTER ALL THE IDEOLOGICAL, POLITICAL AND SOCIAL UNREST OF THE SIXTIES, IS NOW TRYING TO CREATE, IF POSSIBLE, A NEW CODE FOR EVERYDAY MORALITY, FOR PERSONAL BEHAVIOUR, AND FOR A NEW LIFESTYLE.'

It is understandable that Esprit's roots should lie in California; there are few places in the world that can claim to have been exposed to such a tumultuous succession of foreign fashions and lifestyles, from flower power to religious sects, from the environmentalist and anti-nuclear movements to the advent of the yuppies around Silicone Valley.

For architect and designer Kuramata there is no doubt that the concern owes its existence and success to its comprehensive design that attends to every detail. 'FOR ME ESPRIT IS THE DAY, NOT THE NIGHT. THE IMAGE IT PROJECTS IS A CAREFREE, RELAXED AND HEALTHY ONE. IT FOCUSES ON A FAMILY, NOT SPECIALLY ON MALES OR FEMALES. IT IS AN IMAGE THAT RUNS RIGHT THROUGH THE COMPANY, FROM THE SHOP INTERIORS TO THE SALES PROMOTION.'

Corporate design is not the finishing touch as in many companies, but the starting point. Understandably Esprit has found it necessary to capture its philosophy in ten corporate commandments, which its designers are required to abide by:

THOU SHALT NOT IMITATE.
THOU SHALT CREATE NO TASTE.
THOU SHALT NOT SEEK AN EFFECT FOR THINE OWN BENEFIT.
THOU SHALT NOT TRY OUT A NOVELTY FOR THINE OWN GAIN.
THOU SHALT NOT USE MATERIALS FALSELY.
THOU SHALT NOT EXPLOIT THYSELF NOR SHALT THOU ALLOW THYSELF TO BE EXPLOITED BY OTHERS.
THOU SHALT NOT HEED THE OPINIONS OF OTHERS, EXCEPTING WHEN THEY BE WISE AND WELLINFORMED!
THOU SHALT NOT GIVE UNTO ANOTHER WHAT HE DESIRETH, UNLESS WHAT HE DESIRETH BE GOOD.
THOU SHALT NOT CONSORT WITH POPULAR TASTE, NEITHER WITH FASHION, NOR WITH MACHINATIONS, NOR WITH THE DESIRE FOR GAIN.
THOU SHALT NEVER BE SATISFIED.

Jaap Huisman

IBM
Tom Watson Sr:
'We want to be the top'

Punch cards piled high, a confused mass of jack plugs, cumbersome office machines – for many people, thinking back to the early days of office automation arouses protective feelings. Especially when they remember that in those days this machinery was looked upon as the epitome of efficiency. Yet these machines were the precursors of the wave of automation that has presently overwhelmed us.

One of the key figures in this automation revolution was Dr Herman Hollerith, a statistician from Buffalo, America. In 1890 it was his job to organize the census, and for this he developed a punch-card machine in order to process the information more quickly. A machine capable of carrying out instructions completely independently was revolutionary at that time.

It was not long before there was considerable demand in the business world for this machine. The inventor was all too glad to meet this demand: in 1896 he established the Tabulating Company, and shortly afterwards the first punch machines were leaving his factory. A sure success, he must have thought.

Early in the 20th century the Tabulating Company experienced strong competition from Powers, a firm producing qualitatively superior punch-card machines. Indeed, this firm was contracted to deal with the 1910 census, and this threatened Hollerith's company with gradual extinction. The ailing company was bought up by promoter Charles Rantlett Flint, who proceeded to merge it with two other firms. Although the production was now expanded to include time clocks and scales that could also calculate the price of the goods they weighed, the future of the business still seemed shaky. Things improved in the 1920s with the arrival of Tom Watson.

Under the guiding hand of Watson, the firm, now called International Business Machines (IBM), booked large profits from the lease of electro-mechanical calculators, which superseded the old punch-card system. Company employees were rewarded with substantial bonuses – something very unusual in those days – and as a result the contracts streamed in. The introduction of the electric typewriter was also a success. Attempts by other firms to

(opposite)
AS/400
MultiSystem,
1988.
(above left)
IBM Italian
headquarters,
design by
M. Zanuso.
(right) IBM Dutch
headquarters,
design by
W. Ellerman;
detail of the
Dutch IBM
headquarters.
(far right)

(top to bottom, from left) Standard Model B typewriter, 1952; daisy wheel, 1983; sphere-shaped typing element, 1961; Selectric typewriter, 1961; Executive typewriter, 1954.

capture the market for typewriters proved unsuccessful. There was a very simple explanation for this: typists who had learned on one particular brand of machine were loathe to switch to another make. And thanks to this *fait accompli,* IBM remained the market leader.

When it came to computers, however, things proved different. An attempt to develop a computer, twenty years earlier, had been nipped in the bud. The probable turnover was thirty computers, and this was insufficient to warrant the outlay. The prospect for computers did not look too rosy, while on the other hand business was booming for calculators. The American firm RemRand took the plunge with the computer and was unexpectedly successful in the 1950s with its firstborn, called Univac. It was not long before this firm had a reputation for being the number one computer producer in America.

Meanwhile the trade press began to wonder when IBM would launch a computer onto the market. In 1949 Tom Watson Jr intimated that IBM was busy developing a computer – which amounted to a declaration of war against RemRand. Thanks to the lack of vigilance on RemRand's part, IBM soon emerged victor from this struggle. In these turbulent times, Tom Watson Jr, who meantime had become president and managing director of the company, decided to develop a corporate iden-

tity. IBM was already known for its service and reliable production; what it lacked was a modern uniform in which not only its products but all its other manifestations could be dressed.

A determining factor for future developments was the contact at this stage with the young designer Eliot Noyes. He had met Watson during the Second World War, when they were glider pilots in the same squadron. There are several different stories about how they met again. One of these recounts how Watson received various folders, sent to him from an IBM branch in the Netherlands, with information about both IBM and Olivetti products. The accompanying text asked him to compare carefully the information provided by these two companies. Having carried out his comparison, Watson's comment was: 'THE INFORMATION ON OURS LOOKS LIKE SOMETHING OUT OF A MEDICINE BOTTLE'.
It was a good illustration of his go-ahead attitude and insight into the importance of corporate identity. Little further is reported except that shortly after, Watson visited Eliot Noyes while he was still working for Norman Bel Geddes. (There seems to be a connection between this decision and IBM's flat-out promotion of its computer production during these years – and a new, fresh identity was an excellent instrument in the struggle – but so far there is nothing that actually substantiates this theory.)

When Watson requested him to develop a design programme for IBM, Noyes recommended recruiting Paul Rand and Charles Eames. That meant that he, Noyes, could devote himself to industrial design, while Rand took care of the graphic aspects and Eames was responsible for exhibitions and films. In the end it was Noyes and Rand who created the IBM identity. These two had voiced their disapproval in the 1950s of designer colleagues like Walter Dorwin Teague, Norman Bell Geddes and Raymond Loewey. For them, design meant streamlining and keen competition. In the years immediately before and after the Second World War this was the translation in material terms of the 'makeable' progress of American society. But Noyes and Rand were more drawn by the sense of quality in European design, that presented a diametric contrast to American notions. Ironically enough, they were above all attracted by the work of Marcello Nizzoli, who was designer for Olivetti.

Eliot Noyes was trained as an architect and industrial designer. During the period that he was curator at the New York Museum of Modern Art he developed his ideas concerning 'good design' that became standard for that museum. Immediately after the Second World War he worked for a short time for Bell Geddes, before setting up as a self-employed designer. Noyes was also consultant designer for, among others, Westinghouse, Pan America and Mobil (the friendly, round petrol pumps that are still used everywhere are his design). His task for IBM was to supervise product design and interior architecture and, as a result of this work, in 1956 he was appointed corporate design director.

His colleague Paul Rand was slightly younger than him and began his career as a typographer for the magazine **ESQUIRE**. He worked as designer on the editorial board as well as creating all the promotion material. Between 1941 and 1954 he worked for Bill Bernbach's advertising agency and then started working freelance. It was at this time that he began work for IBM. The artist Laszlo Moholy-Nagy characterized Rand as 'AN IDEALIST AND A REALIST: SOMEONE WHO SPEAKS THE LANGUAGE OF THE POET AND THE BUSINESSMAN. HE THINKS IN TERMS OF NECESSITY AND FUNCTION, BUT HIS FUNCTION IS UNFETTERED.'

For IBM, a uniform design, channelled into a distinctive housestyle, chiefly had the merit of practicality: it was universally recognizable and represented the high social level at which the firm functioned. In contrast to this was the individual contribution of the designer and the social status of the 'implementer' of corporate identity. In this respect, producing good designs and advertising is equivalent to

Superselectric 1 typewriter, 1985.

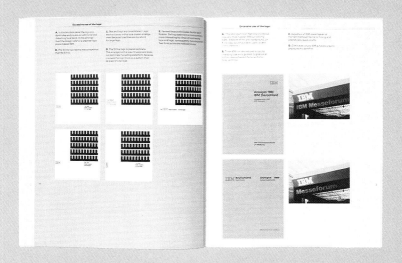

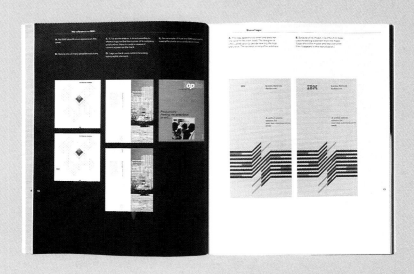

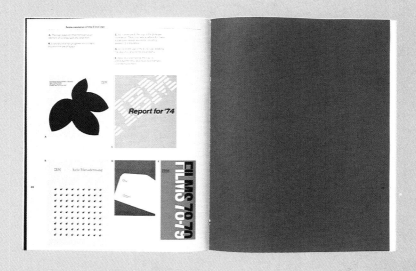

making a personal statement for the general good. And the frequently-made comparison between Adriano Olivetti and Lorenzo de Medici illustrates how raising visual standards can also affect the general environment and make it more pleasant and acceptable.
In their different ways these two Italians possessed great power and influence: the Medici as patron for Florentine Renaissance figures and Olivetti as promoter of Italian design.
The implementation of a corporate identity programme goes hand in hand with a certain social status. According to Robert Sobel, professor in business history, employees of IBM immediately enjoy a certain respect both within and outside their work. The reason is that working for this multinational represents a challenge: though the standards are high, you know that you are pulling out all the stops and are better than any competitor, explains Sobel. This business ethic is based on principles of discipline that have been practised for centuries – amongst others by the armed forces.
This basic attitude was initiated into IBM by Tom Watson Sr: 'YOU'LL NEVER BE A SUCCESS IN ANY UNDERTAKING UNLESS YOU ARE CONVINCED THAT YOU'RE THE BEST IN THE WORLD. YOU HAVE TO PUT YOU SOUL INTO THE BUSINESS, AND THE BUSINESS INTO YOUR SOUL.' Right from the start he realized how important it was to instil a spirit of dedication and diligence into his staff. And more: a code of behaviour. Alcohol was forbidden during working hours as well as at staff social functions. Employees had to wear the IBM 'uniform' – dark pinstripe suit, white shirt, unobtrusive tie; and at the beginning of a meeting it was customary to sing the firm's anthem.

(opposite) Cover and layout of The IBM logo, its use in company identification. (below) Special alphabet, design by Paul Rand.

These examples are now outdated, for with the advent of Watson Jr there came a relaxing of this stern regime and the atmosphere became more informal and congenial. Nevertheless, these rules of behaviour remain illustrative of the spirit that still hovers over corporate culture and which has contributed to the successful image of IBM.

Paul Rand's ideas tied in very neatly with the IBM mentality. His philosophy was 'GOOD DESIGN AT HEART IS SIMPLE HONESTY' and on this basis Rand compiled, instead of an elaborate manual, a handbook with recommendations. This do-it-yourself on design enables about forty different design divisions of IBM to incorporate specific cultural elements of the host country into their design work. Many of these divisions form part of the national publicity sectors, others are recognized Design Centres, responsible for product, interior, exhibition, and graphic design.
Not only did Rand re-style the old IBM logo, he also developed a 'house letter'. This was inspired by the little-used 'City Medium', created by the German designer Georg Trump in 1931 for the Berlin type-foundry, Berthold. Although this is sometimes referred to as a 'special alphabet', in fact this typeface has never been given a name of its own, possibly because it was so little used. Its application worldwide created a good many technical and logistic complications. Indeed, in his 1961 design guide Rand himself advised: 'USE IT VERY SPARINGLY AND DO NOT USE IT FOR TITLES AND GENERAL DESIGN WORKS UNLESS ABSOLUTELY ESSENTIAL'. This recommendation explains why the typeface now scarcely appears in printed matter.
There are several different examples of Rand's re-styled logo based on the City Medium. There is a positive and a negative face, an outline, and an 8-line and 13-line version, each having its own separate function. The two last mentioned are particularly striking: their lines not only hold our attention, they also suggest speed and efficiency. Furthermore, the three letters are connected, producing a strong and coherent effect. The 8-line version is used mainly on packaging and display material, and the 13-line version when special emphasis is needed.

In a new design guide in 1981 the applications of the logo were described with greater precision, partly at the suggestion of Paul Rand who, despite his advanced age, still supervises IBM's printed matter. Partly thanks to his supervision it has been possible to maintain over a long period the design principle of freedom within constraint, and to provide IBM with a coherent corporate image. It is equally important to project this unambiguous image in product design and essential that the consumer can always recognize a product as IBM's. To help designers with this tricky task, there is a fifty-page book providing aesthetic and practical guidelines for the workers at the Design Centres. According to Walt Kraus, present manager of the IBM Design Program,

ABCDEFG
HIJKLMNO
PQRSTUV
WXYZ&

123456789
0?!;:· IBM

Wordt het een gewone PC of Personal System/2?

(top to bottom, from left) Poster for the Dutch advertising campaign 'Will it be an ordinary PC or a Personal System/2?', 1989/1990; accompanying catalogue, 1989; two Dutch magazines for IBM clients: IBM nieuws and Magazine; Academic Information Systems publication; (right) covers and pages from the IBM Bodoni Manual, parts 1 and 2.

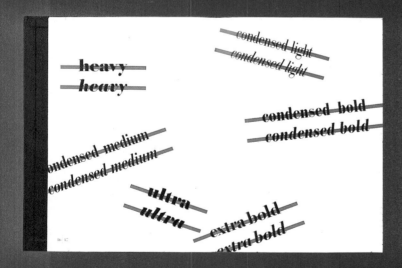

it is doubtful whether a product ever entirely meets the conditions suggested. But he does not want to force his designers into a straight-jacket. 'WE HAVE, OVER THE YEARS, COME UP WITH SOME COMMON SOLUTIONS TO COMMON PROBLEMS.'

Like other colleagues in this branch, IBM sees the design of its products as raising their market value. Inevitably, there is fierce sales competition. But IBM does not let itself be dictated to: 'WE ESPECIALLY RESIST PRESSURES TO CHANGE FOR CHANGE'S SAKE, TO DO SOMETHING THAT IS DIFFERENT THIS YEAR,' explains Kraus. The designs should have a universal appeal, particularly since IBM operates on an international market.
Not only should its products project the IBM identity worldwide, its offices and buildings should also exude a multinational aura. So it was that world-famous architects like Egon Eiermann, Eero Saarinen and Marcel Breuer were assigned various prestigious projects, for example Breuer designed two laboratories, one in La Gauda in France and the other in

Boca Raton in Florida. Such architecture forged the IBM identity into a coherent whole. The corporate identity programme pursued by IBM leaves almost nothing to be desired. It meets the current standards demanded of such a programme, and also has character, style, and personality – all the qualities it expresses in a consistent and self-confident manner. It is generally recognized to be one of the best programmes ever developed for a multinational, and has thus become a prime model for a pragmatic and effective approach in this field.
Possibly this pragmatic approach obscures one danger: the successful formula may appear too goody-goody, and also too inflex-ible. It is quite probable that challengers in the same market area, who have a more light-hearted and possibly more subtle approach, will be able to catch more accurately the mood of the times. But IBM sees no cause for a change of policy within the present cultural patterns. Rightly or wrongly, the glory of the past can never be erased.
Jaap Lieverse, Ronald de Nijs

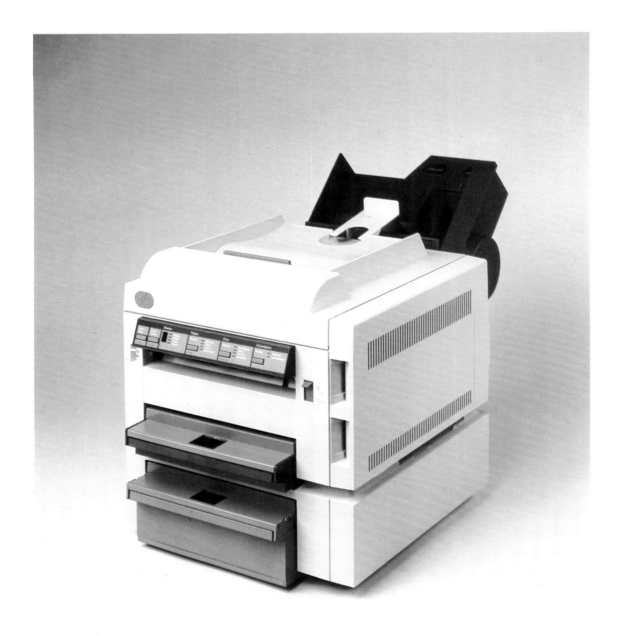

ERCO

Erco
The good and necessary

Top, the south wing of the Erco Technical Centre, with the interior (centre) and the daylight simulation room (bottom).

While not having founded Erco, Klaus-Jürgen Maack is regarded as the creator of the lighting company in West Germany's Lüdenscheid. In 1963 when he entered the family business of its founder Arnold Reininghaus, Maack, a marketing expert from the printing industry, met with a flourishing firm producing kitchen, bathroom and bedroom lighting. None of the products were of exceptional beauty, let alone really different from what other manufacturers of the day were producing. Yet the fittings were apparently good enough to spread light in the homes of many Germans, and in kitchen lighting Erco was even international market leader. The adjustment mechanism of its kitchen lamp, suspended from the ceiling, enabled the so-called pulley-lamp to be lowered to just above the table to produce a small pool of light, or raised high to illuminate evenly the entire space. Every kitchen had one to West Germany's border and beyond, and together with various other manufacturers Erco shared the market in unrelieved likemindedness.

It was exactly this best-seller that the upstart Maack, after briefly studying the market, wanted to throw overboard – to the utter amazement of Erco's personnel, including director Reininghaus, who had only recently taken on his 25-year-old son-in-law. Even though the lamp was the antithesis of what Maack at the time scathingly referred to as the fashion for 'electric baroque' in the lighting market, he foresaw that the period for the harmless pulley lamp was drawing to a close. He pooh-poohed the annual changing collections of the lighting industry. Designs came and went, often before returns on investment could be made. There had to be another way. Instead of following fashionable trends, a light fitting's design should be good enough for at least 10 years. Many years later Maack was to admit that he had no feelers for the kind of fashionable lamps then dominating the market. 'FOR ME PERSONALLY AND FOR ERCO THAT TURNED OUT TO BE A HAPPY COINCIDENCE.'

The lack of an emphatic design to the pulley lamp must have appealed to Maack even then, yet he saw that the possibilities of this particular money-spinner were almost exhausted. Moreover, it was perfectly clear to him that the future did not lie in the kitchen. Postwar development was almost completed, prosperity was rising as never before and Erco's new marketing manager predicted that family life would shift from the kitchen to comfortably furnished livingrooms – a development the company had to remain abreast of if it were not to destroy itself by its own growth. 'THERE WERE SIGNS OF CHANGE IN THE WAY PEOPLE LIVED AND IN THE FUNCTIONS OF HOMES AND OFFICES', Maack said at the time. Changes, for instance, which led to more leisure hours, the appearance of television, and with regard to home and surroundings, necessitated a need for more functional and personal designed environments. This admission marks the death

(opposite, top from left) Stand at the Leipzig Light Fair, 1937; catalogue, 1937; Leuchten catalogue, 1968; house magazine Lichtbericht, 1989.
(bottom) Detail of the glass pyramid, which since March 30, 1989 comprises the central underground entrance to the Louvre in Paris; the lighting element for the structure was specially designed by Erco.

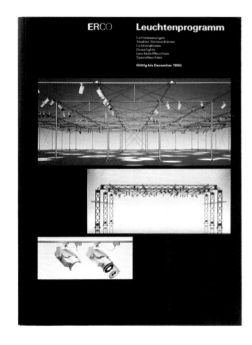

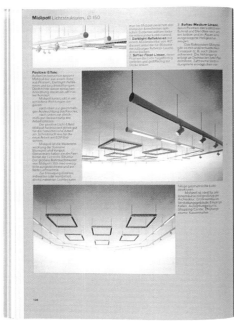

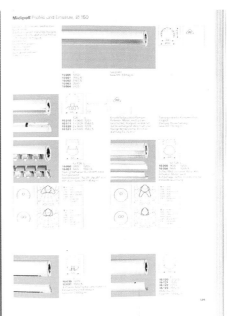

(above) Cover and
inside layout for
Leuchten-
programm
catalogue, 1990.

knell for the pulley lamp and the beginning of a
new Erco, a company thoroughly shaded by
the almost cynical pragmatism of Klaus-
Jürgen Maack, the 20th-century evangelist of
creative lighting. A man once described by the
British architect Norman Foster as amiable,
flexible and jovial, yet at the same time cold,
authoritarian and self-centred.

Erco dates back to 1934 when Arnold Reininghaus, with two associates Paul Buschhaus and
Karl Reeber, founded the Lüdenscheider
Leuchtenfabrik Reininghaus & Co. Both fellow
founders disappeared almost immediately, but
in the middle of the deep 1930s depression
Reininghaus stuck steadfastly to his credo
that one 'COULD NOT LIVE FROM FEAR'. During
the next decade Reininghaus & Co (shortened
to Erco) was swept along on the peaks and
dives of Germany history – slowly but surely
prospering until 1939, subsequently trans-
formed into a war industry and bombed to
smithereens in March 1945. In 1948 production was resumed on the same old footing and
during the Wirtschaftswunder years the firm
with its simple light fittings developed into one
of Germany's leading lighting manufacturers.

The point of
departure of
Erco's lighting
was to illuminate
the architecture
itself, thus the
pyramid at night
becomes a
luminous prism.

Today, Erco has other outlets in Germany plus
operations in 28 countries.

Maack is the first one to give credit where it is
due to his pioneering father-in-law. He was the
one who steered the company through difficult times and made it flourish. He is also the
one who in the early days made a basic resolve
from which even to this day the company has
never wavered. Erco does not target itself
directly at the consumer market, but distributes products indirectly via wholesalers and
more recently particularly via architects who
integrate a lighting system into the architectural concept as a whole. In so doing the
company can demonstrate what is meant
exactly by 'SELLING LIGHT' in various prestigious buildings such as museums and conference centres. No lamps are hung especially for
their decorative function. Instead light is
built-in, sometimes theatrically, sometimes
indistinguishably from incoming daylight.
The preference is also for a narrowly specialist
catalogue for the trade rather than the glossy
folders of the high-street stores.

From consulting Erco's archives its development appears to follow logically from decisions taken at the time by its original founder.
Yet in other aspects, Klaus-Jürgen Maack's
debut marked a break with the past. Since his
appointment – first as the man responsible for
marketing research, product development and
communications, then as director – Erco
gained a new lease of life. At the beginning the
new boss made sure that the emphasis in
management lay first and foremost on a
change in approach to the marketplace.
As quickly as possible he wanted to replace a
product that had to appeal to the fads of the
day with a collection of lighting much more
lasting, made by craftsmen for craftsmen.
After this shift in policy had been implemented, Maack attempted to express the
non-trendy, universal yet specialist nature of
Erco in the way it visually presented itself.
From that moment on, the communications
department was writing a new chapter in
Erco's history.
The period dating from the early 1970s is
distinguished literally by an entirely new
signature. With the help of designer Otl
Aicher, a new trademark for Erco was created:
four capital letters in Univers type going from
dark to light. This design visually encapsulates
Maack's endeavour to have a company not
selling light fittings anymore, but 'light' – a
discovery he owed to Ludwig Mies van der
Rohe and Philip Johnson, designers of the
Seagram Building in New York. There on Park
Avenue he saw the results of their collaboration with three lighting specialists, Kelly, Price
and Goodbar, who concealed Seagram's lighting in the ceilings, thus only allowing the light
itself to make a statement. They had borrowed
this approach from theatre lighting with which
all three, either as technicians or as whizz kids
of the boards, were fully conversant. Their
contribution to the Seagram Building was

Maack's guiding principle when developing the Erco product. Light should not be seen, but should show. Or to use his own words: 'NO LONGER IS THE FORMAL BEAUTY OF THE PRODUCT THE DECIDING FACTOR, BUT RATHER THE SOLUTION TO ANY LIGHTING PROBLEM ONE CARES TO THINK OF.' This way of thinking became the essence of Erco's management style – design was not an aim in itself, it was a means to resolve problems and that applied just as much to the presentation and selling of the products as the products themselves – a folder, for instance, had to be just as carefully thought out as the products it lauded.

This argument applies in an even greater sense to the company premises that recently had a new Technical Centre built by the architect, Uwe Kiessler. The client's brief was that the new building should emanate competence and expertise, it should be a workshop, the 'overalls' as it were for engineers using it. Maack scored through all twenty architects' names on his first list, after each and every one had been caught committing a building 'sin'. It was Kiessler who finally had the honour of creating a building that in Erco style was 'good and necessary' – the architectural equivalent of Univers. Kiessler constructed a 120m-long complex from galvanized steel and aluminum panels with much insulating glass so that the building, particularly at night, flooded the immediate surroundings with light, thus revealing its very nature: a lighting company in the best tradition of the Bauhaus (founded by architect Walter Gropius) and the Hochschule für Gestaltung in Ulm (founded by architect Max Bill), a school which, partly due to Otl Aicher, flourished between 1953 and 1970.

Inspired by the lofty ideals of the Hochschule in Ulm, design has become an essential component of Erco's management philosophy. The company positions itself across the board as being both cautious and goal effective; compliant and self-confident; flexible and headstrong. Aicher's trademark underpins a management style which Erco has rigorously and consistently applied. The Univers, designed by the Swiss, Adrian Frutiger in 1957, is consistently used in all printed matter, whether as lettering for packaging and company cars, the business card of the lighting consultant, advertisements, or for the typography of the house magazine LICHTBERICHT in which architects, engineers and other specialists in the field are kept informed on the newest projects and products. In recent years, Aicher has worked on a new type, the Rotis, and it is intended that this will have a role at some stage in Erco's corporate image.

Univers, which in Germany in particular projects a sense of responsibility (used for government printed matter), quality (used in publishing) and good taste (used in the design industry), was originally chosen because it is the most legible Grotesque. Erco's housestyle

manual states: 'ALTHOUGH IT SEEMS TO MOST PEOPLE THAT THE DIFFERENCES AMONG OTHER TYPES OF GROTESQUE DO NOT VARY THAT MUCH, ERCO, NEVERTHELESS, IS COMMITTED TO STRIVING FOR OPTIMUM RESULTS EVEN AS REGARDS THE DETAILS. A CONSCIOUS INTERACTION WITH DESIGN IS EVIDENT FROM THE TENACITY WITH WHICH DETAILS ARE ALSO HELD UP FOR INSPECTION. IN DESIGN, DETAILS DO NOT EXIST.' Lettering, product design or the design of the corporate image are all subject to the same ground rules: 'ERCO'S DESIGN POLICY FAVOURS SOLUTIONS MADE FROM OBJECTIVE PREMISES. STANDARDS AND STANDARD PROCEDURES ARE PRECONDITIONS RATHER THAN STUMBLING BLOCKS FOR CREATIVITY.' And: 'ERCO'S DESIGN VIEWPOINT IS IN FACT DISTINGUISHED BY THE FACT THAT AESTHETICS CAN DETRACT FROM WHAT IS GOOD, NECESSARY AND IMPERATIVE.' In one of his pastoral forewords in LICHTBERICHT, Maack describes this variation on the 'FORM FOLLOWS FUNCTION' credo as follows: 'WHEN, IN THE DESIGNING OF A FITTING, THE DESIGN IS GEARED TOWARDS THE TECHNICAL DEMANDS AND NOT THE AESTHETIC EFFECT, THEN A PRODUCT IS CREATED WITH THE QUALITIES OF AN INSTRUMENT, WHICH MAKES ITS USEFULNESS IMMEDIATELY APPARENT.' According to Maack his philosophy rests simply on applying the principles of architecture to the development of products. It is no coincidence then that the products are in tune with architecture. In fact Maack makes no secret of the fact that his views are largely in keeping with those of contemporary British architects like Norman Foster and Richard Rogers. Whether a typeface, a lamp or a building, the terminology is always the same: the Good and Necessary. The Erco code on corporate identity stands for no anomalies.

Just as rigidly defined are Erco's housestyle colours. Black, white and grey are the basic colours, with sometimes a mixture of grey and brown chosen for photographs and products. Incidentally, silver-grey cars are reserved for the management, while other company vehicles are painted black, white or standard grey. When Maack commissioned the building of the Technical Centre in Lüdenscheid, it was automatically assumed that the architect would stick to this palette for the building and interior. It meant, however, that copiers, computers and telephones not supplied in these house colours had to be sprayed. Even the housestyle red of the Coca-Cola machine had to capitulate: it was repainted grey on the boss's orders.

The responsibility for executing the housestyle hovers between advertising personnel and product developers. Light fittings, for instance, must conform to highly defined areas of application. They have to be both geschmacks and kulturneutral, accord with the line taken for product developments that Erco has concen-

(opposite) Cover and inside layout of Erco's housestyle manual, 1978.

ERCO ERCO Leuchten GmbH Lüdenscheid

Erscheinungsbild

Richtlinien und Normen

aaaa

Univers 55 Record Gothic Helvetica Akzidenz-Grotesk

allabendlich

allabendlich

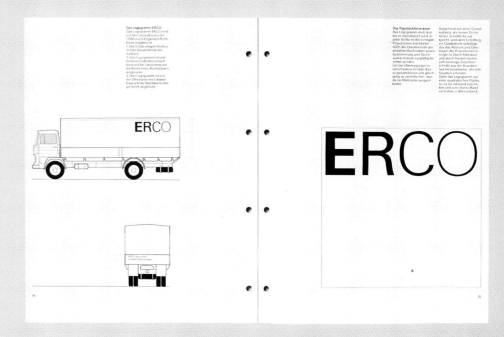

(left) The 52-metre high atrium of the Hong Kong & Shanghai Bank in Hong Kong. By employing an ingenious lighting system it is possible, even on dull days, to allow so-called artificial sunlight to shine through.
(right) For the perceptive viewer, Erco's logo is printed on the lighting fixture of these Optect Strahlers, 1989.
(opposite) In the elliptical lighting fixture above the conference table in the boardroom of the Hong Kong & Shanghai Bank a number of microphones and speakers have been cleverly concealed.

trated on since the radical changes of the 1970s, and meet the requirements of new technology.

Maack leaves no doubt whatsoever that he is the man who takes all the decisions in these matters even when engaging the top names in design. 'THE COLLABORATION BETWEEN CLIENT AND DESIGNER IS SIMILAR TO A GREAT EXTENT TO THAT BETWEEN DIRECTOR AND ACTOR. AND THE BETTER THE DIRECTIONS FOR THE DESIGNER, THE BETTER AND MORE EFFICIENT ARE THE RESULTS.' In the meantime he has evidence enough: Kiessler's Technical Centre, the fittings of international top names like Roger Tallon, Terence Conran, Ettore Sottsass, Shiro Kuramata and Mario Bellini, and the lighting constructions of the Roy Fleetwood/Ove Arup team, plus the collaboration with architect Norman Foster for the lighting of the Hong Kong & Shanghai Bank, where a tailor-made solution was worked out for each lighting problem. Erco was responsible, for example, for the huge mirror which traps natural light and releases it over the massive atrium, and also introduced artificial light that can be reflected via the mirror on dull days. In addition, Erco designed the high-tech chandelier above the table in the conference room. This oval fitting incorporates 48 directed beams of light, 24 microphones, 12 loudspeakers and hovers above the meetings of the capital's bankers like a flying saucer. The extension to the Louvre in Paris, an entrance largely underground after I.M. Pei's design, received a similar exclusive treatment. The emphasis was light yet no light – one way of giving an underground complex the brightness (and corresponding darkness) of a site with daylight. More prestigious perhaps, but not

essentially different from Erco's standard practice of providing lighting for offices, hotels, museums, theatres, banks, supermarkets, airports – for everything in fact save for the average home with which Erco once made its name.
It is just such a company working with outside designers, architects and communication specialists, Maack argues, that needs to protect itself against too many swings in company style by having a consistently developed corporate identity. The spirit of the company must remain tangible and visible. Maack takes the need for a personal style even further. As companies become run on more liberal and democratic lines, the turnover in personnel increases. From this point of view a corporate identity is a safeguard for the mentality an employer wishes to uphold within his firm. For the marketplace it means recognition, familiarity, confidence and credibility.

A company derives from this its self-assurance in the future. In Erco's case all its concepts appear to be synonymous with the views of one man who personifies corporate identity: Klaus-Jürgen Maack, the entrepreneur and art collector who once said he had the same feelings for a well-run company as for a work of art. The man who sees light as his 'MISSION' and who, according to Norman Foster, uses the royal 'WE' when talking, when he really means 'ME, ME, ME.' 'MAACK NOT ONLY WEARS THE PANTS OF THE COMPANY HE MANAGES,' writes Foster 'BUT ALSO APPEARS TO HAVE DESIGNED AND TAILORED THEM TO FIT HIS PERSONAL IDEAS, ENERGIES AND TASTE.'

Gert Staal

Flying Dutchman
poster, ca. 1950.
Studio KLM Paris.

KLM
A history of the future

An aircraft looms out of the distance, following its final glide path, gracefully, effortlessly. Although it is still a long way off, the sky-blue fuselage and the white tailplane complete with a logo can easily be distinguished. The logo suddenly becomes recognisable as the letters K,L and M, the abbreviation for Koninklijke Luchtvaart Maatschappij, **Royal Dutch Airlines.** For an observer, the image conjures up the instant recognition of a reliable Dutch airline at work - an airline which puts the customer first and where quality is a prerequisite. This is the ideal. It means that the company's corporate image and its personality have both been projected successfully.

Since the early years of the airline, it has been a long struggle to ensure that every visual manifestation of KLM, in all its global markets, contributed, in a distinct and uniform style, to an instant identification and a positive perception.

KLM's first logo was designed in 1919 by D. Roosenburg, an architect friend of the company's founder, Albert Plesman. The 'finch', as the device became known, was an attractive but complex design and it failed to meet its basic criteria. A good logo should clearly reflect the company's name, be instantly identifiable and be linked with the observer's perception of the company. After the Second World War, as KLM's route network began to expand rapidly, the need for a clear, recognisable logo increasingly became a commercial imperative.

In September 1951, Plesman gave a presentation at the first international congress organised by the Council of Industrial Design in London. He introduced himself as a 'non-professional':
'I ACCEPTED THE INVITATION WITH PLEASURE, BUT ALSO WITH A CERTAIN NERVOUSNESS BECAUSE I FELT I WOULD BE COMPLETELY SURROUNDED BY EXPERTS ON THIS WIDE AND COMPLEX SUBJECT. I NOW FIND THIS TO BE THE CASE'.
KLM had little to contribute. Its visual image was weak and the message which Plesman thought his company should communicate - what we would today refer to as its 'positioning' - was almost totally absent. Plesman certainly had ideas concerning company 'style' and 'image' but the value of a distinct company identity which would reflect the company's quality, uniqueness, products and people was not fully recognised at that time and his main priority remained the expansion of the carrier's network. Nevertheless, on his return to The Netherlands, Plesman set about trying to improve the company's design performance. In 1952, he commissioned the company's design department to link all the elements of the company to the concept 'service'. The brief was to design an unequivocal corporate identity which would have the blessing of every KLM department.

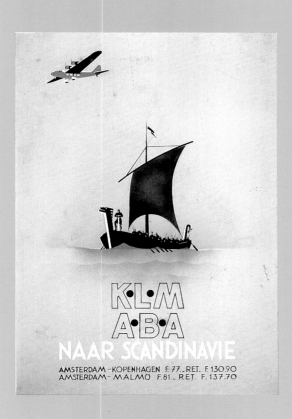

Fly to Scandinavia poster, 1935.

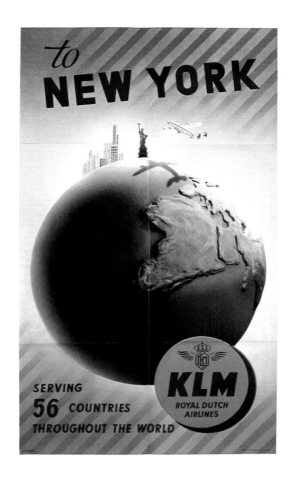

The design department was confronted with a number of fixed design elements on the aircraft: the 'finch' which included the (royal) crown, the Dutch flag on the tailplane (a vestige of compulsory wartime markings) and the name 'Vliegende Hollander/Flying Dutchman' in a blue band along the fuselage. This last item was regarded by Plesman as a good promotional aid and it was used on the first and many subsequent KLM posters. The design department tried hard to find a solution to Plesman's brief but, within the KLM organisation, many others were trying to accomplish the same thing for themselves. The advertising department, for example, continued to use the 'ball and stripe' device wherever possible. The unbounded nature of the striped pattern, however, created problems with its application on other media or various items of KLM's exposure. This, in turn, created a consequent lack of corporate uniformity. The dilemma proved impossible to resolve at the time.

In the late 1950s, in a continuing attempt to simplify and effectuate disciplined uniformity, the possible removal of the national flag from the tailplane was considered. After lengthy discussions the flag disappeared and a new logo featuring stripes, the letters KLM and, for the first time, only the crown part of the 'finch' device was applied experimentally to the tailplanes. The design, however, failed to achieve the desired level of distinction and acceptance and it was discontinued.

Further indecision became apparent when designers Gerrit Rietveld and Raymond Loewy were commissioned to redesign aircraft interiors. Rietveld came up with an interior featuring his customary primary colours combined with grey and white. KLM's Technical Services Department, responsible for maintenance, foresaw problems and the design was not introduced.
The ambitions of Raymond Loewy extended further. Having designed the interior for the Lockheed Electra aircraft, he offered to 'assemble' a totally new house style. His proposals got little support, however, and no further progress was made.

In the meantime, KLM was becoming aware that simply changing the logo was not enough. More was needed. The importance of 'positioning' became clear. How did the company want to be seen? How was it, in reality, perceived?

At this time, with the introduction of the jet engine, a whole new chapter in the annals of civil aviation was begun. The far-reaching consequences of this revolutionary new era in aviation provided added stimulus to the necessity of dedicated thinking about the positioning, world-wide exposure and corporate identity. A number of measures were taken which, within a few years, initiated the creation of a powerful company house style.

KLM entrusted its international advertising campaign to the creative minds of David Ogilvy's American agency. The campaign was preceded by an international study of the characteristics of different nationalities and the basic qualities needed to run a perfect airline. Ogilvy, after extensive evaluation, defined his positioning for the airline and laid

Various KLM
posters
throughout the
years:
To Prague, 1935
(far left);
To New York, 1947
(left);
Fly to the Far East,
1954 (above);
Convair liner,
1950 (above
right).

the framework for the advertising concept: 'KLM, THE RELIABLE AIRLINE MADE BY THE CAREFUL, PUNCTUAL DUTCH'.

During this same period, a British designer, F.H.K. Henrion, held a seminar on company house styles for KLM's management. Assisted by KLM's designers, he demonstrated the visual and conceptual flaws and inconsistencies of current design items while stressing the vital commercial importance of a coherent house style as a management tool: 'FOR A COMPANY OF KLM'S SIZE AND DIVERSITY, AN INTEGRATED EFFORT IS NEEDED TO COORDINATE THE MANY SEPARATE ITEMS ALL BELONGING TO THE ONE CORPORATION TO ACHIEVE COHERENT AND CONTROLLED RESULTS OVER A LONG PERIOD'.

Henrion was asked to provide a framework to promote KLM's brand name within the context of a total house style. This house style should be consistent and uniform, instantly recognisable everywhere in all its visual manifestations, communicating the image of a reliable airline.
He also made full use of the image study findings. He came to the conclusion that 'the crown' was the most important design element but, at the same time, the one which presented the most problems. The image of a crown has traditionally always been a symbol of royalty. In Henrion's view, the KLM crown should be the prominent, distinctive and characteristic symbol of a modern company - suggestive not only of 'regal' but, above all, the reflection of 'quality'. He visually subdued the background and restyled the crown itself.

His design was founded on 'Gestalt' ideas of perception. These assume that people's mental processes reduce everything they see to simple forms. For example, when looking at the complex structure of a wrought iron fence, people will concentrate on the simple horizontal and vertical lines, ignoring the curls and loops. Henrion maintained that the more straightforward and symmetrical something is, the better it can be recognised, remembered and recalled. This is all the more important if the observer's perception is influenced by distance, poor weather conditions and busy surroundings. Henrion argued that a complex image like a crown painted on an aircraft would not be readily recognisable at a distance, in the fog. Moreover, during the check-in procedure, the crown is unlikely to be noticed by a passenger's normal cursory glance at the tickets. These arguments were sufficient motivation for him to drastically reduce the traditional KLM crown down to its 'simple form'. The modern crown was created by reversing the original design. The crown's bars were replaced by the space between them reproducing its external form.

In 1964, the first house style manual was officially presented in which the implementation and execution of KLM's new logo was specified. A House Style Committee, under the chairmanship of the former head of Passenger Marketing, Jan F.A. de Soet, super-vised its launch, emphasising the importance of a consistent house style, positioning the company as a modern, reliable airline which puts quality above all else. The pay-off line was, and still is, 'THE RELIABLE AIRLINE'.

The committee was discontinued in 1965, and for several years there was no special body accountable for the house style.

The thread was picked up again in 1970. KLM's Marketing Department recommended that the company's name should urgently be given more prominence at a time of greater competition in a globally expanding market. More people were taking to the air but their choice of airline had never been so great. More than ever, a strong identification programme was needed as a strategic tool to clearly set the company apart from the crowd. Henrion was consulted again.
He proposed dropping the striped background, making greater use of the two shades of blue and enlarging the logo.

In 1981, KLM decided to re-introduce a consultative body which would resume the responsibilities of the former House Style Committee. De Soet in particular, then vice-president, was convinced that discipline, strict adherence and persistence were the key to the successful implementation of a company's house style. The company's logo, the light and darker blue colours and the stress on 'reliable' were powerful and they worked. He defined design as:
'..... A STRATEGIC DISCIPLINE OF THE FIRST ORDER AND A PRIMARY MARKETING TOOL IN FIERCELY INCREASING GLOBAL COMPETITION. FOR THE OUTSIDE WORLD, DESIGN IS THE ONLY VISIBLE DEFINITION OF THE CORPORATION, ITS NAME, ITS FACE, ITS PERSONALITY, ITS PHILOSOPHY, ITS VALUES, ITS PRODUCTS AND ITS PEOPLE WHO STAND FOR BEING RELIABLE, PUNCTUAL, CAREFUL AND FRIENDLY.'

For that matter, he directed that KLM should emphasise its identity even more strongly. 'EVERY ADVERTISEMENT, EVERY PROMOTIONAL ITEM, EVERY TIMETABLE, EVERY PIECE OF EQUIPMENT IS AN INVESTMENT IN KLM'S NAME AND IMAGE IN MARKET PLACES ALL OVER THE WORLD. ALL EFFORTS MUST BE CONCENTRATED ON CONSISTENT USE OF KLM'S TRADEMARK AND THE STANDARD COLOUR BLUE. THESE ARE ELEMENTS OF VISUAL COMMUNICATION, OF PUBLIC PROJECTION'.

Consequently, that same year, the Dutch advertising agency P.M.S.v.W. was asked to develop the communication concept for KLM's advertising campaign. That campaign should have one distinct, consistent image world-wide, be in-line with the corporate house style as well as adaptable for various messages and different cultures. In addition, it should leave room for creativity at a local level, be convincing and also be adaptable for long-term use. Because external communication is, by definition, also internal, and vice versa, the concept should be suitable for both internal and external communication requirements. It should, of course, automatically produce an instant link with KLM in the mind of the customer.

A year of preliminary sketches and designs finally produced the logical and simple answer - the power of the obvious. Blue, the colour of sky, the colour of KLM, would be the carrier of the message.
'I ALWAYS WONDERED WHY KLM PLANES ARE THE COLOUR OF THE SKY'
'BEING THE WORLD'S FIRST AIRLINE, THEY HAD THE FIRST CHOICE.'

(opposite page, top and middle) Pages from the house style manual, (opposite page, bottom) The application of the house style to stationery and vehicles.

The geometry in the layout of the KLM logo.

House style manual

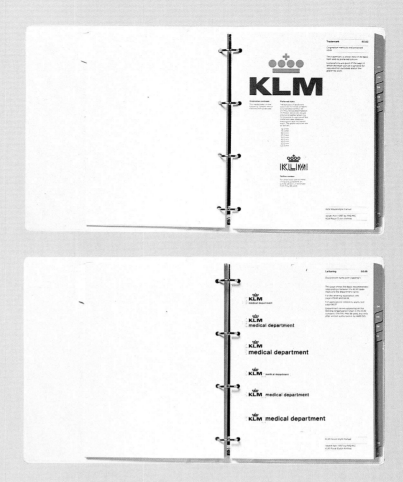

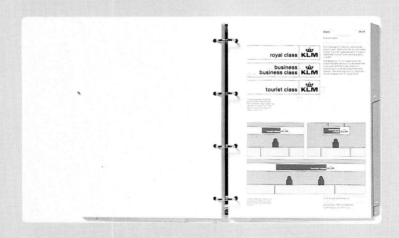

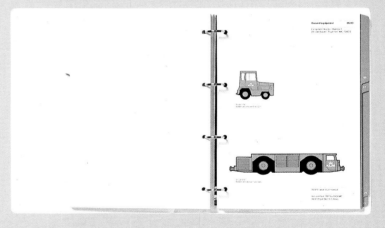

"I always wondered why KLM planes are the colour of the sky."

"Being the world's first airline, they had the first choice."

"KLM creates memorable meals for Royal Class guests."

"Good taste travels well!"

The advertising message itself would be in dialogue form across a blue sky crossed by a small aircraft. That dialogue concept was flexible enough to handle practically any communication need, both internal or external, as well as being adaptable to local conditions abroad.

The house style blue was to play a bigger role. In 1985, it was featured in the redesigned interiors of KLM aircraft. All seats were upholstered in a tasteful, dark blue, the classes being distinguished only by fine, coloured stripes in the middle of the seat and by distinctive head-rests.

On October 7, 1989, the airline's 70th anniversary, new uniforms were introduced for KLM's female staff . By April 1990, KLM's service staff - 8,800 employees on the ground and in the air, in 149 cities and 77 countries all over the world - were wearing the new uniform. Like its forerunner, which dated from 1982, it was designed by the French fashion house of Nina Ricci. The colour, of course, remained the same, as it has done for the last 19 years - bright blue.

All these steps indicate that Henrion's ideas had borne fruit and KLM managed to orchestrate its world-wide application. **'DISCIPLINE AND STRICT ADHERENCE TO THE INSTRUCTIONS OF KLM'S HOUSE STYLE MANUAL WILL BUILD AND REINFORCE THE IMPACT INSTEAD OF DILUTING IT, SAVING MARKETING MONEY INSTEAD OF WASTING IT'.**
A small number of house style elements have been properly and consistently applied across a range of thousands of design items.

All of KLM's design related activities are now dealt with by the Corporate Design Group, established in 1981 under the chairmanship of De Soet. Top management's commitment and continual monitoring prove to be essential. The design group comprises representatives from marketing, advertising and sales promotion, buildings, architecture and industrial design. The group has two

coordinators; one responsible for house style, advertising materials, uniforms and aircraft exteriors, the other for interior and exterior design of buildings, aircraft interiors and such things as catering supplies. Regular contact is maintained with Henrion's office, which now operates under the name Henrion, Ludlow and Schmidt, and with the P.M.S.v.W. advertising agency.

The house style manual gives directives for the use of the logo, colours and lettering. The logo is reproduced in its purest form together with stipulations regarding the use of other sizes and colours. Wherever possible, the logo should be reproduced in two shades of blue - light for the crown and darker for the letters KLM. The letters should be in the house type-face and form a coherent whole with the crown. The manual also specifies the application of house style on ground items, the design and furnishing of sales offices, the typography and layout of stationery as well as making provision for special cases such as KLM Cargo, KLM Party Service and KLM Helikopters/General Aviation.

KLM logo, Arabian style.

The interior of a KLM reservations office showing the wall divided into time zone panels (left). The time zone wall in detail (right).

The interior of a KLM aircraft and the cabin attendant's uniform (left). Even the Catering Services staff are 'packaged' in KLM's house style (right).

Henrion stressed the fact that a house style should be capable of being used for many years. This implies that there must be room and flexibility for adjustment to developments in the world's markets, consumer life-styles, fashions and trends in products and services. Henrion, Ludlow and Schmidt designed 'visual sub-identities' for KLM's subsidiary activities. KLM Party Service, for example, has two variations on the standard logo. One only uses the dark blue and adds the words 'party service' to the crown and KLM. A red dot over the 'i' of service is the only colour element introduced. The second allows 'party service' to be printed in silver with the dot in dark blue.

KLM's house style, in effect, packages the product - 'Service'. The central players on KLM's stage are its personnel, and they are also 'packaged' in a uniform which conveys KLM's image of 'quality' to the public. Addressing the staff in 1982, De Soet said; 'IN EVERY PRICE CATEGORY, PASSENGERS EXPECT FROM ALL AIRLINES SAFETY, PUNCTUALITY AND RELIABILITY. THAT HAS TO BE REALISED, COME WHAT MAY, BUT IN THE END, IT IS THE ATTENTION TO DETAIL, THE PROFESSIONALISM, CARE AND FRIENDLINESS OF THE PEOPLE WHO PROVIDE THE SERVICE TO OUR CUSTOMERS THAT CAN, AND MUST, MAKE THE DIFFERENCE.'

KLM is aware that its own belief in design, advertising or publicity is, in itself, insufficient. It must practice what it preaches and deliver what it promises. The concept of 'quality' is the pivot around which everything in the airline business revolves in the 1980s and 90s. In 1983, KLM launched a far-reaching and integrated programme to improve quality in every facet of its activity. The programme has continued to gain momentum as demanded by KLM's mission. This states that the company is firmly set on course to position itself as an airline operating world-wide, from a European base at a level placing it among the world's top quality carriers, offering professional service at competitive tariffs to passengers and shippers who will not be satisfied with less

than the highest quality levels, ensuring a **reliable, punctual** product and a **careful, friendly** service.

Rapid political change is currently being felt across the globe and, in the near future, these changes will have enormous consequences for civil aviation. Additionally, European, American and Far Eastern carriers are all in the throes of rationalisation, trying to confront the crippling competition within the industry. KLM must take account of all these developments if it is to respond adequately to the threats and potential of the future, remaining in the top league of the world's best airlines.
An important part of that response is KLM's house style - a style that reflects its excellence and uniqueness. The quality of its design radiates the quality of the company, its products and the people behind it. Addressing his management, earlier this year, De Soet, now KLM's president, said;
'HOUSE STYLE IS A VITAL STRATEGIC WEAPON IN THE MARKET PLACE, A BINDING ELEMENT AMONG KLM COLLEAGUES IN 77 COUNTRIES.
TOGETHER WITH OUR PEOPLE IT IS THE MOST VALUABLE ASSET, WORTH BILLIONS OF DOLLARS.
IT SHOULD BE GUARDED AND DEFENDED. IT IS DISCIPLINE AND YOU ARE PERSONALLY ACCOUNTABLE. DON'T PLAY AROUND WITH IT OR DEVIATE FROM IT. DON'T WASTE AND DESTROY KLM'S FIGHTING CAPITAL. ADHERE, INVEST AND ADD TO IT'.
After 40 years, the consistent organisation and implementation of KLM's corporate identity is a reality. The realisation remains a process of supervision from the top, discipline and constant fine-tuning.

Colin Wells

The development
of the KLM logo
(from left). The
'finch' from 1919.
'Ball and Stripes'
from ca. 1950.
'Ball and Stripes'
from 1958. 'Ball
and Stripes' from
1961. The
simplified design
of the new logo
makes it easy to
apply to large
surface areas
such as the tail
and flank of a
Boeing 747-400
(bottom).

Kodak
New electronics out of
a yellow box

Kodak's photographic products always seem to have had the same sunny red, yellow or orange packaging. Their cheerful wrapping reflects the outburst of colour that came with the discovery of celluloid as a vehicle for light-sensitive emulsions.

Red and yellow were the colours Kodak originally donned a century ago. Although one of the two colours always dominates, red and yellow became the multinational's inseparable insignia. Recently a touch of grey has been added to point out that the company also has an Imaging Systems division and deals in more than cameras and rolls of film.

Armed with the slogan 'The right combination', the Rochester-based concern is preparing for its second century, which will see the marriage of their photographic and electronic activities. The synergism of these two technologies will be used to produce floppy discs, microfiches, X-ray films and optical discs. The traditional roll film will be revamped to transfer and manipulate information in addition to storing and filing it.

How simple everything was only two decades ago. Jaunty jingles like 'Make a gift of a Kodak' would ring out in many tongues from wirelesses all round the world, and teenagers and pensioners were snapped Instamatic-ally and with apparent ease, judging by their beaming faces. It was child's play. The Instamatic was a follow-up to the popular Retina in the 1950s, which had succeeded the Box Brownie that Kodak's founder George Eastman had brought on to the market around 1900. The Brownie sold for the price of one US dollar and, at 15 cents, a roll of film could hardly break you. It was a clever move, for it turned everybody into a potential photographer and photography was no longer the privilege of the well-to-do or photography fanatics.

The Box Brownie remained on the market for a remarkably long time, despite its snapshot successors and the fact that photographic developments did not stand still. Further refinement of the finder-less box led to the more manageable pocket camera and the SLR camera with its telephoto or wide-angle lens. But there was an important drawback to making photography so broadly accessible in that the snapshot camera has now virtually exhausted its market potential. There is no household in Europe that does not own one or more cameras.

Early in the 1980s, Kodak hoped to be able to write a new chapter of photographic history with another revolutionary invention, the disc camera, which produces sharper photographs on a disc. In the United States, where instamatic cameras and the results they produce are standard, it did well. But in Europe where people clearly prefer the SLR camera it did not get off the ground. For Europeans the Instamatic is a useful standby alongside the standard SLR.

(opposite, above left) Harris B. Tuttle sr, appears in a 1923 photograph with the 16mm Cine-Kodak movie camera. Tuttle played an important role in the development of the movie camera.

Kodak introduced the Brownie in early 1900.

The SLR's firm footing in Europe can be partly attributed to the strong market position of East and West German cameras, such as Rolleiflex and the Swedish, which in turn paved the way for the influx of Japanese cameras – the Nikons, Minoltas and Olympuses. The disc camera has since discreetly dropped out of sight. Its failure shows that even a wool-dyed corporation can slip up in its own market, particularly in one diversified through the rise of different techniques.

The story of Kodak is the story of George Eastman, a single-minded savings-bank clerk who was obsessed with the 19th-century's magic invention. Eastman was not only fascinated by technique, he also foresaw its commercial potential. He soon set up a distribution network and within five years of opening his Rochester factory he had opened a wholesale outlet in London where later a production line for film and paper was housed.

The company's expansion called for a corporate identity; to begin with it needed a name that was easy to pronounce in any language. Fascinated by the strong impact of the letter K, Eastman decided it had to begin and end with a K and came up with the name Kodak. He had a visionary mind, for Kodak has become a generic name virtually, in the same way as Coca-Cola and Aspirin. Like these makes, Kodak succeeded in penetrating to the remotest of outposts, so that even in the heart of Africa wooden shacks can be found today proudly sporting their 'Kodak Products' sign. The well-travelled name of Kodak was registered as a trademark in the United States in 1888, ensuring its immediate protection in roughly a hundred countries.

During the company's early years, Kodak was written in graceful lettering dictated by the prevailing fashions and it generally appeared in combination with Eastman's name, featured on every product as the inventor and founding father. For a time Kodak's logotype was contained within a small circle along with the initials EKC (Eastman Kodak Camera), but as the company diversified its activities it became necessary to simplify the symbol. To complement this, a simple packaging concept was developed – the red and yellow box.

Before the Second World War the company had already set about streamlining the Kodak logotype and replacing it with a graphic design based on the typewriter letter. The graphic staff initially cornered Kodak in a small black right angle and later contained it in a winged label, as it was known within the company. Other small adjustments followed, but the lettering had been decided on, and the new logo was to be the figurehead of a company anxious to put across a quality image for both its products and service. For in the words of George Eastman, speaking at the company's inauguration, 'QUALITY SHOULD BE AN ARGUMENT TO FIGHT FOR.'

It is rare in the business world for a company radically to alter its corporate image. It is an extremely costly undertaking and causes confusion among consumers and suppliers, sometimes over long periods. Kodak was therefore extremely cautious about updating its corporate image in the 1970s, and for the first time in the company's history consulted outside designers, from the Seleme office in Boston.

In 1980 Joe Seleme thickened the K and implanted the name Kodak, but retained the red and yellow. Detailed instructions – printed in Helvetica capitals – were drawn up on how to apply the rejuvenated corporate image and, more especially how not to, with a long list of abuses to ward off potential transgressors. The yellow prescribed by the B & I (Business and Industrial Unifier) is pantone 123c, the red pantone 485c, and the black is plain black.

The thick K appeared on trucks, flags ('THE CORPORATE FLAG WHEN FLOWN WITH A NATIONAL FLAG SHOULD NORMALLY BE SMALLER THAN THE LATTER'), and on hundreds of thousands of rolls of film the world over. And yet the logo soon started to lose its

(opposite, top to bottom, from left) Eastman Kodak Company Corporate Identity, 1971; Kodak Corporate Identity Manual, 1972; Worldwide B&I Visual Standards, 1987; Retail Identity Standards, 1988; various pages from corporate identity manuals.

(left) An early form of information system. Autographic camera, c. 1915.

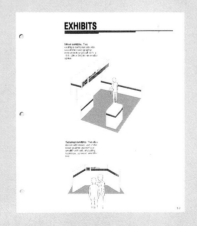

(above) Two
brochure covers.
(bottom right) Two
magazines aimed
for different target
groups.
(bottom left)
Display material
from the late
1970s.

validity: Kodak was confronting image problems; the company was identified too strongly with cameras and films (Kodak is the world's largest producer of films) and not nearly enough with its fast expanding industrial division.

Seleme was called in to sort things out. The Boston design consultants decided to start by simplifying the lettering of the trademark: all the serifs were cut except for the upper one on the A, which was allowed to keep its cheerful flourish; they even went as far as printing Kodak outside the thick K. Finally the logo was underscored with bars of diminishing thickness. This is the logo used by franchise holders or retailers stocking Kodak.

The new Kodak logo bears a strong resemblance to the logo of the Los Angeles Olympics, which shows a star – combined with the Olympic rings – in fast, fading lines, recalling the dynamic and streamlined efficiency of the Olympic organization. The similarity is arguable: the Olympics are an ideal springboard for new photographic technology, for an improved film like Ektacolor Gold, or an even handier video camera. Kodak was the main sponsor of the 1988 Seoul Games. Not only do the Games ensure great exposure during the event, they also offer the sponsor benefits afterwards. This might be in the form of award-winning World Press Photo pictures of some important, impressive or emotional sporting moment.

It was unfortunate that the 1984 Olympics in Kodak's home country coincided with a slump in the corporation's financial situation. Kodak missed these Games. The honour of the main sponsorship went to Fuji. The Japanese had gradually forced Kodak into a defensive position. The ultralight compact camera, improved photocopier and instant camera (which gave Polaroid a considerable head start) brought on the market by Kodak's Japanese and domestic

rivals made these highly competitive. Kodak missed out all round. Losses were put down to the company structure. The hierarchy of the Great Yellow Father, as the company is known in Rochester, had been pyramidal for too long, with a small top management too little inclined to make way for new blood. Also Kodak was an organization run more by technicians and engineers than designers, and one keen to keep most things under its own control.

The arrival of Colby Chandler as company director in 1983 brought a complete change of strategy. There were drastic cutbacks in staff and, more important, many companies were bought up, Sterling Drug being the Great Yellow Conqueror's biggest conquest. Kodak no longer shuns its unbeatable 'enemies' but solicits their collaboration instead. Their Japanese competitor Matsushita produces an 8 mm camera for Kodak and the matching video tape is made by TDK Electronics, another Japanese corporation. The Kodak colours have seemed slightly diluted since and speed appears to be a new theme evolving alongside the quality concept.

The corporation has grown from a strongly centralized, homogeneous enterprise into a ramified organization with autonomous subsidiaries. To be able to distinguish better between the corporation's various divisions, the logo was rejuvenated. The way Kodak was retailed seemed to put across too biased an image of the concern. It did no service to the corporation's other, wholly different, technological branch. The company felt stuck with the leisure label, caught in the yellow pages between the angling clubs and swimming pools. How many consumers know, for instance, that Kodak brought out a duplicating machine called Verifax as early as 1953? The machine was fairly primitive – it required a matrix and a fluid and a good deal of patience – but it was a novelty and it sold rather well within a limited market. (Today Kodak proudly claims to be the only manufacturer of a photocopier, the Ektaprint, that can make colour copies from a black-and-white original, and at an astounding speed too.)

For many years the Kodak emporium was built on a single commodity and its derivative products, and it is to these that it owes its fame. It was not until the 1970s that the multinational cautiously embarked on diversification. In 1971 Kodak bought up Spin Physics which specialized in audio-visual recording technology. Practically every professional video tape recorder or tape recorder in the world is fitted with Spin Physics recording heads.

An important step forward was Kodak's takeover of Atex, a leading manufacturer of word-processing equipment for the graphic industry. Atex is the lifeline for many major newspapers, including **THE GUARDIAN** in Manchester, the **NEW YORK TIMES** and Amsterdam's Perscombinatie newspapers, **DE VOLKSKRANT, HET PAROOL** and **TROUW**. With Atex within its doors, Kodak could concentrate on consolidating its graphic sector.

In 1988, just after Kodak had created its powerful pharmaceutical branch by taking over Sterling Drug, the new Bio-science division found itself in the limelight by fabricating artificial snow for the Winter Olympics in Calgary, where organizers had to contend with an unprecedented lack of snow on the pistes. One can hardly imagine a better form of publicity for a company division otherwise invisible to the public eye.

These entirely new branches – broadly speaking the pharmaceutical, technological and electronic activities of the corporation – needed a distinctive identity of their own. Thanks to Seleme, a small revolution took place. The red and yellow were forced to share their ground with grey. The logo remained but it was underscored with a grey and a yellow line and accompanied by the slogan 'The new Kodak vision'. The grey and yellow lines referred to the specialist fields of the new branches: grey was for the pharmaceutical, chemical or research divisions; yellow for the divisions related specifically to photography.

The new corporate identity enables the various subsidiaries to operate more independently and allows them more creative leeway. This applies to every corporate division, whether they make plastics, X-ray films or batteries. Each division operates with a considerable degree of autonomy, provided the main strategies and Kodak image are not violated. Though Kodak has rapidly developed into a many-headed monster, it continues to lay down the principal strategies from its Rochester head office.

In every country the Kodak House, and in particular the Photographic Division – still that part of the company the consumer sees – is sanctioned to set out its own national advertising and promotional strategies. It is here that the gulf between the United States and Europe is most marked. Advertising methods in America are more forthright and aim at a quick return, whereas on the Continent they involve irony and puns, and underplay in TV commercials.

The revamped corporate identity has raised the subject of the corporate statement for the 1990s and the 21st century. Kodak wants to get away from the image it traditionally tried to transmit of Mum, Dad and the Kids having fun with and in front of the camera. Instead Kodak takes us to exotic corners of the globe ripe for Kodacolour exposure. Today's **ZEITGEIST** is individualistic and dynamic and this is what the concern's corporate image must put across. Young people, who were a logical target audience in the 1960s, are no longer the only consumer targets for the arrows of advertising; experience has taught that they prefer to spend their money on personal computers and ghetto blasters rather than on cameras.

If Kodak is obliged to update its corporate identity frequently it is because the market is forever shifting and target groups are increasingly difficult to define. By the end of the 1970s it was no longer enough for Kodak's corporate identity to be strong and monolithic. It was too limited, too directive. Moreover the company has to be vigilant if it is to cope with the competitive assaults from such increasingly aggressive rivals as Fuji. The Rochester giant has apparently been seated on its throne too complacently for too long, like Philips, Holland's sedentary moloch, which found it had grown too weak when the time came for it to stand its own ground.

For Kodak the revolution has yet to start, a fact heralded by the crisp appearance of the company's corporate identity. This second revolutionary round will entail integrating photography and electronics. Kodak is armed with a variety of products as it embarks on this digital era, where attention is focused on recording information on discs or microfilms, and exchanging, duplicating and manipulating image data.

Kodak claims to having always been a company of inventors – a strong image that it is keen to keep. The giant tends to be slow off the mark when it comes to design with nothing very spectacular to report in this area. Nameless in-house designers continue to fashion the face of Kodak's merchandise. Design does not appear to be Kodak's strongest asset: the company seems unable to come up with designs for its cameras, photocopiers and word processors which are appealing to the imagination. Kodak could do with someone like Raymond Loewy, who expressed The American Dream so admirably. Unlike Xerox, Hasselblad or IBM, Kodak cannot claim any historic milestones along the road of design. The Brownie is the one exception: it is no coincidence that this handy little box camera is as old as the concern itself.

Photography has been described as writing with light, a definition which has a decidedly antique ring about it. Photography was an invention of the 19th century and it was then that it reached its creative heights, providing the first images of a society which people had been hitherto unaware of. Before then most painters had only portrayed the wealthy. With his invention of the film roll and its cinematographic extension, the film reel, George Eastman can be accredited with making photography a medium of the people.

With its black-and-white and colour films, micro and X-ray films, and now, on the eve of a new century, optical discs for laser-registered information, Kodak's impact and import is immense. However extensive and diverse its present range of products, the corporation still likes to be linked with its little yellow box. And thanks to Kodak, a colourful community has indeed posed, pranced and paraded in front of the magic lamp. But the genie has gone out of the magic yellow box and today there seems little chance of it ever returning.

Jaap Huisman

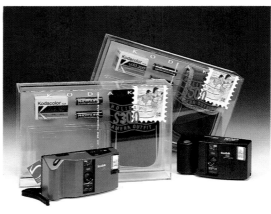

(left) Kodak Ektachem DT-60 equipment for blood analysis, 1987. (right) Two compact cameras, 1989. (opposite) Fanlight for a video cassette, 1984; torches, 1988; disposable cameras, 1988/1989, (left) Kodak color control patches, 1977.

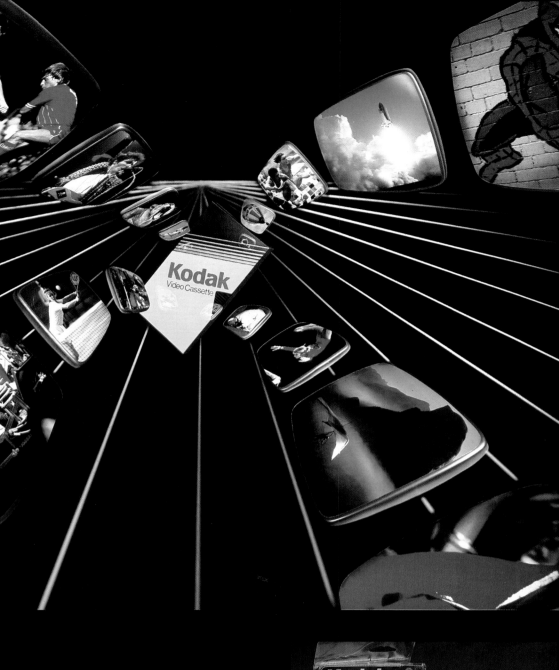

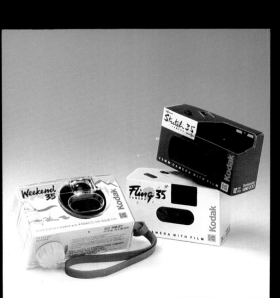

Volkswagen
Cars as a statement of style

So eagerly does the publicity department of Volkswagen AG talk in figures that after a time all those millions start to make you feel dizzy. No fewer than 20 million Volkswagen Beetles are sold worldwide, overtaking the T Ford model to become the best-selling car of all time. In 1987 the total number of cars produced since the company began in 1938 reached 50 million. And the Golf, launched in 1974, has become just as much a desired globetrotter as its illustrious predecessor. In their 1988 annual report, its producers announced that sales had topped 10 million. For six years in succession the Golf has been Europe's most widely sold car. All impressive figures. Yet figures with a dark side to them.

In 1945 Volkswagen lay in desolate ruins. The large contingent of forced labourers – 8000 of the 12000 workers in 1944 – from various occupied countries, had returned home.
The indigenous employees who had no other choice but to remain had more likely than not become homeless during the closing year of the war. The Stadt des Kraft durch Freude Wagens in northern Germany, erected to demonstrate the superiority of great German thinking and now humiliated, paid the toll for the hysterical inflated ego of the Third Reich. British occupying troops now called the tune in this area close to the Russian zone. As in many other German cities, Wolfsburg's industry, which had worked loyally to its dying breath on Hitler's war effort, was flattened.

Ferdinand Porsche's dream, like that of his great protector, was shattered. Seventy-thousand war vehicles and truckloads of components had not been sufficient to prop it up. During the mid-1930s, the Austrian engineer, along with Nazi sympathizers, was heading for a glowing future. No one less than the Führer believed in his idea of an affordable car for everybody and that belief was backed up by the sound of money. Until this point, Porsche had peddled his design to no avail. Daimler, Benz and the Auto Union all wanted to work with Porsche on developing sports cars, but saw no point to this strange compact car for ordinary folk.

However, in the political scheme of the national socialists, the car builder's design was heaven sent. Porsche was able to show Hitler practical ready-made technical drawings, which was very convenient considering the Reich was in a hurry. Legend has it that Hitler himself put together the list of requirements for his new propaganda instrument. According to the demands of the day, it would be a streamlined car, not cost more than 1000 Reichsmarks, have space for five passengers, and be capable of 100k an hour on a low petrol consumption. The car would be classless and thus a symbol of a collective national culture. After a familiarization trip to the United States in 1936, Porsche had already concluded that a yearly production of one million cars was feasible. (This figure in fact was only reached in 1961.)

(opposite, above) Golf Cabrio dashboard, 1989. (centre) Rows of beetles at the ready in 1947 to serve no longer the army but the man-in-the-street.

(above) Aerial view of the Wolfsburg plant from where the Volkswagen was to conquer the world.

In 1946, only a year after the start, the 10,000th Volkswagen was delivered. Employees painted slogans on its bodywork which tell a tale of postwar austerity and hardship: '10,000 cars and too little to eat – could you stand it?' But there were more encouraging slogans too: 'We're on the road – we're coming – out into the wide, wide world!'

In 1937 the head of Deutsche Arbeitsfront (DAF) received 30 million Reichsmarks and orders to start building the car, factory and surrounding ribbon development. In a no-man's-land on the edge of the town of Fallers-leben, Hitler laid the first stone of the future Volkswagen factory on 23 May of the follow-ing year. In that same year he conferred the German Prize on Porsche, together with avia-tion engineers Heinkel and Messerschmidt and autobahn king Fritz Todt. He also chris-tened this new creature. It would be called **KRAFT DURCH FREUDE** and every German by saving up savings points could become the possessor of this advanced motorcar.

The vehicle became the symbol of limitless freedom, the savings card a passport to the stars. '5 MARK DIE WOCHE MUSST DU SPAREN - WILLST DU IN EINEN AUTO FAHREN' a 1938 poster for the car announced, but the promise was never kept. Everyone saved like mad – in that same year deposits already stood at 280 million Reichsmarks – but there was to be no driving. The frozen accounts were suddenly made worthless when the factory had to suspend production of the Volkswagen in order to make itself useful for the war effort. The small number of cars already produced came into the hands of those Nazis who had warmly supported the project, and Porsche and his associates had to modify the design to suit the new circumstances. Two types of mili-tary jeep were built onto its chassis, the Kübel-wagen which transported Erwin Rommel's triumphant African troops and the so-called **SCHWIMMWAGEN**, an amphibious version. Moreover, in the years to follow the factory would also produce components for the V-1 bomb.

This dark period in history was essential to the success of the Volkswagen after the war, something the management of the company is only too aware of, according to the recent work of historian Hans Mommsen. He investigated the company's history, the efforts of the forced labourers and its links with the regime. Ferdi-nand Porsche, he concludes, was indeed loyal to Hitler but was no Nazi. He used the friendship of his fellow countryman to realize

his dream of producing an affordable car. He was an opportunist, not a criminal. When Volkswagen celebrated its 50th jubilee, Mommsen was right in saying, 'GERMANS SHOULD REALIZE THAT THE PRESENT FAVOURABLE ECONOMIC CLIMATE IS PARTLY DUE TO THE ARMS INDUSTRY OF THE NATIONAL SOCIALISTS.' The German art historian Gert Selle pulls together the historic threads even tighter: 'IT IS BITTER IRONY THAT THE VOLKSWAGEN AS THE BIGGEST FANTASY OF ALL THE THREATENING PRODUCTS OF NATIONAL SOCIALIST CUT-THROAT POLICIES, SHOULD NOT ONLY APPEAL 15 YEARS LATER TO THAT EXACT SAME DREAM, BUT BECOME THE ICON OF THE GERMAN REPUBLIC ON THE WORLD MANUFACTURING FRONT.'

It is indeed true that the Beetle has become the face of Germany: consistent and reliable, but also obstinate, tenacious and successfully present all over the world. In the rubble of 1945 it did not in the least look like the car that would ever attain such status. Under the supervision of the British Major, Ivan Hirst, the basic necessary repair work to the factory was carried out. During this time the remaining workforce had to have swimming trunks on the job in order to dive for machinery components which after their dismantling during the final year of the war had been hidden in the water surrounding the factory. English jeeps began to be repaired and the first Beetles assembled by hand, which due to a lack of light transport were much needed for controlling the occu-pied zone. While the British had no wish to own the Volkswagen factory, in September 1945 they took a step that was to save it: 20000 cars were ordered for the Red Cross, for the Post Office and for the allied troops. Still there was no private individual that could relate to the grey-green Beetle and according to car manufacturer Henry Ford it was better it remained that way. Besides, being only 15k from the present border with East Germany, he saw no chance at all for a car plant. However, the factory, born out of a depression, was to be more viable than anyone could imagine. In the meantime the **STADT DES KRAFT DURCH FREUDE WAGENS** was renamed Wolfsburg, where not the good humour of 1938 but the collective bitterness of 1945 created a tremendous explosion of effort that was to be symptomatic of the postwar industrial development of West Germany.

Increasingly more Beetles left the plant – thanks to the indispensable support of the Marshall Plan – and when the British appoint-ed Heinrich Nordhoff in 1948 as director their duty had already been done. Within the year Nordhoff even became director of the entire German factory due to the Allied Military Forces surrendering confiscated possessions. The Beetle could now be improved – according to Nordhoff it had as many things wrong with it as the number of fleas on a dog –, the plant streamlined and Nordhoff, who was to reign until 1968, realized that if he wanted to main-tain the close contact between the factory and

(opposite) Covers and inside layout of VW corporate identity manuals.

Volkswagen
Identifikationsprogramm

Volkswagen
Identification Programme

**Heft 1
Richtlinien zu den
Grundelementen:
Zeichen, Schrift, Raster**

**Volume 1
Guidelines for
basic elements:
symbol, typeface, grid**

Volkswagen
Identifikationsprogramm

Volkswagen
Identification Programme

**Heft 3
Richtlinien zu den
Grundelementen:
Fotografie**

**Volume 3
Guidelines for
basic elements:
photography**

Volkswagen
Identifikationsprogramm

Volkswagen
Identification Programme

**Heft 6
Richtlinien
für die Anwendung:
Farbklima der
Bürogebäude und
Produktionsstätten**

**Volume 6
Guidelines
for implementation:
colour scheme
for offices and plants**

Volkswagen-spezifische
Grundelemente

Specific
Volkswagen elements

Typografische
Zuordnungen

Typographic
layouts

Kombination
von
Schriftgrößen

Combination of
type sizes

Subline

Headline

Subline

Headline

Subline

Headline

Richtlinien für den gemeinsamen
Auftritt der Marken

Guidelines for the joint
appearance of the brands

VOLKSWAGEN AG

VOLKSWAGEN

Der Fotostil im Layout

The photo styles and the
layout

Der Golf.

Der neue Passat.

Der Polo.

Das Golf Cabriolet.
Das Golf Cabriolet Quartett.

Der neue Corrado.

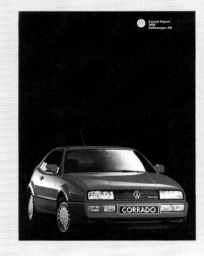

**Bunte Mischung. 64 Golf Cabrio
für Individualisten.**

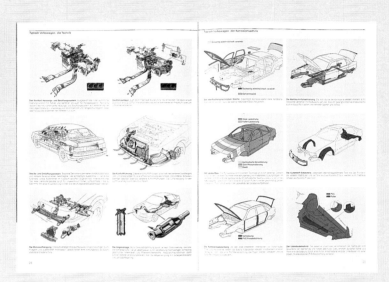

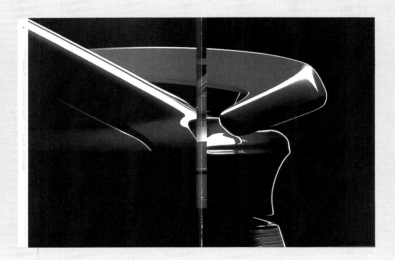

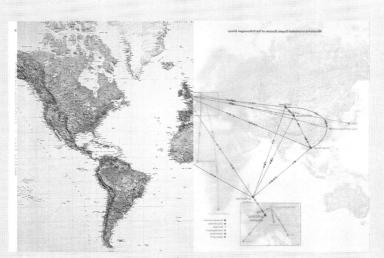

its workers something had to be done for the cultural life of Wolfsburg. Exhibitions and concerts had to turn it into an artistic centre for the region.

Although during this period there was no company style whatsoever, the close ties have remained an important element in management policy at Volkswagen. Staff and workers, dealers and garage owners are all allies in as standard an enterprise as possible – Volkswagen had to be big, become bigger and be the biggest. During the early 1960s, when labour was scarce in northwest Germany, for instance, VW workers from Italy were brought over and housed in a specially built Italian 'village' next to the factory. In 1970 this settlement was converted to a modern neighbourhood of flats with local services and to this day it is still bound up with Volkswagen AG. Training facilities, a medical centre and various recreation clubs for personnel were all organized by the factory.

Initially, the postwar recovery of Volkswagen was limited to its homeland, but by 1947 the first Beetles had already been exported to the Netherlands and two years later the Dutch importer left for New York with a few models destined for an exhibition on German industry. The acceptance of them was slow, notes a company brochure entitled **AN IDEA THAT MADE HISTORY,** yet slowly but surely 'THE BEETLE, AS A CLASSLESS CAR, TOOK ITS PLACE AS A PRACTICAL AND UNCONVENTIONAL VEHICLE WITH HUGE POSSIBILITIES AMONG THE HEAVILY CHROMED ROADSTERS. THE CAR BECAME THE DARLING OF INDIVIDUALISTS, THOSE WHO PREFERRED UNDERSTATEMENT AND THOSE WHO WERE NOT IN A POSITION TO BUY GLIMMERING LUXURY.' It is worth mentioning here that the Beetle-driving public in no way comprised 20 million individualists and lovers of understatement.

After all, the car for the common man was designed as a mass-produced article and as a mass-produced article it has triumphed. Granted the car had a wilful expression to it, but once the world had become used to the Beetle's appearance there was not that much recognizably individual about it. The car belonged just as much to a working-class area in Berlin as the sophisticated centre of Barcelona; in New York no less than in São Paolo. The fanning out of VW multinationals across all continents confirmed the international image of the model. From that moment on, what the aura of the Beetle conveyed became automatically that of its manufacturers too: solid without too many airs; sometimes bordering on the point of blandness. 'VOLKSWAGEN - DA WEISS MAN, WAS MAN HAT', goes the current slogan of the company. Surprises are ruled out.

Volkswagen was the Beetle even in the 1960s when sales figures were clearly starting to decline and the company had to concern itself with a successor. Amid the singing of Nordhoff's praises this was one note of criti-

cism of his policy. So rigidly had he stuck to fine-tuning the success of his monoculture that he had overlooked to present Volkswagen with a new 'Beetle'. Its symbol had become too overpowering to allow room for a new one. The fact that the factory was able to continue for so long without a clear corporate identity is a logical consequence of the car's unique symbolic value. Its characteristic body, which in subsequent versions never really changed, was continually recognizable partly because for many years only one egg was put in the company basket. Even when Type 2 was introduced – the Volkswagen minibus in 1950 taken from a sketch made by the Dutch importer Ben Pon – the original Type 1 remained the bearer of the Beetle name. Every advertisement displayed it, preferably frontal with its 'laughing face' photographed – an image which was carefully cultivated and which eventually was attributed with almost human characteristics in Disney's films about the headstrong Beetle 'Herbie'. Apart from this there were no more gimmicks and no stream of competitive models in own collection. If new technical developments cropped up, which they often did, these were realized in Type 1 without visibly modifying the car. This was the reason perhaps why the management at Volkswagen found it so difficult to accept a new model. Even when the sun began to set on the Beetle they had trouble choosing a successor. Giorgetto Giugiaro was commissioned to design a new model in 1969, and in 1971 the Golf made its first trial runs. In 1977 this car received the designation Gute Form from the German Ministry of Economic Affairs, even though initially Volkswagen had had some objections to this compact car from Ital Design. It was thought that Giugiaro's style was too modern and as a compromise the colourless Passat was launched in 1973. In 1974 when the factory was unable to keep its head above water any longer there was no other alternative: the Golf had to be launched even if it meant the demise of Volkswagen. Since the unexpected success of the Golf pulled the factory onto dry land, Volkswagen's policy appears hardly to have changed. This showpiece too has retained its compact appearance through the years, even when in

The popularity of the 'beetle' reached its zenith in the Disney films in which he was dubbed 'Herbie' the headstrong beetle.

1983 the Golf's form was modified in order to penetrate a more up-market segment. For a shift in policy did take place at Volkswagen during the last decade: particularly through its cars' designs it is aiming at a definitely up-market group. It is not the people with savings stamps that sell the Golf, but those with plastic cards. Advertising campaigns put the emphasis on the pioneering role of the company. What VW does today, many others do tomorrow, is the message. With this the company is also pencilling in the desired profile of its customers – people who appreciate innovation, who want to be in the lead. Even if they are with ten million others, they still comprise an avant-garde group. Moreover, new directions within the company have taken care that a monoculture like that with the Beetle can never happen again. Since the lean years of the 1970s, when both creative stagnation and the oil crisis came simultaneously, Volkswagen now works with more models for various segments, and for the first time in its history produced its first sports car, the Corrado, at the end of the 1980s. Alongside the Golf, the Passat, the Polo, the Jetta, and the many vans and cars produced by the amalgamated Seat and Audi plants, this sports car must also safeguard Volkswagen's future.

At Volkswagen new models are seldom developed for their spectacular design and the factory refrains from associating a particular brand of car with a designer's name. Since Ferdinand Porsche, the models have remained anonymous. The Golf and the Seat Ibiza came from the drawing board of Giugiaro's Ital Design, but the VW empire does not use this as an additional selling point in its marketing. Instead the emphasis is on technical innovation developed by its own draughtsmen. A neutral stand appears to be of greater significance than personal glory: every car, after all, is the result of a collective effort – exactly like Heinrich Nordhoff had espoused in his philosophy of the company in the postwar years. Giugiaro may claim the honours for his concept of a new compact car, but it was thanks to the staff at Volkswagen that the car was driven by a perfect engine, that a diesel version was developed, and that the efforts of the marketing department made Golf an overwhelming commercial success. Teamwork, in fact, based on the factory's tradition. The difference between Volkswagen today and that of Nordhoff's time is its unprecedented diversity. There are numerous versions of one model, whereby each is targeted at a specific market segment, be it simply designed or exceptionally distinguished, practical or ostentatious. More recently, Volkswagen serves the big-city cowboys with a heavy pick-up, the Taro, that appears to be more robust than its American counterpart – wide wheelbase, sits high and with that indestructible macho look of the late 1980s. This is no car for your average Volkswagen driver, but undoubtedly a model with a specific following. The diversifying of Volkswagen undoubtedly stepped up the need for a recognizable corporate identity. Since the 1980s Wolfsburg is no longer a one-horse town and the world had to realize there was only one captain at the helm. Consequently a so-called **IDENTIFICATION PROGRAMME** was drawn up. From that moment on, printed matter, sign-posting, car plants, showrooms and publicity were all bound by the same directives. Printed matter was designed on a fixed grid, Futura and Univers types were used exclusively, blue, grey and an occasional red became the house colours, while in layouts for advertisements and brochures a liberal amount of blank space was required. Photographers were briefed only to photograph the cars from the front or rear or at an angle of 45 degrees sideways on. These could be taken in a bare studio, in a studio with only a few props, or in a more documentary form in an actual situation. In the housestyle manual the application of the different types of photographs is elaborated upon and suggestions made for combining one or more approaches. Every directive is aimed at clarity of image. Colour in drawings is only used to highlight a technical detail, and a couple of beach umbrellas next to a Golf Cabriolet are simply there to emphasize the personality of the car. The corporate identity, the manual informs, is held firm by a consistent repetition of house elements in style and design. The most repeated and by far the easiest to recognize is the Volkswagen trademark: a white V and W piled one on top of the other, encased in a circle on a clear blue background. This logo remained untampered with throughout the entire development of the housestyle. In essence Volkswagen, since 1985, has added little more other than to lay down a few rules to make sure its broad range of activities are properly coordinated without changing the character of the company.

What has been achieved is that Volkswagen South Africa (which in its annual report announced increased profits yet again of 24 per cent) presents itself in a similar way to Autolatina, VW's plant in South America, that the factories in Wolfsburg and Westmoreland Pennsylvania draw one line with one another and that Audi is just as conscious of its clients as Seat or Volkswagen itself. The Audi housestyle is practically the same, apart from the use of a more classic lettering to reach customers – instead of Univers, the Times is used for all printed matter.

Despite all the rules and regulations, the spirit of Volkswagen is still ensconced in the Beetle. In one advertisement depicting an old early 1950s model, viewed from the rear, the caption reads: 'IN 20 YEARS TIME, YOU'LL THINK THE SAME ABOUT OUR GOLF.' That will never prove true. Volkswagen was, and will always be, the Beetle, the non-starter that became a hit – like a child who despite having a handicap, or even because of it, can still become popular. No housestyle can ever beat that.

Gert Staal

Fahren Sie ihn – oder nur so was Ähnliches?

The organization of a
corporate identity programme

The organization of a corporate identity programme

Introduction

A company or organization is like a person: it 'dresses' and communicates, and it has a certain style, in short a corporate image. This image exists in the minds of all those who have to do with the company, including the personnel (and potential employees), clients, private shareholders, financial backers, the media and even politicians and environmental groups. But instead of one indivisible image, a company in fact has different images among different groups. An investor, for example, sees it in a different way from a consumer or major customer, although there is some overlap between these groups. An investor will also go to a department store and then becomes a consumer.

Obviously, a company wants to have as much influence as possible on its image, and corporate identity is a useful aid in achieving this. The concept of corporate identity is generally associated with the style the company adopts when facing the outside world: the logo, letterhead, uniform, etc. But it also includes how telephone calls are answered, how complaints are dealt with and the kind of service provided. The corporate identity covers all these visual and non-visual elements.

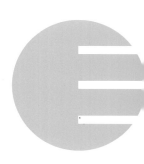

Airlines recognized the value of a corporate identity programme many years ago. The basic products they offered were almost identical so it was in their interest to differentiate themselves by offering better service, greater comfort and a clearly identifiable visual programme. The same is true of banks, which also needed to establish a clear identity because of the decisive importance of their image with the public.

There may, however, be other reasons for initiating this type of programme: target groups may have changed or expanded, or the company may have been involved in a merger. Such changes may also lead to minor or major adjustments to the programme, an additional reason being that visual elements like the logo have become outdated or no longer represent the desired image.

A programme is sometimes instituted or modified in the interests of greater efficiency, but despite the positive side-effects this does not in itself provide an adequate long-term basis for a corporate identity programme. The same applies to the cost-saving effect of rationalizing the stock of forms in use. The idea is to eliminate all the superfluous forms resulting from poor organization. But this is a one-off operation, and so is the reduction in costs. The amount saved can be calculated, but the ultimate benefits of a corporate identity programme are much more difficult to measure. The costs of an advertising campaign can be set against the short-term increase in sales of a product or service, but in the case of a corporate identity programme the results will only be evident in the long term and, most important of all, after it has been consistently implemented. Moreover, it is hard to quantify benefits in the form of greater attractiveness to potential employees and major investors, etc.

As already mentioned, it is vital that the corporate identity be consistently implemented, and this is particularly important in the case of the visual elements. A food company that transports its products in dirty trucks makes a poor impression on the consumer. This kind of programme must be concerned with the 'smallest' details.

The days are almost gone when the managing director, who rarely had any knowledge of design, had a large say in determining the look of a company's printed matter. A corporate identity programme is now run by managers who are more concerned with organization and communication than with design. Good design alone does not guarantee a good programme; what matters is its effective implementation.

This brings us to the heart of a corporate identity operation. Internal and external communication, also known as corporate communication, largely determine the objectives and starting points of the corporate identity programme. The degree to which a programme can be successfully carried out depends on the internal organization.

These two aspects, organization and communication, will be considered in detail in later sections dealing only with the visual part of a corporate identity programme. They must be thoroughly understood and mastered if the visual part is to be optimally effective. The interplay and balance between them determine the content of the programme and how it is put into effect.

Once these aspects are understood, a start can be made on the real work: the development of a corporate identity programme. All the phases of this development process are dealt with here in detail. It is up to the reader to translate them in terms of his or her own company or organization. In the end it is a question of how carefully the programme is carried out, and unfortunately, or perhaps fortunately, there is no simple recipe.

Organization and communication

Before turning to organization and communication, we must first consider the culture of a company. This largely determines the internal organization and communication and hence the development of a corporate identity programme.

Company culture as the heart of an organization

Every employee will have to follow consistently the rules as regards corporate identity imposed from above, certainly in matters where he will often want to have his own say. Whether or not this goes smoothly will depend on the culture which exists within every company.

A good example of an organization whose whole formula is founded on the company culture is the giant hamburger concern McDonald's. Through its franchise system, it has 9000 restaurants spread over four continents, so that no set of rules or corporate identity programme could possibly make the whole operation uniform and identical. This is, however, the image that McDonald's wants to project to the public, and this is achieved through a company culture based on mentality, atmosphere and identification with the enterprise. Accordingly, the most important task of the McDonald's management, at the level both of the whole concern and the individual restaurant, is to define and direct the company culture.

Any organization that does not have a cohesive culture promoting its interests will find it very difficult to implement a corporate identity programme. The reason is that the company culture largely determines to what extent and at what speed such a programme is effected, and thus its ultimate success.

If the company culture is to be improved or structurally changed, a large budget will be required for internal motivation programmes. A recent example is the chemical concern Akzo, which adopted a new corporate identity in 1988. Up to then Akzo had been a collection of independently operating subsidiary companies, each with its own identity, but now it wanted to present itself as a single concern. Large amounts were invested not only in a new logo for the whole company but also in internal motivation programmes for the personnel.

Organization and responsibilities

There are two sides to the concept of organization in relation to corporate identity. The first concerns the company as an organization and the second how the corporate identity is organized within the company. Of course, the former significantly influences the latter. Together with the company culture, both determine the quality and range of the corporate identity. This identity has to be made to measure for a company and the method of organization must be adapted to it.

In organizing a corporate identity the following aspects have to be considered:
- private company or government body;
- centralized or decentralized management;
- products or services;
- national and/or international market.
These aspects define the character of the organization. The tax department requires more organization and regulation than, for example, a florist's. It is easier to carry out a corporate identity programme for a company with all its production concentrated in one country than for one with production units all over the world. In some cases the organization of the company may be so complex that it is decided to carry out only a limited programme. In any event, setting up and implementing the programme will have effects throughout the company and so clear agreements on tasks and responsibilities are required.

Generally speaking, the *content* of the programme is the responsibility of top management, preferably the chairman of the board (where there is one). In practice it will be delegated to a management department. This should be the corporate communications department, which can combine this responsibility with its tasks in the fields of internal and external communications. This responsibility includes the monitoring of the general application.

Responsibility for *implementation* can best be given to a separate department which is in charge of developing, applying and continually modifying the corporate identity, in cooperation with the logistic departments. If such a department does not yet exist, it will have to be created. It can be at the management level, but in practice it is also sometimes at a lower level. Apart from being responsible for implementation, it also has the job of drawing attention to incorrect applications. Any measures that may be needed as a result can then be taken either by this department alone or jointly with the corporate communications department.

There is an important reason for separating responsibility for content and for implementation. Because the department in charge of implementation has a service function, it is not desirable that it should combine this with a responsibility in the field of content such as monitoring. Experience shows that this kind of combination generally does not work in practice: if a department sees that its wishes are not met, it will stop using the services of the department in charge of implementation. This deadlock will undermine the strength and effectiveness of the corporate identity programme.

In principle neither of these responsibilities belongs with the marketing department. The demands and conditions set by marketing are essentially different from the requirements of a corporate identity programme. The marketing department is generally concerned with achieving short-term objectives, whereas corporate identity is a long-term matter. In advertising, for example, the marketing requirements would soon prevail over those of corporate identity. Given that marketing makes its own demands of advertising, the part played in it by corporate identity must be a matter for consultation. The rules thus arrived at will have to be observed by the marketing department as part of a proper external communication strategy.

The communication strategy

All of a company's activities must conform to its objectives, and the same applies to a corporate identity. The internal and external communication strategy forms the link between the company objectives and the corporate identity objectives. It is essential that the company objectives be clearly understood before any activities in the field of corporate identity are undertaken.

The concepts of continuity and profitability are generally at the heart of company objectives, but they also cover such matters as core activities and social policy. One company which has long shown great concern for these aspects is Olivetti. It operates a primary social and ethical policy, based on an overall plan for production and production conditions which is closely related to the social circumstances of the employees. Olivetti's corporate identity, which is an extension of this policy, has long been regarded as a model.

The internal and external communication strategy establishes the desired image and how it is to be achieved. This image may differ from the one prevailing among target groups, and in that case the difference should be eliminated with the aid of the communication strategy. By aiming at synergy in all its manifestations, the company can retain greater control over its identity and hence its image. The communication strategy lays down in what ways and in what form the company wants to communicate with its target groups.

The objectives of the corporate identity are derived from this strategy. One of the purposes of this direct linkage is so that if the strategy changes this will lead where necessary to modification of the corporate identity. The stated objectives are most important in maintaining corporate identity. They might be: providing a service, being innovative and offering reliability, etc. But any competitor might quickly arrive at very similar objectives, so this is an opportunity for a company to stand out by emphasizing its special qualities. The statement of objectives is also required in order to assess results and particular manifestations in relation to corporate identity. In other words, developing a corporate identity forces a company to begin by taking a good look at itself: what does it stand for, what does it want to achieve, and which communication strategy is the most suitable?

The question of internal communication deserves special attention. The aim, after all, is that the rules of the corporate identity programme should be understood, accepted and hence applied. This process will be smoother in, say, Japan, where company loyalty tends to be strong, than in Europe, where there is more emphasis on the individual. Less communication and organization will be needed where there is a cohesive company culture than where it is weak or completely absent, as in the case of a newly established business. Internal communication informs the personnel about the underlying motives, how corporate identity is organized and who is responsible for what. A wide range of methods can be employed for this purpose, from personal letters to staff magazines and departmental presentations. These activities are an extension of the motivation programmes mentioned above.

Once the method of organization and the internal and external communication strategy have been decided, the development of a corporate identity can begin.

The development process

Developing a corporate identity programme can throw a new light on various routine matters. Familiar procedures are suddenly open to discussion, and in some cases the employee's contribution may now be limited to applying the corporate identity rules. The chatty staff magazine which was meant for internal consumption but was also read by outsiders, the individual business card in a different format leaving plenty of room for notes, and the business gifts displaying the logo so attractively but in a slightly different colour are all now outlawed. Any negative reactions to such changes must of course be met sympathetically. If careful consideration is shown towards the personnel during the development process, the changes can result in a positive attitude throughout the company. Shock then gives way to the feeling that follows a thorough spring-cleaning.
Developing an identity is not a one-off event but a continuing process: a corporate identity does not stand still any more than the company does. There are four phases in this process: orientation, design, implementation, and application and monitoring.

The orientation phase

In this phase the company's behaviour towards all its target groups is thoroughly examined. Together with the corporate communications department, the top management arrives at a *plan of approach* for the development of a corporate identity programme. This will include the objectives, the development strategy, the planning, the budget for development costs, an estimate of the costs of implementation, and an organization and communication model. The plan of approach can best be drawn up by the departments which will later be responsible for content and implementation, since they have the knowledge required at their disposal. It is a good idea to involve the organization and marketing departments in drawing up the plan at an early stage. In many companies the mix of marketing and corporate identity in commercial manifestations is a crucial point.

During this phase it will become clear that help from outside experts is essential. In the first place, the very fact that the company knows itself best makes it difficult to take an objective view. In the second place, specific expertise on organization and communication is often not available within the company. The outside experts initially work under the corporate communications department. After the plan of approach has been approved, they come under the *'corporate identity work group'.*

An important part of the plan of approach is an inventory of all the current manifestations of the company. A study of this material is particularly valuable: when everything (good and bad) has been brought together, the lack of coherence may be obvious, and the overall effectiveness must then be questioned. This can be the most persuasive argument in those cases where the department responsible feels the need for a new corporate identity programme but the board still has to be convinced.
This inventory also provides an insight into the size of the development project and the amount of work involved. By checking the material against the rules applying at the time, one gets a

good picture of which departments either deviate from them or do not observe them at all. Additional research into the reasons for this is extremely useful because they can serve as criteria for the corporate identity to be developed.

After the plan of approach has been approved, the board of directors sets up a *'corporate identity work group'* (referred to hereafter as the 'work group'). This includes representatives of all the departments which will be directly involved in the corporate identity programme, such as corporate communications, design, marketing, finance, purchasing and the logistic services. This broad base is necessary in order to resolve any problems that may crop up when the programme is carried out. Above this work group there is a 'steering group' which approves the decisions taken and bears the final responsibility on the basis of company policy and the objectives of the corporate identity as stated in the plan of approach. This steering group includes representatives of all the important company divisions and is chaired by a director.

One of the work group's first tasks is to draw up a *programme of requirements* based on the corporate identity objectives. The designers will later be given their brief on the basis of this programme and it also serves as the criterion for judging results during the development process. It can be divided into seven groups:

1 historical requirements (relating to the past and the continuity of the company);
2 organizational requirements (relating to the company structure and type of organization);
3 communication requirements (relating to the internal and external communication strategy);
4 economic requirements (relating to the budget and the available time);
5 quality requirements (relating to the present image and the existing competition);
6 technical requirements (relating to normalization, standardization and the means to be used by the company);
7 social requirements (relating to company culture).

It is only after this programme has been drawn up that the work group can decide which other outside experts should be involved in the plan of approach, and in particular which designers. It is important to choose a design agency that is competent and experienced in the field of corporate identity and that suits the character and philosophy of the company. In many cases outside expertise in advertising, communication, public relations and corporate identity itself will also be required. The development of corporate identity is a long-term business, and so both the design agency and other outside experts should be available for a considerable period. This should extend beyond the development and introduction phases since their help can be especially valuable when later modifications are made.

The budget for the costs of introduction can now be determined. A significant part will be reserved for external experts. While these costs are substantial, they are as nothing compared with the overall introduction costs, certainly not when set against the savings made by rationalizing the stock of forms in use, the different types of stationery and other printed matter. (A corporate identity operation almost always has a rationalizing and in the long run cost-cutting effect.)

The costs of introduction are substantially affected by whether changes are all done at once or only as and when replacement is necessary. In the latter case something is only produced in the new corporate identity when the old stock is finished or when, for example, a company car must be replaced. This means that only design costs are incurred; other costs, such as printing, are not included in the budget because they would have had to be met anyway when old stocks were replenished.

Introducing the corporate identity in one go means that stocks and assets also have to be written off in one go even though they still have some value. Stationery, packaging materials, business gifts, signs on buildings and company vehicles, which must be relettered or even resprayed, are all affected. Introduction therefore becomes a very expensive business. The disadvantage of introduction on a gradual, replacement basis is that both the old and new styles continue to be seen side by side for a long time. This confuses business partners and the public. It can also lead to problems in internal communication: in the early phase many employees will hear a great deal about the new corporate identity but see very little of it. From the point of view of communication, introduction in one go is much to be preferred. Of course it is possible to steer a middle course between these two alternatives. Depending on the budget, priority is given to changing certain manifestations, leaving others to be done when replacement is. This approach may be the solution if a particular effect has to be achieved by a certain date, for example because the company has changed its name or become independent or because of competitive considerations.

In the case of a change of name or legal status, the obvious choice must be for introduction in one go. In many countries it is even an offence for a company to present itself under anything other than its correct name and legal status. The question of the name to be used and those of the various departments is one of the things that the work group must have decided before the designers can start work.

In practice every working unit that consists of more than one person will quickly feel itself to be a group or department. It will give itself a name and use this on stationery and other matter internally and externally. This problem is immediately encountered in every design phase. Consistency in the use of names is essential: good design cannot sort out a tangle of obscure names in an obscure structure. Decisions on names will have to be confirmed by the steering group. Leaving the problem to the designers will only lead to delays in that phase. Moreover, this is the company's responsibility, not that of the designers.

The design phase

In this phase the visual elements, the *design system* and the *application rules,* are developed by the design agency in cooperation with the work group and the other outside experts. To enable the designers to form a picture of the company, all the material collected by the work group during the orientation phase is made available to them. At the same time the work group gives the designers a brief based on the programme of requirements drawn up earlier. In this way the designers acquire a clear view of the company and the desired corporate identity. If anything remains unclear, they should be given an opportunity to carry out their own research and to talk to people at all levels in the organization, from the top management to the shop floor.

After this preliminary phase the design agency can start work on developing the basic elements of the corporate identity, which will then be tested on various kinds of material. This is done in cooperation with the work group, in a continual process of development, testing and modification. The design agency and all other outside experts maintain contact with the company through the work group, of which they are in fact external members. It is important to ensure that outside experts are commissioned only by the work group; this will prevent people being given contradictory commissions that might delay the whole process.

Once the project has been running for some time, the importance of a single channel of communication will become apparent. Because of the frequent contact between the design agency and the logistic departments, the latter will be inclined to bring the agency in to deal with every little problem. This is most undesirable: it cuts across the work group's priorities and makes it impossible for the design agency to follow a sound approach.

The design phase consists of several stages. The agency presents its proposals, which are examined by the work group, and then if necessary new proposals are made. When the designs have taken a definite shape, they are assessed by the steering group. This is an important stage and the steering group should exercise direct control at this point, bearing in mind that it will be responsible for the content of the programme in future.

The design of the elements of the corporate identity-the logo, the colours and the typography-is followed by the design system for the elements on the various kinds of manifestations. This system sets out the design rules for groups of material and the application methods for the relevant elements of the corporate identity programme. For example, in the case of product brochures it lays down which formats may be used, whether they are horizontal or vertical, where the logo is to be placed and against what background colour, the typography of the text and how photographs and illustrations are to be positioned. This is not something to be treated lightly, since in the future many of these application methods will have to be used by employees with no design training and without the help of the agency. So the design system, which provides the basis, must be clear, and it must indicate what cannot be changed and where there is room for manoeuvre. A clear explanation will help the layman to understand the problems. The system can be tested through pilot schemes using small print runs. The work group and the steering group assess the interim results on the basis of the programme of requirements, so that modifications can always be made. Apart from the quality of the separate elements, the main concern should be with the coherence of all manifestations-they must all reflect the same spirit.

A great deal of time must be reserved for developing the individual elements and the design system. If insufficient time is allowed, and if final designs are made prematurely to meet the introduction date, the quality will suffer. There is the danger of looking for solutions for each individual form: a logo that looks very good on letter paper may be a complete failure in a sign on a building. However, there are relations between these different forms, and this must be taken into account well in advance.

It should also be borne in mind that suppliers may have a limited production capacity and that deliveries may take some time. If a company wants to replace all its neon signs in one go by a certain date and the supplier can only produce a limited amount, extra charges can be expected.

Contact between the design agency and the logistic departments at too early a stage can lead to designs being regarded as final when they are not. There have been cases of printed material not being ready for the introduction date because the design used did not conform to modifications made in the meantime. So the pallets with the material go straight from the printer to the incinerator. Good planning can prevent this by setting the right priorities and allowing the design agency enough time to develop a proper system.

In addition to the design system there are the *application rules* based on the organization of the company. They cover such matters as which departments are entitled to their own stationery and how the names of those departments are to appear on it. It is also necessary to establish what should be done when neither the design system nor the application rules provide a solution. When will initiatives taken by employees be welcomed and when not? To which person in a certain department should they go when there is a problem? These rules establish how the corporate identity programme is organized within the company: who is responsible for what, and what to do in various situations.

After the elements of the corporate identity, the design system and the application rules have been decided, they can be set out in one or more handbooks.

The function of the handbook

The handbook plays a central role in the introduction and application of the corporate identity. As already stated, the contents comprise the corporate identity elements and the design system developed by the design agency on the one hand, and the application and organization rules originating from the company on the other. Compiling the handbook would seem to be a straightforward job, and so it is often left to the design agency. The result is a very attractive looking book containing a course in design based on the elements of the corporate identity which is only intelligible to designers. The handbook should, however, be suitable for all users within the company. The user should be able to consult it when developing or ordering material. When required, it should set out the correct procedure for ordering or point out which logistic department should be used. It should be more like an owner's manual for the corporate identity programme. Many of the users will be more concerned with the application and organization rules than with the design. The handbook should of course be a perfect design example of the programme, but the contents must be largely a matter for the work group. Work on the design cannot begin until the contents have been determined. Ideally, the handbook should take the form of a folder or loose-leaf binder containing separate sections. Only a few users at the management level will need to have the complete handbook, and many users at lower levels will not need more than a few sections. Another advantage is that you do not have to wait until the whole thing is finished: the most important sections can be printed and issued first. All that is required is a binder to keep them in. Because of the low print run, handbooks are relatively expensive and so tend to be given only limited distribution, with the result that the application of the corporate identity is also limited. So the use of separate sections, more carefully distributed, is to be recommended.

Wider distribution of the sections will have the desired effect of acceptance of the corporate identity throughout the company. Whereas, for example, in the past only the head of the garage had the handbook, now each mechanic can have the section about the lettering on vehicles. A further advantage is that when changes are made to the corporate identity programme only the relevant sections of the handbook need to be replaced.

Of the various media for communicating the visual part of the corporate identity programme, print still provides the best quality. Video may also be used, but the quality of reproduction on a screen is as yet inferior. Nonetheless the electronic age has its uses in the communication of application and organization rules, and there are also disadvantages to using handbooks. Although they are looseleaf, in practice they are often not updated quickly enough. They may bear the user's name and a number, but after a while no one knows where to find them. In fact, a handbook belongs to a particular job rather than to a particular person. The department in charge of carrying out the corporate identity programme is often not informed when there is a change of personnel. Communication between this department and the users is not always what it should be.

So it is a good idea to put the application and organization rules in a database which can be consulted by all employees through a computer network. This can also be used to provide constant communication between the department in charge of the programme and the personnel. At the same time, the printed handbook will continue to play an important role in the application and monitoring of the corporate identity programme.

The introduction phase

The introduction phase begins when the basic elements have been finalized, the design system has been established, and the application and organization rules have been formulated. In other words, when the corporate identity programme is ready for large-scale implementation. The date for introduction should coincide with the point at which the handbook is made available to the users.

If the introduction takes place too soon there will be confusion because the programme has not yet finished 'crystallizing'. The users will find it difficult to follow the application and organization rules properly. As a result it is all too easy to make mistakes, and the first material is likely to present a prominent but bad example. Mistakes in interpretation may also be made during the production of the material.

An orderly introduction depends on internal communication as well as the handbook or other (temporary) guides.

The personnel should be prepared well in advance through the company's channels of communication. The board of directors can play an important part here: they can motivate the personnel by expressing a clear view of the objectives and by convincing them of the importance of the application rules. Regardless of whether the introduction is gradual or all at once, it will require a formidable logistic effort. For the work group this is the busiest phase. The central concerns are budget control, planning and coordination. The best method of coordination between the logistical departments and the designers is to divide the various company manifestations into groups and to have a separate work unit, consultation structure and schedule for each group. A member of the work group should always take part in these consultations to ensure that there is coordination between the work units. The results produced by these units should be regularly seen and discussed by the whole work group.

The application and monitoring phase

This phase is one of the last and does not really belong to the development process. The corporate identity programme has now been integrated into the company. The work group and the various work units have been disbanded (the former's tasks are taken over by the department in charge of implementation). The steering group remains in existence and continues to exercise control, intervening when necessary. It is assisted by the department in charge of implementation, which supervises and advises on corporate identity matters. The steering group is also assisted, as regards the content of the programme, by the corporate communications department, whose job is to ensure that it is in line with the internal and external communication strategy. This department is also responsible for internal communication and monitoring. The first keeps the personnel alert when they are applying the programme, and the second detects when things go wrong.

By continually collecting material of all kinds, the corporate communications department retains an overall view and is in the best position to monitor progress. Material is always checked against the objectives of the corporate identity, and thus against the internal and external communication strategy. It is advisable to involve the design agency in this process. If it is necessary to intervene, this should always be done on the basis of the corporate identity objectives. Monitoring is much easier if the purchasing and ordering of material is done through one central department. Control is also improved if the same printers are always used. All that then needs to be done is to ask them to send samples from each print order to the corporate communications department. A corporate identity programme must be continually monitored and where necessary modified. In short, the development process is a continuing process.

Alex Visser

IMAGE

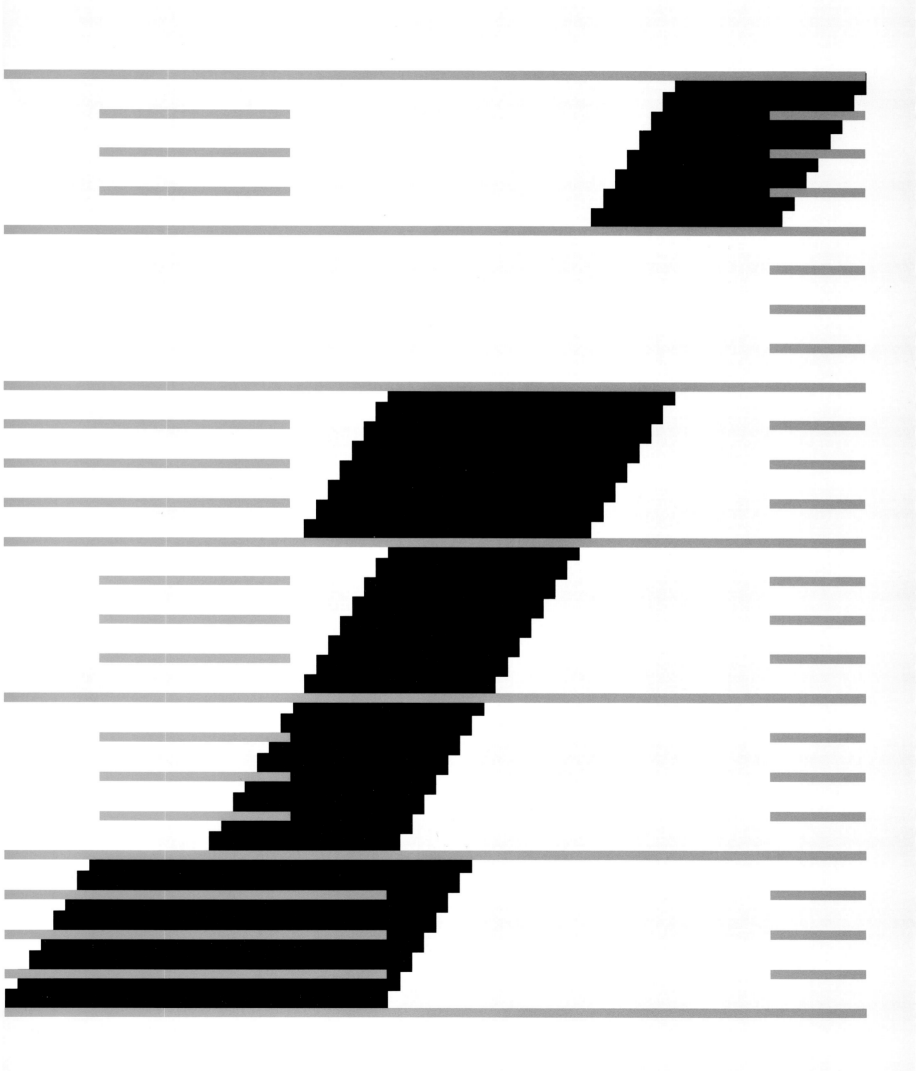

Contents

Introduction

A housestyle can never be a ragbag of separate constituents. It originates out of a matured concept that has to lead to a coherent whole. A housestyle rests on coordinated designs, often referred to as a 'programme'.

The above observation implies that the designs should never lose sight of the fact that the various housestyle elements of a company's presentation should possess one and the same tone. Writing paper, lorry or calender – on a number of points it should be possible to trace them all back to the same basic ingredients; they should have the same 'feeling'.

For those designing a corporate identity this makes heavy demands. From the beginning a frame of reference has to be determined, how much or how little freedom can be given to each individual design. The originator of the housestyle has to guard that others loyally follow the concept through to the end.

At a certain point so much was happening in the development of housestyles that norms and directives could be anchored into a manual. The horizontal pages of this book include such a manual. Not from a known, established organization, but one in relation to a fictitious company we have christened IMAGE.

This theoretical manual is reproduced on the right-hand pages, its style is technical: aimed at practical use by experts who can use it as reference. The left-hand pages give a more general view, background information and consideration on what is dealt with in the manual. These are undoubtedly more accessible for readers less familiar with the manual's jargon.

The trademark

The trademark
Image's trademark consists of two
elements: the basic house layout and
the trademark itself (the italic letter
'i'). It can be entirely reproduced by a
typesetting machine, and has the
advantage that it retains its sharpness
no matter the size.

The trademark is a symbol, the most essential means by which
a company visually manifests itself. It is a signal –
'YOU ARE DEALING WITH US, WITH OUR PRODUCTS OR OUR
SERVICES,' like the well-known star of Mercedes or the logotype of Coca-Cola. Trademarks can be divided into various
categories. The main ones are symbols like the shell of Shell
and the logotypes like the fixed signature of the IBM mark.
In daily usage the two types are often confused.
Within the complicated legal constructions of organizations
nowadays, many companies have more than one name. There
is the familiar shorthand version used in day-to-day conversa-
tion: Philips, for instance, next to Philips Lighting Manufacturers PLC or Philips Holland Ltd. The everyday name is cast in
fixed graphic form and becomes the logo (type).
The Image trademark is an 'I' in italic and as such is one of the
many that fall between logo and logotype. The 'I' may stand for
Image but you only realize this through a learning process.
It could just as well mean 'Italy'or 'Inspiration'. You can place it
in the same category as BP's mark – two yellow capitals on a
green shield – what this means has simply to be 'learnt'.
Trademarks are a product of their time. No matter how much
the designer tries to create an enduring trademark this is often
superseded by changing trends and fashions. Trademarks such
as AEG's or Olivetti's have been modified numerous times since
they were created.
For a company a trademark is an extremely good thing and this
justifies the efforts involved in having it legally protected
against imitation by third parties or misuse. This protection
takes place through company registration agents.
The branches and geographical reach of the trademark are
important factors when registering. A registered trademark
can be used for a certain period of time and for a certain area.
The huge number of trademarks in circulation both for companies and products makes the designing of an original one a
difficult and – for the pre-registration investigation by a patent
office – an uncertain business. With logotypes, or a combination of logotype and symbol, one can often avoid this problem,
assuming that the everyday name of the company is original.
Originality is often lacking when this name exists out of three
letters such as BBC. This is no easy starting point for a unique
logotype.
Designing trademarks is no simple matter. Its smallest and
largest application can vary enormously in size. A designer has
to be well aware of these practical situations. One example of
the problem of scale is when you drive into Paris from the North
on Autoroute No. 1 and see how much supportive tubing
(visually undesirable) holds together the new trademark of the
chemical giant AKZO on a block of flats. Yet this same trademark has to be capable of being printed a centimetre wide on
the curve of a ballpoint pen...
Besides this, a designer should not make a design too dependent on the use of more than one colour. It should, whether
being photocopied in black and white or distorted by a fax
transmission, be able to retain an acceptable quality and recognizability. Clients are increasingly demanding that a trademark
should be suitable for being produced via the limited resolution
of a laser printer. Although technology is developing apace,

Sizes
The trademark can be typeset in
various sizes or enlarged linearly.
The unit of length chosen for this
imaginary housestyle is the inch.
The example opposite shows a
trademark one, two and three inches,
respectively.

this demand circa 1990 still presents restrictions with its
design.

It is important for a company to guard that a trademark is
properly executed and reproduced. Much has been gained
once a company is in control of a trademark's total realization
and prescribed sizes (during the printing process). It means,
especially for a decentralized organization, the need to have
perfect reproduction models or negatives available or, better
still, to be linked to a computer data base. Production using
such a data base is a guarantee of maintaining quality in all
sizes in which the trademark will appear. As far as size is
concerned, a designer can sometimes be taken by surprise, like
the author of this piece who saw his logo for a Dutch local
council blown up to 10 X 10m on the banks of a roundabout and
filled in with white and blue violets.

With a trademark, as with so many other designed objects,
form and content go hand-in-hand. Sometimes the form can
have an unambiguous message like the shell motif of Shell;
other times there appears to be no direct link between what
you see and what it is supposed to represent, like the pop-art
type diamond logo of Renault. By consistent and regular use a
trademark becomes recognized among the target group.
Logotypes when they are used in entirely different cultures
with other alphabets may have to be translated in to, say, Ara-
bic or Chinese. Cultures can also make special demands on an
international trademark. The Christian cross presents the Red
Cross with problems in the Islamic world, for instance.
One must guard against using designs and colours which could
be unacceptable in other parts of the world.

Today a trademark is not the static item it originally was. Trademarks can now be chosen in moving form. This is frequently
the case on TV where the logos of the various networks are
dancing around the screen. Because of the new media the
animation possibilities of a trademark have become an additional requirement. How does a trademark behave in a filmed
building-up or breaking down of its constituents, when turning
loops or when seen in perspective? Just how flexible a trademark can be has been well demonstrated down the years with
Bibendum, Michelin's rubber tyre man, who despite all the
tricks he has to perform for his boss remains recognizable at all
times.

Use of colour

Colour is an optical phenomenon with a strong associative and psychological effect. Colour is a primary component of a housestyle, even if you dismiss it altogether and use black and white. Then such a choice could convey restraint, sobriety, sternness, an aversion to any kind of frivolity. At the same time this presents the designer with the challenge to convey successfully a different meaning entirely with black and white: the chic of Chanel no. 5 for instance.

Colour is a prominent aid for recognizability, which is a housestyle's objective after all. Truly exclusive colours are difficult to realize, especially if you only have one secondary colour in the first place alongside the almost inevitable use of black for the typography. Shell's colours of red, yellow, black and white are an exception. In general, housestyles out of financial considerations have one main colour. Any additional colour is a recurring factor in the printing costs, and moreover it is crucially important whether the colour flows directly from the printer's ink pot or can be achieved by colour separation (the colours being magenta, cyan, yellow and black, the basic ones for full-colour printing). For many pure – and for a housestyle the most attractive – colours, their reproduction in full-colour printing is often no more than an approximation of the exact colour balance. The result is that for printed matter with colour reproductions one or more secondary colours should be added to the four-colour process.

The psychological effect of the colour black has already been mentioned. It is clear that colours have an associative effect and that the connotations are not the same all over the world, but are culturally determined. This is a complicated matter for multinationals which should be taken into account when drawing up housestyles. It is no mere accident that Lufthansa, after the Second World War, decked itself in neutral blue and yellow shades, thus disassociating itself from the national colours of West Germany.

The following practical example speaks volumes on the possibilities or otherwise of colour in housestyle. In the mid-1960s the Belgium Generale Bank had a fairly flimsy corporate identity with a strong and intensively used logo. With this they neglected to make a real colour choice. The result was a black and white affair, sober in tone, that they tried to pep up in the 1980s by applying Bordeaux red to interior- and display elements. This colour has a somewhat passive personality and when used in printing, moreover, can easily become brownish or purplish or subsequently dirty-looking. An awkward circumstance was that in the meantime the combined competition had insured themselves with good serviceable bank colours. Clear red was the only colour still 'free', but in Belgium it has definite left-wing connotations. In the final count the Bank could be convinced of the use of much clear red combined with a small amount of bright blue. This produced for the banking world in and around Belgium a new positive colour image, free from associations with France or the Netherlands which use equal quantities of red and blue in their national flags. And with the presence of blue, the red in the housestyle no longer means 'left-wing'.

Colour specification is carried out almost universally within the codes of the internationally known printing-ink system of Pantone (PMS). Regarding the ability of these colours to be translated into paint quality for spray cans and brushes, we refer you to what is said about this in the section on Fleet marking. The contrast between black ink and white paper cannot be surpassed in printing. Small size typography in other colours leads inevitably to a less sharp contrast, thus reducing the impact of the information. The result is that the role of house colours is largely limited to strengthening the individual identity of the housestyle. Combined with this, they also enhance the aesthetic appreciation of printed matter. The house colour, often printed separately, can be pre-printed in large amounts where it has fixed positions on the logo, writing paper, invoices, etc. Incidentally, in many Western countries printing technique is such that orders can largely be run on multi-colour presses whereby a second, third, or even fourth colour no longer sends costs soaring as much as they used to. Often the client still has to get used to all these changes: printing technology has developed at a spanking pace, making exact colour control possible.

Use of colour

The use of colour is an essential component of a trademark. While this is discussed at length in the following section, it is worth describing here the colour combination.

Generally speaking the logo is reproduced in black and blue. For special applications there are other possibilities. For internal stationery use can be made of a one print run. In that case the trademark is printed in black. It has also been designed for diapositive use.

The house colours are Pantone Process cyan and black. They are applied to all interior and exterior elements as background colours and/or in the trademark. These colours are part of the international Pantone Matching System (PMS). It is known how every colour in this system can be mixed from Pantone's basic colours. This means even when working with various printers, the results will be the same when using Pantone colours.

Material

Paper is the most widely used medium by far for house colours. It is important to make sure how it has been produced and, in particular, to pay attention to the degree of whiteness. The colour plates reproduced here are on wood-free, matt, machine-coated paper.

ISLE COLLEG
RESOURCES CE

Typography

UNIVERS 39

UNIVERS 45
UNIVERS 46
UNIVERS 47
UNIVERS 48
UNIVERS 49

UNIVERS 53
UNIVERS 55
UNIVERS 56
UNIVERS 57
UNIVERS 58
UNIVERS 59

UNIVERS 63
UNIVERS 65
UNIVERS 66
UNIVERS 67
UNIVERS 68

UNIVERS 73
UNIVERS 75
UNIVERS 76

UNIVERS 83

GKty
GKty

**Some differences
between Helvetica
and Univers**

Typography
Univers type is used exclusively for the housestyle. On pages 178 and 179 are examples of the range of type size used from this family: 7 point Univers was chosen for captions, footnotes, references etc. and 9 point Univers for body text.

One point extra white was given for the line spacing, giving us, for instance, 7/8 points, 9/10 points and 12/13 points. For some typesetting machines the line space setting is in millimetres: 7 points = 3mm, 9 = 3.75mm, 12 = 5mm etc.
Line space setting was +1 (spacing codes are based on Berthold typesetting machines).

Typography is written visual communication. The term can mean anything from a few lines of type required for a poster to the extremely complex text treatment required for a major reference work. Typography is thus one of the tools of the housestyle designer. The choice of type and the way it is used in printed matter can be a characteristic factor in the total visual corporate identity. Within the enormous number of type families we can distinguish between type suitable for chunks of body text alongside the more numerous families more suited for headings and display text.

Type families for body text are available in a wide-ranging assortment varying from Light Condensed to Expanded Bold. The Univers, the house letter of Image, has an exceptional choice of no fewer than 22 gradations, far more than one would be reasonably expected to use for giving text the necessary accents. Most housestyles have three type families at the most and in a limited number of gradations. Too many type variants would damage the instant recognition of the typographic image of the housestyle. A corporate identity also prescribes the choice in size of type which may be used and general type-setting instructions which form the basis for the treatment of text, including justified or ragged setting, column widths, when to use all-caps and how much interlinear spacing. Typography is not only a question of letters and numbers, but of other print-ed items like lines, bands, borders and symbols.

Among the huge choice of type families – produced by many manufacturers on various systems – there are many qualities and permutations. It is often advisable when choosing a house type to specify from which system it should be drawn.

For centuries typography was carried out using its own measuring system in which words like cicero, didot, pica and points belong. While points is still widely used for text size the metric system has won hands down when it comes to line spacing, column widths, white spacing and the margins around the type area.

In the first instance individual lead or wooden letters were the basis for typography, later there was competition from mecha-nized type cast as individual letters or in lines. The technique made gigantic strides to photosetting and subsequently arrived at the electronic phase. Next to these increasingly advanced high-tech systems, more choice became available with the arrival of the somewhat unprofessional self-adhesive lettering and in recent years with desk top publishing or DTP computers, relatively cheap and accessible to relative layper-sons and when properly used providing a good substitute for mreal' typesetting systems. This is a development that has taken the market by storm and which will also demand a role in many a corporate identity programme. Because DTP is user friendly for those not trained in typography, it holds risks in maintaining the high standards of typesetting. For the time being housestyle designers would do well to point out the risks involved to quality when using DTP systems.

During the typesetting process, like any other human activity, mistakes can be made. Correcting proofs has two major func-tions: that marked instructions on the manuscript have been properly carried out and the text properly reproduced, on the one hand, and that it is the correct text, on the other.

The responsibility for this often lies with the authors of the text or with others untrained in typography. For corrections to be carried out effectively it is important to use special correction marks. That is why many housestyle manuals include the well-known page of standard symbols for correcting.

The typeface

In visual communication type has two roles: it aims to draw attention and then retain that attention. For the first role, that of being eye-catching and inviting, different rules apply from in the second role of conveying more extensive, detailed information. The enormous range of available type families covers both functions. There are thousands of types made which are suitable for headings, short intros and logotypes. Much more limiting, however, are the number of type families suitable for body text. Headings, by definition, feature more prominently and are bigger in size. Body text is composed from type that is suitable for the ease with which it can be read.
For housestyles there is the overriding tendency to restrict the number of type families used. This is understandable, for it gives the housestyle a uniform look and makes it instantly recognizable. The house type for Image is the Univers and from the many permutations of this family both the letter for headings and body text was chosen. It is no accident that Univers was created by the Swiss/French typographer, Adrian Frutiger, at the same time as the world was being flooded by the first wave of housestyles: 1965 to 1975. A rich assortment of type was ready for the new technological age.
The Univers family is so wide ranging that only insiders can identify the special family features. Sanserif, disciplined and straightforward, is a type created for objective information. This implies that most Univers variants, with the exception of the somewhat extreme gradations, do not excel at drawing attention. Such a neutral type as Univers does not really contribute to the unique character of Image's housestyle. It is a good choice, but many companies have used it before Image.
The often mentioned Dutch output of government housestyles is chock-a-block with Univers applications.
In this respect the Univers family is similar to the somewhat older Helvetica, which also has many gradations and enjoyed much popularity between 1960 and 1980. Univers and Helvetica are the Volkswagens and Opels of visual information. Respectable, reliable and widely known, no vehicles for romantic travels or with which to impress. These are the major forerunners of the corporate identity epoch. Sanserif appears to be synonymous for efficiency, orderliness and modernity. Later on Frutiger introduced a type family under his own name regarded by many as the successor to Helvetica and Univers. Recently, this was followed by the launching of his Avenir family.

Nevertheless a housestyle does not limit itself to sanserif. The Egyptian-looking types with serifs the same thickness as the vertical part of the letter such as Rockwell, Serifa, Glypha,

Lubalin Graph and Clarendon can rejoice in their manifold applications. They form a synthesis between sans face and serif, are a pleasure to read and interesting for headings.
This does not mean that classic type families should be dismissed. Housestyle designers are very much aware of the aura, say, of the time-honoured Bodoni, attributed with being dignified, reliable, conservative and having class. The demand for these 'values' has led to contemporary variations: attractive new type families which build on the design principles of the classic book types.
Some housestyles successfully marry a sans face with a serif. The one should not exclude the other. The choice of type is of fundamental concern when drawing up a housestyle. Once that ingredient is chosen then 'everything is still possible with the typographical layout – the way the text is 'served'. Combined with this it is essential that the type used in printed matter and advertising is in harmony with one another – something which it is not always easy for the client to keep a watchful eye on.

Univers 55
Medium
Adrian Frutiger,
1957
Haas'sche Schrift-
gießerei AG
H. Berthold AG.

ABCDEFGHIJKLMNOPQ
RSTUVWXYZ
abcdefghijklmnopqrstuvwxyz
1/1234567890%
(.,-;:!i?¿−)·[''„""›‹]
+−=/$£†*ß§&
äÅÆÖØŒÜäåæıöøœßü
ÁÀÂÃÇČÉÈÊËÍÌÎÏĹŇÑÓÒÔÕ
ŔŘŠŤÚÙÛŴŴÝŶŸŽ
áàăãçčéèêëíìîïĺňñóòŏõŕřš
úùûŵŵýỳÿž

Univers 65
Bold
Adrian Frutiger,
1957
Haas'sche Schrift-
gießerei AG
H. Berthold AG.

**ABCDEFGHIJKLMNOPQ
RSTUVWXYZ
abcdefghijklmnopqrstuvwxyz
1/1234567890%
(.,-;:!i?¿−)·[''„""›‹]
+−=/$£†*ß§&
äÅÆÖØŒÜäåæıöøœßü
ÁÀÂÃÇČÉÈÊËÍÌÎÏĹŇÑÓÒÔÕ
ŔŘŠŤÚÙÛŴŴÝŶŸŽ
áàăãçčéèêëíìîïĺňñóòŏõŕřš
úùûŵŵýỳÿž**

**Univers 57
Medium
Condensed
Adrian Frutiger,
1957
Haas'sche Schrift-
gießerei AG
H. Berthold AG.**

ABCDEFGHIJKLMNOPQ
RSTUVWXYZ
abcdefghijklmnopqrstuvwxyz
1/1234567890%
(.,-;:!i?¿–)·['',""›‹]
+−=/$£†*ß§&
äÅÆÖØŒÜäåæıöøœßü
ÁÀÂÃÇČÉÈÊËÍÌÎÏİĹŇÑÓÒÔÕ
ŔŘŠŤÚÙÛŴŴÝŶŸŽ
áàăãçčéèêëíìîïİňñóòŏõŕřš
úùûŵŵýỳÿž

**Univers 67
Bold condensed
Adrian Frutiger,
1957
Haas'sche Schrift-
gießerei AG
H. Berthold AG.**

ABCDEFGHIJKLMNOPQ
RSTUVWXYZ
abcdefghijklmnopqrstuvwxyz
1/1234567890%
(.,-;:!i?¿–)·['',""›‹]
+−=/$£†*ß§&
äÅÆÖØŒÜäåæıöøœßü
ÁÀÂÃÇČÉÈÊËÍÌÎÏİĹŇÑÓÒÔÕ
ŔŘŠŤÚÙÛŴŴÝŶŸŽ
áàăãçčéèêëíìîïİňñóòŏõŕřš
úùûŵŵýỳÿž

In general, bodytypes are measured in the typographical point size. The sizes of Berthold Fototype faces can be exactly determined. All faces of same point size have the same capital heigth—irrespective of their x-heigth. In hot metal and many other phototype-setting systems the capital heigths often differ

In general, bodytypes are measured in the typographical point size. The sizes of Berthold Fototype faces can be exactly determined. All faces of same point size have the same capital heigth—irrespective

In general, bodytypes are measured in the typographical point size. The sizes of Berthold Fototype faces can be exactly

In general, bodytypes are measured in the typographical point size. The sizes of Berthold Fototype faces can be exactly determined. All faces of same point size have the same capital heigth—irrespective of their x-heigth. In hot metal and many other phototypesetting systems the capital heigths often

In general, bodytypes are measured in the typographical point size. The sizes of Berthold Fototype faces can be exactly determined. All faces of same point size have the same capital heigth—irrespec-

In general, bodytypes are measured in the typographical point size. The sizes of Berthold Fototype faces can be exactly

In general, bodytypes are measured in the typographical point size. The sizes of Berthold Fototype faces can be exactly determined. All faces of same point size have the same capital heigth—irres-pective of their x-heigth. In hot metal and many other phototype-setting systems the capital heigths often differ considerably from one face to the other. For measuring point sizes, a transparent size

In general, bodytypes are measured in the typographical point size. The sizes of Berthold Fototype faces can be exactly determined. All faces of same point size have the same capital heigth—irrespective of their x-heigth. In hot metal and many other phototype-

In general, bodytypes are measured in the typographical point size. The sizes of Berthold Fototype faces can be exactly determined. All faces of same point size

In general, bodytypes are measured in the typographical point size. The sizes of Berthold Fototype faces can be exactly deter-mined. All faces of same point size have the same capital heigth—irrespective of their x-heigth. In hot metal and many other photo-typesetting systems the capital heigths often differ considerably from one face to the other. For measuring point sizes, a trans

In general, bodytypes are measured in the typo-graphical point size. The sizes of Berthold Fototype faces can be exactly determined. All faces of same point size have the same capital heigth—irrespective of their x-heigth. In hot metal and many other photo

In general, bodytypes are measured in the typographical point size. The sizes of Berthold Fototype faces can be exactly determined. All faces of same

In general, bodytypes are measured in the typographical point size. The sizes of Berthold Fototype
faces can be exactly determined. All faces of same
point size have the same capital heigth—irrespective of
their x-heigth. In hot metal and many other phototype-
setting systems the capital heigths often differ

In general, bodytypes are measured in the
typographical point size. The sizes of
Berthold Fototype faces can be exactly
determined. All faces of same point size
have the same capital heigth—irrespective

In general, bodytypes are
measured in the typographical
point size. The sizes of Berthold
Fototype faces can be exactly

In general, bodytypes are measured in the typographical point size. The sizes of Berthold Fototype
faces can be exactly determined. All faces of same
point size have the same capital heigth—irrespective
of their x-heigth. In hot metal and many other
phototypesetting systems the capital heigths often

In general, bodytypes are measured in
the typographical point size. The sizes of
Berthold Fototype faces can be exactly
determined. All faces of same point size
have the same capital heigth—irrespec-

In general, bodytypes are
measured in the typographical
point size. The sizes of Berthold
Fototype faces can be exactly

In general, bodytypes are measured in the typographical point size.
The sizes of Berthold Fototype faces can be exactly determined.
All faces of same point size have the same capital heigth—irrespective of their x-heigth. In hot metal and many other phototype-
setting systems the capital heigths often differ considerably from
one face to the other. For measuring point sizes, a transparent size

In general, bodytypes are measured in the typographical point size. The sizes of Berthold Fototype
faces can be exactly determined. All faces of same
point size have the same capital heigth—irrespective of
their x-heigth. In hot metal and many other phototype-

In general, bodytypes are measured in the
typographical point size. The sizes of
Berthold Fototype faces can be exactly
determined. All faces of same point size

In general, bodytypes are measured in the typographical point
size. The sizes of Berthold Fototype faces can be exactly determined. All faces of same point size have the same capital heigth—
irrespective of their x-heigth. In hot metal and many other photo-
typesetting systems the capital heigths often differ considerably
from one face to the other. For measuring point sizes, a trans

In general, bodytypes are measured in the typographical point size. The sizes of Berthold Fototype
faces can be exactly determined. All faces of same
point size have the same capital heigth—irrespective
of their x-heigth. In hot metal and many other photo

In general, bodytypes are measured in
the typographical point size. The sizes
of Berthold Fototype faces can be
exactly determined. All faces of same

The basic grid

The basic grid is an aid to achieving continuity in the arrang-ement of text and pictures. In its simplest form this can give coherrence to the individual pages of a brochure or catalogue. More obvious is the grip such a grid can have on a housestyle: 'family' ties between individual elements can be better controlled during the design and production process.
The basic grid provides an orderly and unchanging basis, the simplicity or complexity of which gives the designer freedom or restrictions. In one sense this grid is similar to the lines on a tennis court: it does not affect the creative style of play, but creates order and determines boundaries. Moreover, in this case it is the player himself/herself, the designer, who draws up the ground rules at the beginning of the housestyle operation, even if these are made bearing in mind the stated requirements of the project.
Housestyle printed matter falls in two groups: consumer stationery and advertising. With letters and invoice sets many factors are involved and there is a strict hierarchy of information which requires a basic layout with an intensive lineal design that offers space for additional and varying text, printed or otherwise. A standard layout for advertising purposes can have a much looser structure because the contents are less detailed.
A grid shows clearly the relationship between type page (cut off standard page sizes such as A4) and the type area – the type page minus unprinted margins above, below, right and left. Within the type area a fixed division is made to indicate interlinear spacing in the length, and column size in the width. The designer would do well to have a clear image first of the sort of information that has to be arranged on the page and, on the strength of that, produce the basic framework. Borders outlined on the layout can be used to determine the size and positioning of text and pictures. Between columns there should be a free zone, the intercolumn space, otherwise the texts will crush one another and be illegible. The standard practice is an intercolumn space 4.5 or 5mm wide for an A4 page. Similarly, many layouts choose to have certain rules governing space in a vertical direction so that where necessary it can remain blank. These rules indicate preferable place marks to separate text from pictures and determine the preferred size of illustrations.
It has already been mentioned that a basic grid is an important instrument for the orderly design of printed matter. Through its singularity, originating from the ground rules composed for the project, it can contribute greatly to recognizing the way a company visually expresses itself. It means that designers do not have to sit in front of a blank sheet of paper for every new brochure or document, but can base designing and detailing within the framework provided by an already given layout system. In this case it is usual to have available pre-printed sheets of the grid onto which the design for text and pictures can be arranged. This is also a useful reference for typesetters and printers to check whether type and pictures are positioned correctly as well as to instruct third parties on the standard basic practices for the typography. This makes the calling in of other designers and printers – without risking jeopardizing the standard 'look' of the product – a much more controllable busi-ness.

To make it perfectly clear, flexibility or otherwise of the grid will determine the size of the design units. Here it must be realized that uniformity and recognizability are sacrificed in proportion to the increase in intricate design embroidery. A good layout will fall somewhere between being flexible and having a recog-nizable identity. Working with a grid should not lead to dogmatic design practices so that it becomes a straightjacket. It should be experienced as an important and pleasant aid that puts the accent on the creative process where it belongs – on the good use of freedom within a framework. A housestyle, by definition, has certain authoritarian features and in practically all cases is hemmed in by rules. A grid provides a theoretical reference for the practical work.

The basic grid
The basic grid used has been drawn up in inches. The reason for this is that often a combination is made from typeset text and printed text (from a typewriter or computer printer), making this layout suitable for any possibility. The layout has been designed on the most widespread paper size in use: A4. All other layouts are derived from this (see below). The layout is divided vertically into 1/6 inch units. This distance equals line space setting 1 on a typewriter or printer.
Horizontally the A4 layout is divided into one inch units. Typewriter text is based on the number of characters per inch (10, 12 and only rarely 13 characters per inch). By making use of inch-columns this text can always be put into columns, no matter the number of characters per inch. The most commonly used pitch (characters per inch) on a typewriter or printer is 10. The broken lines are based on this. Every one-inch column is divided into 10 1/10 inch units, whereby the last serves as a white space between columns.

The set column widths are directly
derived from the inch columns. Below
is an overview of the link between
layout columns and set column
widths.

Number of layout columns

1	2	3	4	5	6	7	8

Set column width in inches

8/10	1 8/10	3 8/10	4 8/10	5 8/10	6 8/10	7 8/10	8 8/10

Set column width in millimetres

20	45	70	95	120	145	170	195

Set column width in didot

4½	10	15½	21	26½	32	37½	43

Sizes

Standard printing paper sizes are the A and B series, with A series preferred. The ratio length/breadth is such that when the paper is folded into two the ratio remains exactly the same. This has advantages for instance when reducing, while standard A sizes are suitable for filing systems and photocopiers. The sizes most used are A4, A5 and A6.

Bearing in mind international agreements concerning standardization, it is recommended that sizes from the A series be used. In so doing we conform to decisions taken by the International Organization for Standardization (ISO) and the Dutch Standardization Institute (NNI) as laid down in Recommendation ISO/R 216-1961 and NEN 381-1962.
The above-mentioned recommendations for technical reasons, however, are not subscribed to by the United States, and we shall return to this later.

A series
Given in mm

A0	841 x 1188
A1	594 x 841
A2	420 x 594
A3	297 x 420
A4	210 x 297
A5	148 x 210
A6	105 x 148
A7	74 x 105
A8	52 x 74
A9	37 x 52
A10	26 x 37

B series
Given in mm

B0	1,000 x 1,414
B1	707 x 1,000
B2	500 x 707
B3	353 x 500
B4	250 x 353
B5	176 x 250
B6	125 x 176
B7	88 x 125
B8	62 x 88
B9	44 x 62
B10	31 x 44

Correspondence

In corporate life the letter is still an extremely important medium. Letters deal with transactions and contracts, appointments and dismissals, loans and claims, people and things. A letter is a messenger, a tangible statement, explanation or query. Adding certain details to a sheet of paper gives it the potential of a document. It goes without saying that a certain visual status is attached to such a function: the 'messenger' must present itself in a proper manner. The document-type look of a letter is derived from announcing the statutory name of the company (usually repeated in the signing off) often – and here the housestyle rears its head – printed under the company logo.

In the letter head all manner of addresses and information appears. Sometimes the names of banks with bank numbers are added and there are special positions for the name or the department handling the correspondence, reference details or the subject under discussion. Always mentioned is the Chamber of Commerce registration number and in some countries even the amount of deposited capital. Letter head design partly depends on national postal directives. There are standardization institutes which concern themselves with this and propose recommendations for disseminating the necessary details that have to be stated. However worthy standard practices may be, they do not contribute very much to producing writing paper which has an individual appearance, while this is all important for a housestyle.

The typography of a letter can include a number of other details: marks to indicate the position of margins, where to start and end the letter, where to fold, perforating marks, etc. Certain companies feel a need to have special luxury quality writing paper for management purposes. More expensive paper is chosen and the colour in the logo is often replaced by a blind stamp.

A standard layout for writing paper, especially for multinationals with many overseas branches, is an urgent requirement from a corporate identity viewpoint. By having identical stationery the interrelationship of the various divisions is convincingly conveyed.

A basic stationery set should consist of standard size writing paper of A4 size (Imperial size in the US), follow-on paper, envelopes, compliments slips to enclose with documentation, and business cards. Visually all these elements have much to do with one another as they are used either together or as substitutes for one another.

The arrival of word processors and automation have made new demands on writing paper. A printer, for instance, can have certain consequences for the choice of paper thickness and finishing touches like blind stamps can create problems.

The starting point for address and other details as well as the space for signature, etc. are pre-programmed in the wordprocessor and that also dictates the position of margins and suchlike.

The designing of writing paper is one responsibility; correctly filling in the pre-printed data is just as important too. Within the context of the housestyle the concern should be to have design and typing on paper of the same uniform quality.

In earlier days there used to be typing instructions drawn up. Today the word processor and printer takes care of much of the meticulousness required in the carrying out of correspondence.

The writing paper

Writing paper
The layout for the writing paper conforms to NEN 1026: 'Writing paper, invoices and postcards' 1984 and ISO 3535. The first two lines of the layout form an upper margin of 13mm and are not used. The left-hand column of the layout is also a margin of 32mm and is only used for sender's name, space for address, and marks to indicate where letter should be folded and where the last line of type appears. These marks are printed in blue, are 0.25mm thick and 1/10 and 2/10 inches long, with a line space setting of 1/6 and 1/24 inch. The company name Image is in caps, 16 points and positioned on the third line. Sender, address and bank info is 9 points caps and lower case References are 7 points caps and lower case.

By beginning all printed or typed text 32mm in from the margin, the letter appears orderly and well-presented. The letter head is so designed that when using a window envelope the layout for the address is clearly visible. The one-inch trademark is in the fourth column. The marks are in blue and the trademark and all other texts are in black.

The layout for the second sheet is the same as for the letter head. However, only the marks for where the last line of type appears and the left-hand margin for sender's details are printed. These blue marks are typical of the company style and as such can be recognized as originating from the company, hence reproducing the trademark again is unnecessary.

Writing paper is more than a fundamental tool for correspondence; it has 'character', no matter what the quality or context. Even if blank it says something about the mentality of the user. How well has the letter head been designed? What has been left out in the heading and what has been included? What about the colours used? How restrained or showy is the total image? Is the design daring or conservative, refined or crude? In the light of present-day trends writing paper as a separate expressive form is more or less outdated. Everywhere the interrelationship between the different levels of presentation is common and writing paper is part of a larger coherent whole. In recent years a pre-printed fax form is added to the traditional correspondence set. It is a substitute for writing paper, has appropriate spaces for relevant details related to the fax message and thus far as a relative newcomer has largely been excused from conforming to housestyle principles. There is no valid argument for this widespread misguided view: a fax message belongs automatically to leading communication media.

Sometimes the relevant information that has to go into a letter head is so extensive that it is not possible to place it all on one side of a sheet of paper without affecting the amount of space left over for content. This can be the case when the names of all the partners of a large firm of accountants or lawyers have to be mentioned, or when registered terms of delivery have to be stated. The reverse side of the paper does not always afford a way out as it is realized that here any text is less noticeable and both sides of a sheet of paper cannot be photocopied at the same time. Photocopying is the lot of much correspondence nowadays. Many companies find adding a secondary colour to the printing of the letter head a valuable asset as it immediately identifies the original letter from the photocopy.

In less progressive organizations one still finds paper of a smaller size like A5. The supposed advantages, largely in the fact that less paper is used, are far outweighed by the disadvantages. One need not be embarrassed about sending a short letter, letters do not have to appear longer than they are. However, separate production and extra storage, the need for non-standard envelopes are all clear arguments against: a word processor has just as little interest in A5 as the filing systems. Archaic elements like this are fortunately being eliminated with the increasing use of a corporate identity.

The follow-on sheets of writing paper should reflect the design of the first. This is often confined to reproducing a scaled-down version of the trademark or logotype with markings for date, subject matter, etc. The choice of paper is an important factor for the presentation of a letter. As well as numerous bond paper types there are also heavier qualities with a watermark, giving the impression they have been handmade and coming in a variety of shades. Sometimes a darker colour of paper is at the expense of an effective contrast with what is typed or printed onto it and makes photocopying complicated. Although the amount of company correspondence can be considerable, the careful selection of good quality writing paper is a responsible expense in every way. The drafting and production of letters in an organization is already a fairly expensive process in which the price of the writing paper itself is a subordinate factor.

IMAGE

Number, Streetname
Code, City
Code, Country

Your letter of	Your ref.	Our ref.	Tel. ext.	Date

Subject

Telephone number   Bank account number
Telefax number   Registration number
Telex number   Chamber of Commerce

IMAGE

Number, Streetname
Code, City
Code, Country

Your letter of	Your ref.	Our ref.	Tel. ext.	Date

Subject

Telephone number   **Bank account number**
Telefax number   **Registration number**
Telex number   **Chamber of Commerce**

The business card

Business cards
The business card is 106 x 74mm and is divided into 3 ½ columns using the same layout as for the writing paper. The left-hand margin is 4/10 inch, in which the blue marks appear for user's business and private address. The tradename is in the third column. Immediately under is the name (on 10th layout line) and function (on 16th layout line), preceded, left, by blue layout lines. The text has a line space setting of 1/6 inch, and like the trademark is printed in black. All lines are printed in blue.

When drawing up a housestyle it would be difficult to find any subject more discussed than that of the business card.
This is not difficult to explain. The housestyle is judged by the management of a company and it is precisely in these circles that the exchanging of business cards has taken on an almost ceremonial character. The card personifies its holder. Its design and what is mentioned on it contribute to the bearer's status. Once handed over, the small piece of printed card takes on a new life in the albums in which 'each other is saved'. Small wonder that a business card is a sensitive subject.
What is stated on the card is nearly always a bone of contention between company and individual. Out of corporate consideration it is important to put trademark and the statutory name of the company plus relevant address. Yet how relevant 'relevant' is remains a point of discussion. Postal address alongside visiting address, phone and telex numbers, but what about telex, fax and telegram details? How far does one go with titles, functions and names of departments? What about private numbers or even addresses?
All this information has to be incorporated onto a card – unlike Image's – that is the same size of a bank or credit card. Double cards can solve this problem but can get squashed when inserted into holders. On the other hand a vertically designed business card is a solution when there is a lot of text. By presenting the text in columns with white space in between, much text can be positioned. Unfortunately many managements experience this as an infringement of the corporate code which tacitly prescribes horizontally designed cards.
A business card then is mainly a compromise whereby the management itself often deviates from the standard rules – less text, more 'status' – but for others imposes strict directives on what should be stated at an operational level for the company on the cards.
If one wants to eliminate undisciplined growth and that is surely one of the objectives of a corporate identity then ordering and production should be arranged centrally, for instance, via the Purchasing Department. It is also recommended that the text for the cards is standardized on an order form so that modifications and restrictions on the user are recorded from then on.
All that remains is a question of design and choice of card. It is possible for the logo in the house colour to be printed in huge quantities so that it is available on demand. Once it has been arranged, in accordance with policy, who is admitted to the ranks of card bearers then nothing more stands in the way of enacting the ritual the Japanese have given to the rest of the world.

IMAGE

Number, Streetname
Code/City
Telephone number
Telefax number

Home address
Number, Streetname
Code, City
Telephone number

Name

Function

IMAGE

Number, Streetname
Code/City
Telephone number
Telefax number

Home address
Number, Streetname
Code, City
Telephone number

Name

Function

Business forms

Memos, invoices, etc. are tools for presenting information in an orderly fashion. A well-presented form provides the receiver of the information with a clear point of reference. It goes without saying that such a well-presented form can be traced back to the organizational structure of a company or department. The efficiency of office procedures stands or falls with this. Organizations are in the grip of memoranda. To outsiders it is amazing to experience every time how companies are controlled by forms: enormous stockpiles used to record the day-to-day operations of a company. It is precisely in this area that a rewarding task awaits the designers of a corporate identity. Combing through, shortening and improving business forms is a logical consequence of striving for standardization within a housestyle. Designers can support the client in this more or less organizational task, or leave it in the client's hands entirely. Next to an official form circuit, known and sanctioned by the management, most companies operate a second unofficial one.

A serious approach to a housestyle requires the registering of the entire stockpile of internal and external forms, both from the official and the black circuit. This stockpile should be classified and analysed one by one for their validity, relevance and function in the administrative process. Often a high percentage are unnecessary, outdated or can be combined. Reducing the magnitude of this stockpile leads to considerable savings in production, administration and processing time. Forms are distinguished by their design and content. Good design is pointless if this does not go hand-in-hand with clear, unambiguous language. Memos require a certain editorial care: they should be preferably couched in the normal everyday language of the form-fillers rather than in that of local government. Improvements to the existing stock of business forms is an extensive part of a housestyle operation, but in itself can produce more than cost-effective results. During the last decade the designing of forms has developed into a wide specialism in which organization experts, language specialists and designers can play a role. For the housestyle designer familiar with the problems surrounding form-filling, design of forms presents the opportunity to express the company housestyle. Colour, logo, typography and style details can all be used in creating a stock of forms with recognizable housestyle features.

The size of a form is often dictated by administrative equipment and varies between A5 and A4 on the one hand and the non-standard size of perforated continuous forms on the other. How they are filled out – by hand, typewriter or word processor –has consequences for their basic layout, both in the width (appropriate space for pica orientated widths of printing machines), and for the vertical carriage (interlinear spacing). A proper approach to business forms should also include a watertight ordering procedure: who may organize the stock of sets and what conditions does their organization have to comply with? The greatly varying content of the individual types of forms makes it complicated to pinpoint all possible directives in the housestyle manual. Housestyles tend to give no more than principles concerning size, layout, typography and use of lines. The often huge consumption of NCR sets within a company justifies appointing someone to take charge of these, who designs them himself/herself or commissions someone else to do it. Desk top publishing can – if in the right hands – assist with improving and controlling the stock of NCR sets.

For many years at international level there have been intensive discussions among standardization committees concerned with both a standard layout for business forms as 'paper information carriers' and for electronic information. These committees have available basic layout units for business forms so that their design can be brought much more into line with one another.

It is a popular misconception that internal forms would be able to duck en masse the rules concerning housestyle. A well-developed internal housestyle form gives a staff member the feeling that he/she is taken just as seriously as the firm's external relations.

Trade documents

The designs for NCR sets etc. illustrated here are all based on recommendations in NEN 2059 'Trade documents' and NEN 3516 'Designing forms'. These norms conform to ISO 6422 'Layout key for trade documents' and ISO 8440 'Location of codes in trade documents'. All this information is laid down in the 'United Nations layout key for trade documents', published by the UN in 1982. The format is designed on two standard paper sizes from the A series: A4 (210 x 297mm) and A5 (148 x 210mm).

Basic layout

The already described layout has been retained. The 9/10 columns are divided in two by a 1/10 inch white space, providing a more flexible make-up. Thus the layout gives 16 4/10 inch columns with a 1/10 inch white space in between each time. The column width is geared to four positions of American elite typewriter type size of 1/12 inch (10 and 12 pitch respectively) and five positions of German Perl according to DIN 2107.

Margins

The upper margin is 13mm and lines with the first continuous horizontal line of the layout. Similar to the writing paper, the first column is left free, creating a left-hand margin of 20mm. This column is only used for the housestyle lines, marks for folding and for the centre of the page. The right-hand margin of 12.25mm is also left free. The margin below lines with the last but one line of the layout. The white space between columns 9 and 10 marks the centre of the type area of 175 x 275mm.

Stationery design

Sender's particulars begin at the left-hand margin, 13mm in from the top of the page and are preceded by the layout lines. The trademark is in columns six and seven. The name of a form is given in the ninth column in nine point semibold. Under the sender's details, on the 11th line, is a 0.25mm line across seven columns indicating the space for the addressee. This deviates somewhat from that of the UN layout key because of the place of the window in the now accepted ENCS/6 and EAS envelopes according to NEN 1025. These envelopes will eventually be modified to fit the UN layout key.

Two lines below the name of the form are the marks indicating spaces for date, number, references etc., which run down to the 11th line of the layout. Here there is space for a second address if necessary. Below left, on the last line of the layout, is the form number in seven point Univers 57.

This layout is for standard details which appear on all business stationery. The rest of the layout can be done according to need and in close cooperation with the department responsible for the company housestyle. The following examples - an invoice on A4 and an order form on A5 – illustrate how various business stationery can be designed using the basic layout. The use of the central axis between columns eight and nine makes for order and good presentation. An invoice may be typed or printed. When filling in an order form by hand, writing guidelines are required. This means that a number of details important to the design of any form need to be known beforehand, such as handwritten or typewritten completion of forms, method for reproducing, filing system and possible binding system.

Typography and use of colour

All text is set in Univers. For business stationery there are two types of text:
- Continuous body text for introductions and explanations. This is set in nine point Univers 55, in caps and lower case, with a line space setting of 3.75mm. Where necessary Univers 65 can be used for small headings or text which needs to be accented.

- Text which indicates the information required and where this should be filled-in. This is set in seven point Univers 57, in lower case with a line space setting of 3mm.

The aim of having two different texts is that after completion of a form the body text reads like a story, as it were, supplemented by the informative text. The latter is then not so necessary any more and can be set in a more modest type size.

Two types of lines are also used:
- marks to indicate an appropriate space on a memo etc. These are 0.25mm thick and as long as the width of the space.
- writing lines on forms, memos etc. completed by hand and requiring a signature. These are 0.1mm thick and as long as the width of the space.

In general only horizontal lines are used. Markers indicate the top of the space. A space is not enclosed by a line.

The vertical layout of forms/ documents is achieved by splitting the markers by 1/10 inch.

All text is printed in black, lines in blue on a white background. For simple internal memos both text and lines are in black.

Divergent sizes

Earlier we touched on the importance of international standardization for paper sizes. Taking into account the many divergent sizes still around, we illustrate here the layout in question for a housestyle in a non-standard A or B paper series.

Illustrated is a paper size that is used most in the United States: 216 x 279mm (8½ x 11 inch). The upper and left-hand margins are the same as the A4 and A5 size, in accordance with the UN layout key. Here too columns one and 16 remain unused, so that all the spaces on the forms, memos etc. are in the same positions as on the standard size papers. This produces a wider right-hand margin, so that the type area is centred in the width, which creates a symmetric design. The details at the foot of the forms, memos etc. are placed five lines higher than on the A4 size. This layout makes it possible for it to be copied without any problem from this divergent paper size to standard A4 size.

IMAGE

Number, Streetname
Code, City
Code, Country

Original invoice

date

invoice number

reference number

consignee

buyer (if not consignee)

notify or delivery address

terms of delivery and payment

specification

quantity   unit price   amount

date

signature

FORM NO.

IMAGE

Number, Streetname
Code, City
Code, Country

consignee

notify or delivery address

specification

Original invoice

date

invoice number

reference number

buyer (if not consignee)

terms of delivery and payment

quantity   unit price   amount

date

signature

FORM NO.

IMAGE

Number, Streetname
Code, City
Code, Country

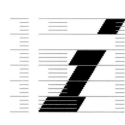

Orderform

date

order number

contact person

telephone

date of delivery

to deliver

signature

FORM NO.

IMAGE

Number, Streetname
Code, City
Code, Country

consignee

notify or delivery address

specification

Original invoice

date

invoice number

reference number

buyer (if not consignee)

terms of delivery and payment

quantity	unit price	amount

date

signature

FORM NO.

Envelopes

Envelopes

Business envelopes need to conform to many requirements. Internationally there are many tight rules governing size, sender's details, what may be printed etc. These need to be strict because envelopes must be suitable for automated processing and should not confuse scanning machines. It is obvious from this that if an envelope has to conform to the aforementioned norms it should not have an outrageous appearance.
A straightforward envelope has been chosen, which includes trademark, lines and details of address.
The design is for all envelopes regardless of size.

The envelope illustrated here is the smallest one used in the company style. It is 110 x 220mm and has a 110 x 30mm window to the left and a 20mm left-hand margin. Size and layout is in accordance with NEN 1025, 1978 and ISO 269, 1976. The envelope is identified with the code EAS/6V. Below an overview of other sizes and types is given. The 13mm upper and 32mm left-hand margins illustrated on p 199 are used for all sizes and within these are the house markers for sender's details.
The trademark is in the fourth column similar to the writing paper.
All envelopes are white and can be printed blue (making them opaque) on the inside.
Text, lines and trademark are set the same as for the writing paper. Lines are blue, text and trademark black.

Sizes
A-series
(Size in mm)

EA3	312 x 441
EA3/2	156 x 411
EA4	220 x 312
EA4/2	115 x 312
EA5*	156 x 220
EA6*	110 x 156
EA6*	110 x 156
EA7	78 x 110

* Envelopes with a window are indicated as follows: EASV, EA5/6V and EA6V.

Within the area of improving efficiency, as well as the question of economics, there is hardly a more rewarding side to a corporate identity project than a company's stock of envelopes. Unless the company already has someone in charge of printed matter there is mostly an abundance of sort, size and quality, a jungle in which a hatchet can generously go to town. Envelopes are no more and no less than containers for letters and documents: transporters of paper, in other words. With the general acceptance of standard paper size, both for letters and drawings, the way has been cleared for strictly limiting the variety of envelope sizes. If you have a small range of envelopes for folded standard size writing paper and illustrations, you have enough for practically any situation. In many old stocks one still comes across envelopes suitable for quarto and folio sizes which do not fit anymore into current standard sizes. The cabinet envelope EA5/6, with or without a window, is the most elementary type. The window is chosen for efficiency – it prevents double work and enclosing the contents incorrectly. Nevertheless there are branches or departments of a company for which a window envelope is an unsuitable, too 'cheap' choice and thus closed envelopes are used.

In most cases the basic set of envelopes comprises an EA5 type into which A5 or a once folded A4 sheet of paper fits and an envelope for unfolded A4 post, with or without a flap to give more volume. Add to this a lightweight airmail envelope, perhaps a special size envelop for continuous forms and another A4 hardbacked one, then practically all needs are covered.

When establishing the type of envelopes to use, a choice has to be made concerning paper quality, the design of the flap and the window, the material for the window and the pattern printed on the inside. It is worth remembering that in daily business practice the postroom or the secretary's desk is where an envelope winds up. Many envelopes never come under the attention of the addressee. This could be a reason to concentrate on quality and the ease with which it can be dispatched rather than expend energy on its exclusive design and printing.

All the same, should an 'own' non-standard envelope be needed there are enough possibilities – depending on the total required – to modify the design with personal touches like one's own choice of pattern inside the envelope (non see-through).

When printing envelopes it is important to take into account local postal regulations. The zones in which printing or non printing is allowed have still not been completely standardized internationally. Worse still, envelopes with windows (window to the right or left) are subject to national postal restrictions. This makes the standardization of writing paper and envelopes for international corporate identities a problem. It is standard practice – and when using commercial envelopes, cheaper – to print all the necessary details like address and name of sender on one side – the front – of an envelope. Some organizations allow the name of the sender to appear in the window of the envelope and thus achieve considerable savings in printing and control costs. One avoids the double appearance of the logo: pre-printed on the envelope and repeated in the postmark.

IMAGE

Number, Streetname
Code, City
Code, Country

IMAGE

Number, Streetname
Code, City
Code, Country

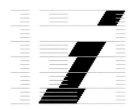

Publicity

Publicity
Here examples are included of various media which can be used to reach divergent target groups. Within the context of the housestyle, use can be made of additional promotional design elements, such as a square, circle or triangle.

The visual communication of a company falls into two main categories. The first is the more or less permanent side comprised of a fixed core of consumer printed matter – stationery sets, forms, etc. – while the other is of a more varied nature and has to do with promotion – the publicity required in order to focus attention on the product or service of a company. It is difficult for adequate publicity to flourish in a situation where the consumer is not given any new impulses. A déjà-vu experience is not very stimulating, at the most it is only an acknowledgement. While a corporate identity is aimed in the first instance at continuity in the design of all elements, incorporating these into ongoing enticingly orientated publicity is an important point for attention. How can one provide these 'fresh messages' with the unmistakable features of their sender? When a company supplies external and internal relations with a house magazine this has to comply with two interrelated criteria. If it is not to be experienced as an incidental publication it should have visual continuity. It may evolve in the course of time, but in essence every issue should be able to bridge the gap between itself and each of the preceding issues. A magazine is one of a series, with certain recognizable features both in form and editorial style for its readers. This is exactly something for a housestyle, for it deals with continuity.
The above criteria are largely required of an annual report – also a magazine type publication, but published less frequently. Precisely with this type of medium aimed at financiers, banks, press, government, business relations, staff and job-seekers, a confusing visual presentation should be avoided. Standard features and quality impress shareholders more!
In the design of brochures, leaflets, catalogues and price lists a choice has to be made continually between a restrained or an innovative approach. To what extent the housestyle should be emphatically present is a matter of knowing the market.
Packaging certainly falls under publicity too. It can so happen with a product that corporate identity remains in the background in the interests of the brand. That depends entirely on the sector in which the manufacturer or distributor operates. With supermarket products there are different for those of considerations than with spare car parts in the dealer's stockroom or pharmaceuticals in a chemist's shop. Just how much a housestyle comes to the foreground varies from case to case. Shop attributes like displays, posters and streamers will all have to go through the sieve of the housestyle. The volume of publicity material will often decide whether this is produced by the company's own design studio, whether it falls under the studio responsible for the housestyle, or winds up at an advertising agency or packaging specialists. Again it remains the task of the management to give directives on how far a corporate identity should be respected.

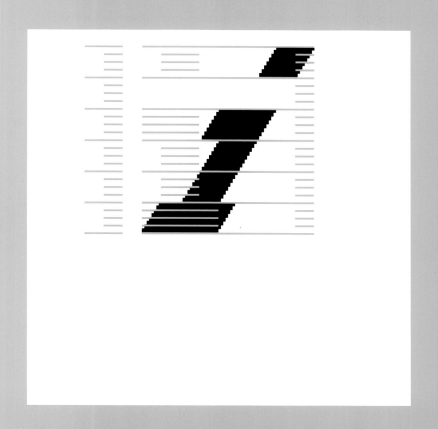

Advertisements

Companies mainly advertise in newspapers, magazines and telephone and trade directories. Advertisements inform about products and services or recruit personnel. Nevertheless what an advertising medium represents can rise above its direct function. Within the reference of a housestyle, advertising is a constantly recurring presentation in which the message reaches further than simple content. By using a consistent style of advertising the company is brought positively anew under the attention of a broad public. Housestyle elements play an active role in advertisements in perpetuating the public image of a company. Thus within the directives of a housestyle a standard layout for advertisements belongs. Tradename, logo, use of house type, certain borders and style elements lend a recognizable signature to advertising.

For personnel ads and straightforward business type announcements there will be little discussion on the desirability and the effectiveness of maintaining housestyle elements. Nevertheless in recent years, for high-level functions a need has arisen among companies employing a housestyle to pep up the emotional value of a personnel ad by using a more pretentious type far removed from a businesslike, functional one. The same need is to be found among many advertising agencies when it concerns a type family for eye-catching advertisements. That is why in many housestyles there is an area of tension between a disciplined type on the one hand for informative printed matter and a more emotive one on the other for advertisements.

The upshot of all this can mean that the marketing and advertising experts of a company have the extra task of making sure that housestyle and advertising do not become too much estranged. After all, a company does not stand to gain anything by appearing one minute in jeans and the next in a morning coat.

Advertising is more than a question of placing advertisements. The media and everything that goes with it is much more versatile. An important medium is the TV spot, more traditional is the cinema screen or the advertising film. For these media, too, the same applies that trademark, logo, house colours and typography borrowed from the housestyle help enforce the standard look.

For an organization with a decentralized approach it is vitally important that, from the point of view of housestyledesigned ads, clear directives exist and visual aids are supplied to ensure and uphold the company style. Large multinationals with a wide geographical spread of branches would do well to choose carefully type for headings and text. It is difficult to maintain a housestyle in less developed countries when one has a too exclusive choice of type.

Advertisement budgets – precisely because of placing expenses – can command large sums of money. A tight policy with regard to size, permitted white space (visually important anyway), desired text size, etc. can have a curative effect on budgets. A housestyle is an excellent tool with which to control such details.

Action campaigns have a limited reach. They demand a carefully selected media agenda and timescale. In many cases content and visual image after a period of a year or so will have to change tack altogether. The image of an ad – the photographic and illustrative approach – can also be brought into play to strengthen general recognizability within the terms of the housestyle. One can think here of an image repeated of one and the same person or long-term use of certain design features.

This approach has been used for a long time in the advertisements for KLM by working with fixed blue skies and clouds which have practically become housestyle elements. For as long as the campaign lasts these are constituents added to the housestyle to enhance the image. Thus advertising within the framework of a corporate identity often means the bringing together of enduring housestyle elements with campaign-linked 'shifting' constituents.

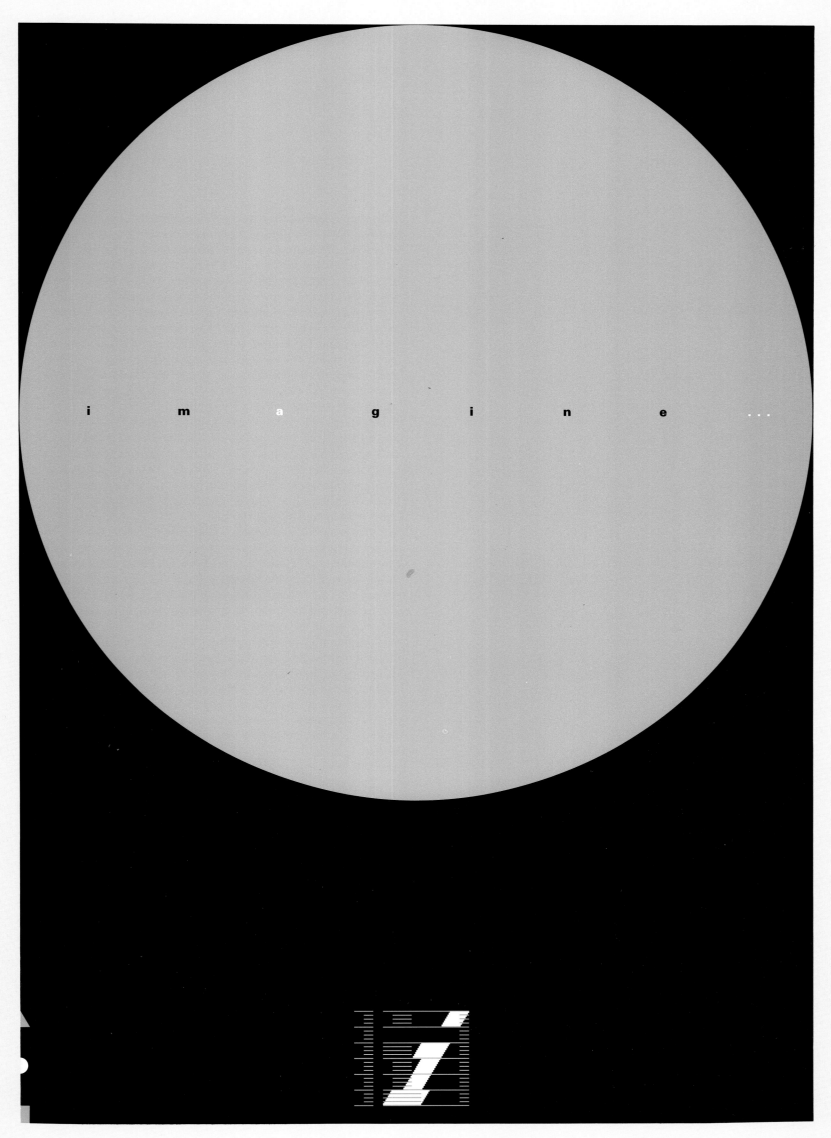

Signs on buildings

The premises of a company is an important factor in the manner in which a company wishes to present itself and house its workers. That applies equally to both commercial businesses and manufacturers. The building or complex has a 'signalling' effect on visitors and passers-by from the way in which the identity of the occupant is made visible. The standard way is to affix the name or logo to the main facade and on those side walls which afford a favourable view when seen from the urban landscape. The size of the signs should be seen in relationship to the desired distance of observation. In addition architectonic circumstances play a role. The lettering in many countries is subject to the rules of planning committees: you cannot do everything everywhere.

If a building should remain clearly observable in the dark or in bad weather then the signs should be illuminated or one can choose illuminated advertising. The latter falls into two main categories: illuminated boxes – box-type elements lit up from within by fluorescent lighting, and individual letters and signs in neon – internally lit through neon tubes or so-called chain light (linked halogen lamps).

With large illuminated boxes, which mainly have a translucent front of acrylic sheeting like Perspex, problems can often occur through the seams used to exceed the maximum sheet size. Cracks can appear which admit light, or overlapping which results in a darkening of the colour. The way in which cable is laid can also present problems, especially with individual letters. It would be wise to avoid visible cable.

With illuminated advertising the difference between so-called day and night value – what you see when – should also be taken into account. It may be necessary with certain logos to adjust the positioning of the letters in connection with glare. The thick sides of the letters or sign can be opaque or translucent, in a contrasting colour – the secondary house colour for example – or have the same day value as the fronts of the letters.

At street level, sign or logo can be affixed to wall plaques (by the main entrance to the building for instance) or used as window lettering (shop fronts). Here, too, optical requirements play a role. Strangely enough, white window lettering is in nearly all cases the most noticeable because windows have a dark surface. Window lettering is produced in the same way as fleet marking, using self-adhesive lettering which can be rubbed off. Wall plaques can be part of the sign system, but in that case they should harmonize in design and appearance with the rest of the signing.

The name plate should include more than just the everyday name and logo. It is correct here to state the statutory name of the company. Wall lettering is a bone of contention between architecture and communications, producing tension between architect and housestyle designer. Many architects experience lettering as an undesirable addition to their creation. That is why they prefer to do it themselves, but do not always have the background in communications that such a skill demands. This sometimes limited knowledge of the subject, combined with the pet hobby horses of planning committees and the commercial interests of the lighting companies, makes the signing of buildings within the reference of a housestyle a complex task. It is not made any easier if the company has many branches in varied types of premises.

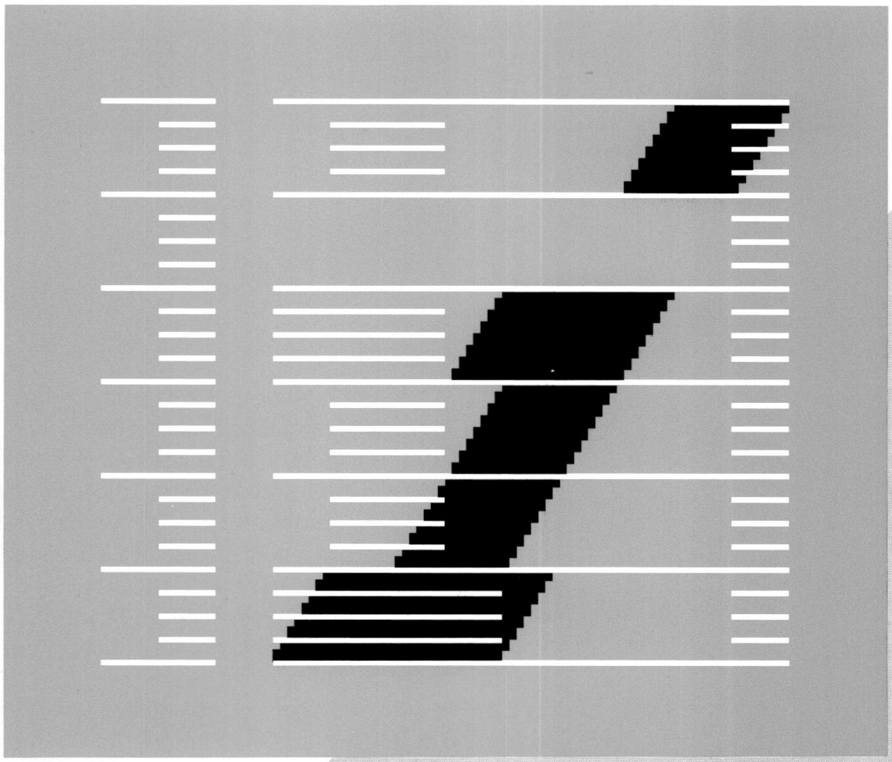

Routeing

Routeing
The white and black trademark on a blue background is a follow-through of the exterior signing of the building. The black triangle is a neutral background for the contrasting white lettering. The blue layout lines help sustain the trademark's rhythm and act as markers for the white triangular arrows.

Routeing is a visual technique for making company buildings and sites more accessible. By means of text or pictographs, mainly affixed to panels or signs, visitors or internal users are led to their destination – from the very first sign to the desk with the personal nameplate of the person they wish to see. A good sign system is a part of the care a company takes in its approach to customers and staff. Indeed, no one wishes to enter a building and feel like a fish out of water.

A sign system can already start with indicator boards along a public highway, routeing to the entrance of the site, marks for the parking area and signs to the entrance and reception. Within the building this then continues in the form of indexing – listing what is where on each floor and signs on how to reach the locations. The housestyle here can be used in the application of house colours and materials and by using the house typography. A specific component of the typographical aspect are the directional arrows designed to harmonize with the type or the logo.

Routeing is developing increasingly into a separate skill. It requires knowledge of buildings, the ability to analyse traffic movements, typographical skills and a broad technical knowledge. Too many signs and boards is just as irritating as too few. The use of pictographs (like the well-known man or woman for public conveniences) has to be carefully considered. How comprehensible are abstract symbols for expected visitors?

At central points in the building there are index boards listing what is where. This begs the question how permanent the information is, how often personnel and departments move around. One should avoid carefully executed signs having temporary and often handmade directions stuck over them. When many changes to the information are envisaged, a mutational system serves well, and is foolproof to avoid unwanted tampering.

There are many industrial produced sign systems on the market. Their design is often neutral and lacks the characteristic features that fit a housestyle in question. However, it is sometimes possible and financially attractive to adapt these systems by using house colours or logo to suit the housestyle. Security considerations can get in the way of a complete execution of a sign system. In that case one has to be restricted to providing signs for the public areas like directions for lifts/escalators, floor and room numbers. In such cases the visitor is 'picked up' and 'led' through the building.

Sign systems are created out of letters, colours and certain materials. They are a part of the total corporate identity and should logically abide by the norms of the housestyle.

RECEPTION DESK

CONFERENCE ROOM

ENTRANCE

LIFT

PARKING

Fleet marking

Fleet marking
Because of the imaginary nature of the company, the designs are reproduced in very general terms. Thus it is an unknown factor what type of transport would be used - private cars, lorries, motorbikes, ships or aircraft. What is important however is that all the various attention-seeking images whether on the ground, on water or up in the air retain the house signature. This is best done by being simple, clear and readable.
The trademark is used in a variety of standard sizes. This has practical advantages when using self-adhesive lettering as the latter can be quickly supplied when new letters are required.
The RAL international colour system is for car lacquers and building paint and is available through many paint and lacquer suppliers as well as car manufacturers.
The specific lacquers chosen for the company style are RAL 5015 (blue) and RAL 9005 (black).

Vehicle livery design is a rewarding part of the housestyle. Fork-lift trucks, all types of carriers, delivery vans and trucks, ships and aeroplanes lend themselves ideally to the colours and logo of a company. Applying these housestyle elements calls for precision in the design and execution process. House-style colours can be printed admirably in printing ink specifications of which the Pantone PMS series is the most wide ranging and internationally accepted system. Conversely, paints and lacquers suitable for decorating land and sea-faring transport are far less internationally coded and standardized. The RAL system for paint lacquer is of German origin and is widely known in Western Europe. The primary and secondary colour samples of RAL are limited when compared with PMS's and are too few, in fact, to provide more nuances of colour in them all. Large paint factories have laboratories where they do their best to approach the printing ink colours such as those from the PMS series. The essential difference between printing inks and spray paint is a certain tolerance. Printing ink is normally used on white paper and has a transparent quality. With paint and lacquer the results are quite different, so it is virtually impossible to make comparable results.
Applying both logo and name and any secondary information onto transport material hardly ever takes place anymore using a skilled hand and brush. It has become a question of expensive self-adhesive films from producers such as 3M, produced by specialized companies in the exact required colour and meticulously cut mainly with the help of a computer. They come on sheets, exactly positioned, and are applied to surfaces using a sort of rubbing technique. Their design is perfect and the durability of this fleet marking often surpasses the operational lifespan of the material it is used on. Their production costs are not to be sneezed at, but then neither are the results. Many companies proceed with the fleet marking side of their new housestyle when replacing old material or during a major overhaul to existing equipment. It goes without saying that one-off, simultaneous fleet marking is best in respect of public and personnel – the latter experience the change of tack first and experience it the most strongly.
We read from left to right. Material moving forwards when looked at from its right side moves against this direction. Should we stand on the other side of a truck or aircraft then we experience the opposite case. This fact can lead to complications with fleet marking. How do you place the logotype in relation to the logo? How does one experience the mirror image of a lion looking left, for instance, on the tail of an aircraft? These are tricky problems for the designer.
The resulting quality of housestyle fleet marking will depend on small details like the lettering on the cabin doors of trailers, the numbering of particular units and the announcement of safety directions, etc. Fleet marking stands or falls according to the willingness to maintain materials and keep them clean.
Well cared for materials make demands on cleaning facilities. Responsibility for this lies increasingly with the person in charge of all the company equipment. Transport material is under the eyes of the general public day and night. It therefore plays a major role in the way a company communicates publicly.

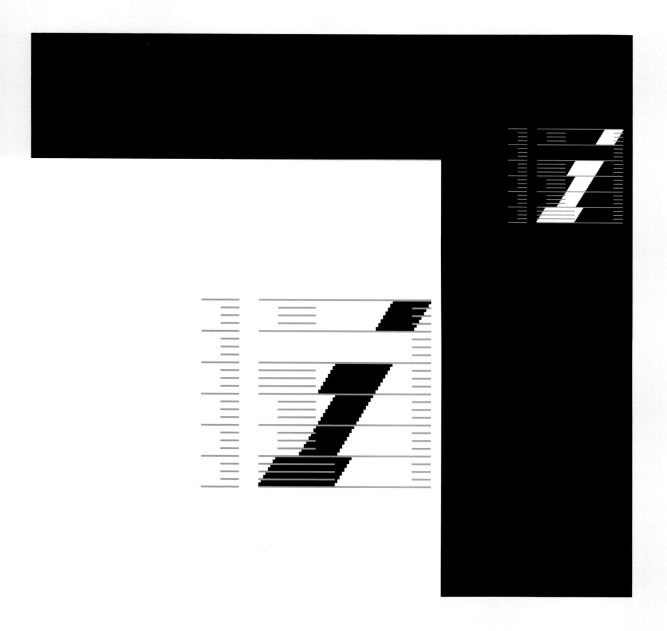

Miscellaneous

Flag
The company flag is a recumbent triangle with a length/breadth ratio of 2:3. The size of the trademark has been adapted to this, its height being 2/3 the height of the flag. The trademark is in the upper left-hand corner next to a left-hand margin 1/9 and an upper margin 1/10 the height of the flag. The flag is white, the lines blue and the trademark black.

The nature of a company determines the extent and variety of its corporate identity. What is the product? How does a particular branch reach potential consumers? What role do personnel play in a firm's image? To what extent do consumers personally visit a company? This will determine the need for industrial clothing and uniforms, sugar bags and cigars, flags and pennants, ties, scarves and other giveaways. In addition, entrance tickets, programmes, maps, parking tickets, calendars, diaries, invitations, Christmas cards, posters, display material, price tickets, receipts and rubber stamps may be required. In short, the number of items which can carry housestyle elements are numerous and wide ranging.
It goes without saying that the wide application of a housestyle strengthens a company's identity and draws together in a consistent manner all its sundry activities. In the service sector such as the airline industry the implementation of a consistent housestyle at all levels is generally accepted. The product in this case is fairly abstract: seats which are shifted from A to B and which in the eyes of the operator have to remain filled. A housestyle can be employed to demonstrate clearly how reliable, safe, comfortable, prompt and affordable an airline is. This leads to an extensive packet of printed matter, packaging, catering products and suchlike which have to be coordinated, designed and produced. A housestyle manual can only give limited assistance in such cases, it can give no more than the norms. From this open-ended aspect of the housestyle all these divergent applications can be periodically modified to suit new demands and trends. This is a permanent point of consideration for marketing and advertising experts as well as housestyle monitors and coordinators.
Another area of attention is that of sponsoring sport and culture. The housestyle here acts as a bridge between company and sponsored object. The presentation of the event, the participants, public areas and attendant publicity are all opportun i-ties for a housestyle actively and positively to represent the company. Housestyle here goes hand-in-hand with well thought out public relations.
Sponsorship breathes life into a housestyle. Using the basic elements as departure points, a company can embroider onto the basic theme and in this way give its visual image new impulses.

Bibliography

This bibliography lists all the works of reference mentioned in the texts as well as recommended reading. It should be said that the case studies of particular companies arose largely out of interviews and consultation of company manuals. Neither these manuals nor data referring to the interviews are listed in the bibliography.

In search of an identity

Barnicoat, J. *A concise History of Posters,* London, 1979

Bos, B. *Indruk, In druk,* Lecturis, Eindhoven, 1977

Broos, K. *Piet Zwart,* The Hague, 1973

Canetti, E. *Massa en Macht,* Amsterdam, 1976

catalogue *Industrie en Vormgeving,* Stedelijk Museum, Amsterdam, 1986

Dirken, J.M. *Leesbaarheid,* Lecturis, Eindhoven, 1976

Elias, N. *Het civilisatieproces,* Utrecht, 1987

Gombrich, E.H. *Aby Warburg,* Frankfurt A/Main, 1981

Groenendaal, M.H. *Drukletters,* Culemborg/Birmingham, 1975

Hammacher, A.M. *Mr. Jean François van Royen 1878-1942,* The Hague, 1947

Hauschild, H. *Die Schrift,* Leipzig, 1951

Hauser, A. *The Social History of Art,* New York, 1975

Hefting, P. *Operatie Bedrijfsstijl,* PTT Nederland NV, The Hague, 1989

Huxley, A. *The Brave New World,* London, 1977

Janson, H.W. *History of Art,* London, 1986

Jencks, C. *Post-Modernism,* London, 1988

Kaemmerling, E. *Bildende Kunst als Zeichensystem,* Köln, 1984

Kennedy, P. *The Rise and the Fall of the Great Powers,* New York, 1989

Lang, L. *Das Bauhaus 1919-1933,* Berlin, 1966

Lepschy, G.C. *La linguistique structurale,* Paris, 1968

McShine, K, *Andy Warhol, a retrospective,* London/New York, 1989

Morris, D. *De naakte Aap,* Utrecht, 1969

Morris, W. *Works,* with lectures and essays, New York, 1934

Neubecker, O. *Heraldiek: bronnen, symboliek en betekenissen,* Baarn, 1988

Ollins, W. *The Corporate Personality,* London, 1978

Pentagram *Living by Design,* London/New York, 1978

Pevsner, N. *Pioneers of Modern Design,* London, 1960

Ramakers, R. (ed) *Bedrijfsstijlen,* Rotterdam, 1985

Richaudau, F. *La Lisibilité,* Paris, 1969

Schultze, J. *Neunzehntes Jahrhundert,* Baden Baden, 1970

Schwarzbauer, G.F. 'Das Prinzip der Wiederholung', *Kunst Magazine,* 1978

Smits, W.C.M. *Symboliek van de kleur,* Amsterdam, 1967

Velde, H. van de *Zum Neuen Stil,* Munich, 1955

Braun

Burkhardt, F. *Design: Dieter Rams,* Berlin, 1980
Forty, A. *Objects of Desire, Design and Society from Wedgewood to IBM,* London, 1986
Henrion, F.H.K., A. Parkin *Design Coordination and Corporate Image,* London/New York, 1967
Spark, P. *An Introduction to Design and Culture in the Twentieth Century,* London, 1986

Royal PTT Netherlands

Boers, W. *Kunst, Kunstenaars en het Staatsbedrijf der PTT,* dissertation for a masters degree in sociology, University of Amsterdam, Amsterdam, 1986
Ginneken, L. van, a.o. 'Kunst en Vormgeving bij de PTT', *Kunstschrift,* 1985
Hammacher, A.M. Mr. *Jean François van Royen 1878-1942,* The Hague, 1947
Hefting, P. 'De Dienst voor Esthetische Vormgeving' in: *Kunst en beleid in Nederland,* Amsterdam, 1986
Hefting, P. *Operatie bedrijfsstijl,* PTT Nederland NV, The Hague, 1989
Hefting, P., R.D.E. Oxenaar 'Achtergronden, wordingsgeschiedenis en inhoud van de PTT-bedrijfsstijl', *Het PTT-bedrijf,* The Hague, 1983
Klinkenberg, J., J. de Bont, H. Lamers 'Een nieuw systeem een oud probleem', *Compress,* 27-12-1983
Pruys, S.M. *De Paradijsbouwers,* Utrecht/Antwerpen, 1974
Reitsma, E. 'Ook in het belastingkantoor, het politiegebouw of postkantoor is kunst', *Vrij Nederland,* 24-7-1982
Rooy, M. van 'Het postbedrijf en zijn esthetische dienst. De erfenis van Jean François van Royen', *NRC Handelsblad,* 4-12-1981

The London Underground

Barker, T.C., M. Robbins *A History of London Transport,* vol. 1 & 2, London, 1974
Barman, C. *The Man who built London Transport,* Newton Abbet, 1979
Bayley, S., *The Conran Directory of Design,* London, 1985
Forty, A. *Objects of Desire. Design & Society from Wedgwood to IBM,* London, 1986
Gsöllpointer, H., a.o. (ed) *Design ist unsichtbar,* Vienna, 1981
Huygen, F. *Brits design, imago en identiteit,* catalogue, Museum Boymans-Van Beuningen, Rotterdam, 1989
Spark, P., a.o. *Design Source Book,* London, 1986
Stewart, R., *Design and British Industry,* London, 1987

Adidas
Catalogue *Sport en design,* Museum
Boymans-Van Beuningen, Rotterdam, 1988
Wissen, H. van 'Drie strepen veroveren de
wereld', *De Volkskrant,* 14-9-1988

Coca-Cola
Bayley, S. *Coke! Coca-Cola 1886-1986: Des-
igning a Megabrand,* London, 1986
Biedermann, U. *Ein Amerikanischer Traum,*
Hamburg, 1985
Industrial Design. Raymond Loewy. London/
Boston, 1979
Olins, W., *The Corporate Personality,* London,
1978
Oliver, T. *The Real Coke, the Real Story,* London,
1986

Esprit
Esprit's Graphic Work 1984-1986, Rodundo,
San Francisco, 1986
Esprit. The Comprehensive Design Principle,
Rodundo, San Francisco, 1989
Huisman, J. 'Werk Sottsass vol nostalgie en
libido', *De Volkskrant,* 11-3-1989
Roodnat, J. 'Met ons gaat het goed', *NRC
Handelsblad,* 24-3-1989
Sujic, D. *From Matt Black to Memphis and back
again. An anthology from Blueprint Magazine,*
London, 1989
Zalm, R. van 'No detail is small', *Design,* nr. 3
1987

IBM
Henrion, F.H.K., A. Parkin *Design Coordination
and Corporate Image,* London/New York, 1967
Maisonrouge, J. *Manager international 36 ans
au coeur d'une multinationale de l'infomatique,*
Paris, 1985
Rand, P. *Thoughts on Design,* New York, 1947
Rand, P. *Paul Rand: A Designer's Art,* New
Haven, 1985
Sobel, R. *IBM, marktleider, ook in de
toekomst...,* Utrecht/Aartselaar, 1986
Spark, P. *An Introduction to Design and Culture
in the Twentieth Century,* London, 1986

Erco
Blauw, E. *Het Corporate Image, Beeldvorming
van de onderneming,* Amsterdam,
1986
Gsöllpointer, H., a.o. (ed) *Design ist unsichtbar,*
Vienna, 1981
Ramakers, R. (ed) *Bedrijfsstijlen,* Rotterdam,
1985

KLM
Arnheim, R. *Art and Visual Perception,*
Berkeley/Los Angeles, 1954
Brinkgreve *De house style van de K.L.M.,* not
published, 1984
Diethelm, W. *Signet, Signal, Symbol,* Zürich,
1976
Gombrich, E.H. *Ideals and Idols,* Oxford/New
York, 1979
Gombrich, E.H. Julian Hochberg, Max Black
Art, Perception and Reality, Baltimore/London,
1972
Henrion, F.H.K., A. Parkin *Design Coordination
and Corporate Image,* London/New York, 1967
Henrion Associates *K.L.M. Royal Dutch
Airlines, Rationale of Crown Recommandations,*
internal publication, 1962
Hochberg, E. *Psychologie van de waarneming,*
Utrecht/Antwerpen, 1966
Nederlandse Stichting voor Statistiek
*Enquêtes inzake staartvlakbeschildering in
opdracht van Koninklijke Luchtvaart-Mij NV,*
The Hague, 1959
Plesman, A. *Industrial Design in Dutch Aviation,*
London, 1951

Kodak
Bicker Caarten, B. 'De grote gele vader is nog
lang niet uitgekiekt', *NCR Handelsblad,*
20-8-1988
The New American Design, anthology, San
Francisco, 1989
*75 jaar Kodak Nederland, Historisch overzicht
van Kodak Nederland,* Odijk, 1988

Volkswagen
Gsöllpointer, H., a.o. (ed) *Design ist unsichtbar,*
Vienna, 1981
Heskett, J. *Industrial Design,* London, 1980
Selle, G. *Design-Geschichte in Deutschland.
Produktkultur als Entwurf und Erfahrung,* Köln,
1987

**The organization of a corporate identity
programme**
Blauw, E. *Het Corporate Image, Beeldvorming
van de onderneming,* Amsterdam, 1986
Bos, B. *Huisstijl: een expressie van kwaliteitszin,*
Deventer, 1986
Hefting, P., R.D.E. Oxenaar 'Achtergronden,
wordingsgeschiedenis en inhoud van de PTT-
bedrijfsstijl', *Het PTT-bedrijf,* The Hague, 1983
Olins, W. *The Corporate Personality,* London,
1978
Olins, W. *The Wolff Olins Guide to Corporate
Identity,* London, 1984
Visser, A. *De PTT-bedrijfsstijl,* T.U. Delft, Delft,
1988

'Image' - a corporate identity manual

Beukers, H. *Op een rij gezet,* Amsterdam/
Veenendaal, 1986
Blauw, E. *Het Corporate Image, Beeldvorming
van de onderneming,* Amsterdam, 1986
*ISO 838 Paper, holes for general filling purpo-
ses-specifications,* International Organization
of Standardization, 1974
NEN 381 Papierformaten, Nederlands Normali-
satie Instituut, Delft, 1962
NEN 1025 Enveloppen, Nederlands Normali-
satie Instituut, Delft, 1978
*NEN 1026 Briefpapier, factuur en (brief)-
kaarten,* Nederlands Normalisatie Instituut,
Delft, 1984
NEN 2059 Handelsformulieren, Nederlands
Normalisatie Instituut, Delft, 1988
NEN 3316 Ontwerpen van formulieren, Neder-
lands Normalisatie Instituut, Delft, 1976, 1981
(supplement)
Oltheten, Th., K. Steenwijk *Ontwerpen van
formulieren,* The Hague, 1977
Proost Prikkels 394, Papier & Zo, Proost en
Brandt N.V., Amsterdam, 1983

Further reading

Bernsen, J. *Design Management in Practise,*
Copenhagen, 1987
Bayley, S. *Natural Design. The Search for
Comfort and Efficiency,* London, 1985
Booth-Clibborn, E. (ed) *The Best in British
Corporate Identity & Design,* New York, 1989
Carter, D.E. *Corporate Identity Manuals,* New
York, 1978
Carter, D.E. *Designing Corporate Symbols,* New
York, 1978
Carter, D.E. *Designing Corporate Identity
Programs for small Corporations,* New York,
1982
Carter, D.E. *American Corporate Identity,* New
York, 1986
Carter, D.E. *American Corporate Identity 2,*
New York, 1987
Deal, T.E., A.A. Kennedy *Corporate Cultures,
The Rites and Rituals of Corporate Life,*
Reading, 1984
Eksell, O. *Corporate Design Programs,* London,
1967
Ellinger, R.G. *Color Structure and Design,* New
York, 1980
Favre, J.-P., A. November *Color and
Communication,* New York, 1979
Graves, R. *Corporate Culture, Diagnosis and
Change,* London, 1986
Gray, J.G. *Managing the Corporate Image: The
Key to the Public Trust,* Westport, 1986
Holmes, N. *Designing Pictorial Symbols,* New
York, 1985

Hurlburt, A. *The Design Concept,* New York, 1981

Jackson, P.C. *Corporate Communications for Managers,* Philadelphia, 1987

Joseph, B. *Corporate Design,* New York, 1987

Marquis, H.H. *The Changing Corporate Image,* New York, 1970

Mollerup, P. *The Corporate Design Programme,* Copenhagen, 1987

Napoles, V. *Corporate Identity Design,* New York, 1988

Oakley, M. *Managing Product Design,* New York, 1984

Olins, W. *The Wolff Olins Guide to Design Management,* London, 1984

Olins, W. *Corporate Identity. Making business strategy visible throughout design,* London, 1989

Redding, W.C. *Corporate Manager's Guide to better Communication,* Glenview, 1984

Rosen, B. *The Corporate Search for Visual Identity,* New York, 1970

Ruch, W.V. *Corporate Communications: A Comparison of Japanese & American Practices,* Westport/Greenwood, 1984

Sauerhoft, S., C. Atkins *Image Wars: Protecting your Company when there's no Place to Hide,* New York, 1989

Schmittel, W. *Corporate Design International, Definition and Benefit of a consistent Corporate Appearance,* Zürich, 1984

Selame, E. and J. *Packaging Power: Corporate Identity & Product Recognition,* New York, 1982

Selame, E. and J. *The Company Image: Building Your Identity & Influence in the Marketplace,* New York, 1988

Simpson, M. (ed) *Corporate Identity: Name, Image and Perception,* New York, 1987

Stockton, J. *Designer's Guide to Color,* Part 1 and 2, San Francisco, 1984

Vedin, B.-A. *Corporate Culture for Innovation,* Brookfield, 1980

Wildbur, P. *International Trademarks Design, a Handbook of Marks of Identity,* London, 1979

Sources of illustrations

Acknowledgements

The publishers have made every possible effort to meet their obligations in connection with copyright. Should there, despite this, have been some oversight, the publishers would greatly appreciate it if those concerned would contact them.
The publishers would like to thank the following companies, publishers and museums by whose kind permission the illustrations are reproduced.

10 Feathers of a parrot. Fred Nordheim, Artis Zoo, Amsterdam

11 Feathers of a parrot. Fred Nordheim, Artis Zoo, Amsterdam

12 May Day Parade, *1987.* ABC Press

15 Sir Winston Churchill. ABC Press

16 The Vatican. ABC Press

17 Seoul Olympics *1988.* ABC Press

18 Cas Oorthuys: 'Olympiad under dictatorship' poster, *1936.* Stedelijk Museum Amsterdam

19 (above) Paul Schuiteman: 'Central Union of Transport Workers' poster, *1930.* Gemeentemuseum The Hague; (below) Hitler Youth in Olympic Stadium. Associated Press

20 Parthenon, Acropolio. Rolf Bos, the Netherlands

21 Amphora. Allard Pierson Museum Amsterdam

22 Donatello: bronze statue of David. David Finn, USA

23 (above) Claude Monet: Garden at Giverny. Stedelijk Museum Amsterdam; (below) M. Cheval, ABC Press

24 (above) 'Delft salad oil' advertisment. Rijksmusuem Amsterdam; (below) logotype of paint dealer Ripolin. *Mart. Spruyt calendar,* Mart. Spruyt BV, Amsterdam

25 Enamel advertisement. *More street Jewellery,* C. Baglee & A. Morley, New Cavendish Books, London

26 Logotype of Medinos Tandcream. *Mart. Spruyt. calendar.* Mart. Spruyt BV, Amsterdam

27 Mc Knight Kaufter poster for London Underground, London Transport Museum

28 'Howdy Friend' poster. Coca–Cola

29 Logotype. *Mart. Spruyt calendar,* Mart. Spruyt BV, Amsterdam

31 (above) Piet Zwart: advertising brochure for Delft Kabels, *1932.* Gemeentemuseum The Hague; (below) An early form of information system. Kodak Netherlands

32 Rietveld Schröder House. Frank den Oudsten and Lenneke Büller

33 (above) Piet Zwart: Nijgh & Van Ditmar advertising brochure, *1931.* Gemeentemuseum the Hague; (below) Piet Zwart: 'Tempo' cigarette box, *1935.* Gemeentemuseum The Hague

34 Evolution of the AEG logo from *1898* to the present. AEG

35 Peter Shire: 'Hollywood' table, *1983.* COPI, The Hague

92 *Imagen Global,* CEAC, Spain
93 all illustrations NASA
94 all illustrations Esprit
95 Esprit
96 all illustrations *Esprit. The Comprehensive Design Principle,* Rodundo, San Franciso
97 all illustrations *Esprit. The Comprehensive Design Principle,* Rodundo, San Francisco
98 above Esprit, bottom *Esprit's Graphic Work 1984-1986,* Rodundo, San Franciso
99 all illustrations *Esprit. The Comprehensive Design Principle,* Rodundo, San Francisco
100 all illustrations *Esprit's Graphic Work 1984-1986,* Rodundo, San Francisco
101 all illustrations Esprit
102 all illustrations Esprit
104 IBM Netherlands
105 all illustrations IBM Netherlands
106 all illustrations IBM Netherlands
107 IBM Netherlands
108 all illustrations IBM Netherlands
109 IBM Netherlands
110 all illustrations IBM Netherlands
112 all illustrations IBM Netherlands
113 all illustrations IBM Netherlands
114 all illustrations IBM Netherlands
115 IBM Netherlands
116 all illustrations Erco
117 all illustrations Erco
118 all illustrations Erco
119 all illustrations Erco
121 all illustrations Erco
122 all illustrations Erco
123 Erco
124 all illustrations The KLM Archive
125 The KLM Archive
126 all illustrations The KLM Archive
127 all illustrations The KLM Archive
128 KLM
129 above KLM, bottom The KLM Archive
130 all illustrations KLM
131 all illustrations KLM
132 all illustrations KLM
133 KLM
134 all illustrations Kodak Netherlands
135 Kodak Netherlands
136 all illustrations Kodak Netherlands
137 all illustrations Kodak Netherlands
138 all illustrations Kodak Netherlands
139 Kodak Netherlands
140 all illustrations Kodak Netherlands
141 all illustrations Kodak Netherlands
142 all illustrations Volkswagen
143 Volkswagen
144 Volkswagen
145 all illustrations Volkswagen
146 all illustrations Volkswagen
147 all illustrations Volkswagen
148 Volkswagen

Index

We have tried to make this index as compact and functional as possible. Page numbers set in bold type indicate that a definition of a term is offered here.

'The Image of a Company' is a project of V + K Publishing,
Laren, The Netherlands, and was initiated by Cees de Jong.

This book was made possible by the support of
Lay-out zetterij Boxem B.V. This typesetting company is a.o.
specialized in corporate identity programmes.

Design by
V + K Design, Laren, The Netherlands
Cees de Jong, Ernst Schilp

Reproduction photography by
Arthur Martin, Bussum, The Netherlands

Typesetting and Lithography by
Lay-out Zetterij Boxem BV, Amsterdam, The Netherlands

Printed and bound in Belgium by
Snoeck, Ducaju & Zoon NV, Ghent

Research work on illustrations by
Paul Hefting, Paul Lempers, Ernst Schilp, Gees-Ineke Smit,
Alex Visser

Texts written by
Ben Bos, Paul Hefting, F.H.K. Henrion, Jaap Huisman,
Jaap Lieverse, Ed Lute, Ronald de Nijs, Gees-Ineke Smit,
Gert Staal, Alex Visser

Editor for Dutch text
Ronald de Nijs

Translators Dutch into English
Karen Gamester, Lynn George, John Rudge, Wendie Shaffer

Editor for English text
Tom Neville, Architecture Design and Technology Press,
Great Britain

Other contributors
Klementine Vis, Braun Netherlands
Paul Hefting, Royal PTT Netherlands
John Reed, London Underground Great Britain
Sheila Taylor, London Transport Archive Great Britain
Franz Brunnberg, adidas West Germany
Jane Sabini, Coca-Cola Great Britain
Yoeki Verkouteren, Esprit Netherlands
Henk van Bork, IBM Netherlands
Hartmut Knauer, Erco Leuchten West Germany
Gees-Ineke Smit & Ies Hoogland, KLM Netherlands
Jaap van der Kleij & Pieter Schoon, Kodak Netherlands
Helga Steinacker & Peter Vogel, Volkswagen West Germany